PATENT TO MARKET SUCCESS

The Step-by-Step Guide to Cashing in on Your Patent

Matthew Yubas

Broadword Publishing
166 London Court
Cardiff, NJ 08234

Patent To Market Success
The Step-by-Step Guide to Cashing in on Your Patent

Published by:

Broadword Publishing
166 London Court
Cardiff, NJ 08234
www.Broadword.com

www.ProductCoach.com

ISBN-13: 978-0-9725521-8-9
ISBN-10: 0-9725521-8-9

Library of Congress Control Number: 2009942043

Printed in the United States of America

This publication is designed to provide accurate and authoritative information with regard to the subject matter covered. It is sold with the understanding that the author and publisher are not engaged in rendering legal, accounting, or other professional service.

This product is not a substitute for legal advice.

Companies and individuals mentioned in the book do not imply an endorsement of their products or services.

For information on bulk purchases, please visit www.Broadword.com.

Contents

PART THREE – SELL OR LICENSE FOR ROYALTIES 81

Acknowledgements

I owe a huge debt of gratitude to everyone who contributed to the creation of this book. Whether you helped with the content, editing, proofreading, or design suggestions, your influence has made the difficult task of writing a book much easier to bear. I would sincerely like to thank those of you involved for the following:

For subject matter advice: Kim Babjack, Dorsey L. Baker, JD, Billy Carmen (Wizard Industries), Howard M. Cohn, JD, Mark R. Malek, JD (Zies, Widerman, Sutch and Malek), David Smith, JD (Tynax), and Matthew Tarnay (Product Development Resource).

For detailed critiques and edits: Kevin Mills, Dan Wolfson, and Evan Yubas.

For content review, critiques, and suggestions: Ann Alger, Margaret Back, Alex Boles, Gary Burns, Otto Glaser (Houston Inventors Association), Susanne Moore, JD, Douglas Rook (Inventors Forum), and Vincent Sellecchia.

The Write Right Critique Group for editing and suggestions: Mary Andrews, Mike Blevins, Jesse Cavazos, Barbara Griffith, Julie Hudson, Patti Johnson, Shayla Szaloy, Joe Trent, Nilah Turner, Bethany Valles, and Marquel White.

And Victoria Vinton for her cover and invention roadmap designs.

The Constitution Protects Inventors

The Founding Fathers of the United States had the wisdom and vision to see the importance of innovation and protection of inventors. The Constitution brought forth the foundation of patent and copyright laws as seen in Article 1 Section 8.

> ### *Constitution of the United States*
>
> *Article 1 Section 8*
>
> *The Congress shall have Power...*
>
> *To promote the Progress of Science and useful Arts, by securing for limited Times to Authors and Inventors the exclusive Right to their respective Writings and Discoveries;*

Introduction

Who This Book Is For

After filing for a patent, many people are confused on the next steps to take. The patent process has a beginning, middle, and an end (having a patent granted). Yet making money from an invention often seems confusing. There are many paths to take, many loaded with pitfalls, and with various opinions on what to do next.

This book, *Patent To Market Success*, is for inventors, entrepreneurs, and everyday people who have filed for a patent and want to successfully get their invention into the market.

Whether your invention is a simple household device, automotive accessory, game, sporting equipment, pet toy, or sophisticated electronic gadget, the guidance you need to sell or license to a company, or bring to the market yourself, is now in front of you.

Patent To Market Success takes the guessing game out of how to proceed to the market. There's a great deal of work to get there, but now, with this book in hand, you'll have a clear path to success.

What This Book Is Not

This book is not a feel good story based on the successes of the past. You won't find fluff or wasted pages. The material is real-world information, precise procedures, and specific guidance to help you make money from your invention. Use this book like a roadmap to move forward and reach your goals.

Organization of This Book

The essence of *Patent To Market Success* is the **Market-Step** process. The **Market-Step** process is a 7-Step system that integrates marketing and sales methods with invention development, legal, and financial techniques.

This process is not magic. The journey takes diligence on your part, but capitalizing on your creativity is now possible.

This book is organized into five sections.

- **Part One** – The vast opportunities available to you; an overview of the 7 steps to get into the market; a method to help you decide whether you want to create a business around your invention or sell to a company; a guide to why products fail and why they succeed; and easy-to-follow market research techniques.

- **Part Two** – The steps and technologies to create a prototype; techniques to create user requirements; how to work with a prototype maker; and methods to gather feedback and improve your invention.

- **Part Three** – The process to sell or license your patent to companies; how to value a patent; creating a Product Proposal to put your invention into the language companies understand; methods to find companies and techniques to contact them; an explanation of license agreement terms; negotiation strategies for the best deal; and how to use agents or consultants.

- **Part Four** – The methods to turn your invention into a winning product; marketing techniques; procedures for developing and manufacturing; tips for packaging, and how to successfully launch a new product.

- **Part Five** – Methods to get your product into retailers, QVC and HSN; little-known methods to market through specialty distribution channels; and how to make sure you're on track and generating additional sales.

- **Appendices** – For more details and advanced procedures, the Appendix covers topics including how to overcome competition; selecting a target market; creating a marketing plan; getting money for your invention; how to start a business around your product; and understanding the details of a licensing agreement.

Each step of the process includes diagrams, descriptions, examples, and exercises. This book takes you by the hand as if you had your own coach leading you personally through each section. And throughout, you'll find Internet resources for additional support.

Believe and Move Forward

You believe in your invention, but perhaps others are less enthusiastic. New ideas are not easily recognized for their market potential. Historically, people have a difficult time accepting new ideas.

Think of the beliefs of the past – the Earth is the center of the solar system, the world is flat, you can't break the sound barrier, you can't run the mile in under four minutes, and there's no need for a computer in the home.

People with a vision for the future are risk takers. They stand out from the crowd and are not afraid to be different.

However, new ideas are just ideas if they sit and collect dust. There's an important difference between – a piece of wood and a baseball bat, a ball of yarn and a sweater, and a piece of plastic and a Rubik's Cube. Success can only occur when you believe in your idea and take action.

You might have doubts and stumble along the way. That's normal and human. If you're stuck or at a plateau, keep at it until something clicks. Keep playing the game until you win. Focus on the end-results and keep moving forward.

What if you're working hard on an unmarketable invention? It happens all the time. As an example, the Palm Pilot was the first electronic organizer to gain mass market acceptance. However, companies had previously introduced several failed handheld devices for over 10 years. The need existed, but part of the problem was timing. Technology wasn't ready and people were still new to personal computers and didn't need another electronic device.

What if you have several product ideas? You need to screen out the ideas that are not marketable so you can focus on creating your winning products. When you research the market, you reduce your risk and increase your potential reward. If you're not quite certain of the marketability of your invention, seek advice from a professional with a product marketing background.

Remember, I'm your Coach and I'm here to assist you. For Coaching and other Services, please visit my website (www.ProductCoach.com).

Best Success With Your Invention,

Matthew Yubas

Inventor Stories

Joe McVoy and Brian Crane

Joe McVoy and Brian Crane turned an idea into a $45 million business.

In 1980, Joe was running a company in the advertising specialty market. While looking for companies to put decals on Frisbees, he met Brian. Brian had a screen printing press and a small business making custom printed souvenirs using a special "prismatic" vinyl. They decided to form a partnership to create new products with Brian in charge of manufacturing and Joe in charge of sales and marketing.

Noticing that people liked their souvenirs with shiny colorful designs, they came up with the idea to apply the same methods to decals for kids. At the time, most decals were rather plain. The new decal had special colorful holographic designs that reflected light into rainbows.

To test the market, Joe took the new decals to several local independent card and gift stores. He offered them 30 day credit terms and they agreed to start with small purchases. To his delight, the products started selling and selling well. Using his artistic talents, Joe created and tested up to 50 different designs. He returned to each store on a regular basis to see what types were selling and to replenish the stock.

The colorful decal became very popular and stores were selling out. Since Joe could only cover so much territory himself, he signed-up an independent sales rep. The rep turned out to be so good, Joe hired him as a full-time employee in charge of sales. Additional reps were signed-up to cover the United States.

To support the sales rep's efforts, Joe took out full page ads in trade magazines. The advertising strategy was to attain additional retailers and distributors. The product became so successful, Joe was featured on the cover of several magazines.

With a strong record of sales, Joe contacted Target. After several meetings, the buyer placed an order. It was supposed to be a $5,000 order for a market test. However, the buyer made a mistake and placed a $50,000 order. When the buyer called a few days later to correct the order, Joe said he was sorry but the order was already shipped. In reality, they hadn't actually fulfilled the order so they scrambled to finish production the next day.

Since Target was originally expecting a small quantity, they hadn't set up a warehouse slot. As a result, all the decal products went directly into the stores. Fortunately kids loved the decals and sold out quickly.

The business continued to grow and within four years the product was in 20,000 retail locations and generating a $1 million a month in sales.

One of their competitors, 3M, offered to buy the company. At that point, Joe and his partner felt they could do better and declined the offer.

The partners continued to challenge each other to grow the business. Brian would say he could make more than Joe could sell. Joe replied he could sell more than Brian could make.

Things were looking great for Joe and Brian, but their luck soon ran out. Retailers bought assortments of their decals without tracking sales performance of each design. The most popular designs sold well and the bad designs didn't, but the stores kept reordering the same assortments. Consequently, they had displays full of products nobody wanted.

At the same time, large competitors began making similar designs and muscled their way in to take over retail shelf space. As a result, monthly sales dropped from $1 million to $250,000 in just one month.

To make matters worse, Joe and Brian were not managing their finances properly. They lacked adequate working capital and had high overhead (300 employees). They cut expenses but it was too little too late. After a few months they had to file bankruptcy.

Joe learned from this experience and soon after built-up a new company. He created a completely new line of school supplies (portfolios, 3-ring binders, spiral notebooks, pens, pencils, and rulers) all made from prismatic and holographic materials. Both Target and Walmart loved the products and placed orders. Due to strong sales, they won an award for "Best New Vendor" in Target's stationery and school supply department.

He grew the company to $6 million in annual sales in only a few years with just 10 employees, instead of 300 like the prior company. However, to finance the large orders, Joe brought-on investors, and in doing so lost control of his company. When the investors wouldn't allocate funds to create more new products, Joe left.

Don't worry, Joe started yet another company – a mail order catalog company selling children's products to doctors, dentists, hospitals, and banks. This time, after building a 10,000 strong customer list, he sold the company to a competitor and got out on top.

To see what Joe is doing today, visit his website www.joemcvoy.com.

Cary Austin

What began as a way to reduce customer complaints, Cary Austin turned an invention into a million dollar business.

In the 1960s, Cary grew up on a cotton farm in West Texas. Being a typical kid, he went to school and helped with chores around the farm.

The family also had a side business of drilling water wells and installing water pumps. As the water business became busier, the family sold the farm.

Cary started working on pumps while he was very young. By the age of 15 he had acquired his driver's license and worked on installing water pumps for customers after school and on the weekends. He learned all aspects of pumping water for rural homes and farms.

In high school, Cary took electronics classes and loved to tinker with mechanical and electronic parts. He built his first computer at the age of 17. Two years later (1980) while attending Texas Tech University, his father was injured in a car accident. Cary left school to help his family run the water pumping business.

The business ran smoothly for a number of years. However, when a customer's water stopped flowing, Cary received calls to come out and repair the system. The unhappy customers would call at all hours of the day or night.

Most of the failures were due to the water pump. When turning on a sprinkler, shower faucet, or irrigation, a water pump cycles on and off to meet the demand. This required Cary to regularly replace water pumps. Even if a pump was still under warranty, he had the labor cost of removing the old pump and installing a replacement. In addition, the time repairing an old system took away from selling a new system.

Cary knew the cause of water pump failures was due to the constant on and off cycles. After years of trying to solve the problem using electronic controlled Variable Frequency Drives, he wondered if a valve could vary the flow to match the usage and eliminate the frequent on and off cycles. By doing so, a water pump would last longer and he could reduce his service calls.

His first attempt of a solution was a home project. Using a shut off valve lever he opened it enough to let a little bit of water flow through the plumbing. He noticed right away the pump turned on and off less frequently. But the next morning, his early rising wife Karen rousted Cary out of bed at 5 am with shampoo in her hair because the shower didn't flow enough water. It was clear that more testing was needed.

The first real prototype was made from a standard pressure regulating valve. Cary drilled a small hole in the middle to flow a small amount of water on a constant basis. He installed the prototype and it appeared to work as planned.

Karen thought he had a marketable invention and should file for a patent. However, Cary thought the idea was too simple and surely someone else would have thought if it first. They made an appointment with an attorney not knowing what to expect. The attorney did a basic search and suggested he file for a patent.

A few months later, Cary discovered a problem with the design. Sediments from well water had clogged the hole in the valve and made the invention useless. He finally figured out a new solution but the design for the patent was wrong. With additional attorney fees, a new patent was filed.

To test the invention in real situations, Cary went to his current customers to ask if he could install a new device for free to improve the life of their water pumps. They all agreed. As a result, his business profits went up 20%. Since the water pumps lasted longer, his repair costs declined dramatically. This was the encouragement he needed to know his invention was for real.

During the next year he sold pumping systems with his new invention as part of the package. Because his parts and repair costs would be less over time, he could charge a lower price than anyone else in town.

After making sure the design worked properly in the field, he sold the service business to focus on creating and selling his valve products. He found a contract manufacturer to produce a small quantity to offer for sale. The product was named the Cycle Stop Valve (CSV) because it stopped the need for a water pump to constantly cycle on and off.

To spread the news, he exhibited at industry trade shows. The new invention caused quite a stir among the retailers, service installers, and pump manufacturers.

One pump company was so interested, they invited Cary to visit their company for a demonstration. Cary anticipated it could be a big breakthrough if this well-known company packaged his valve with their water pumps. After the meeting, Cary called back regularly to see if they planned to order his product. They kept stalling. Finally Cary gave up hope of selling to a big company and moved on to marketing direct to customers.

Years later a former employee of the pump company told him what really happened. A company wide meeting was called to discuss the situation. Since the Cycle Stop Valve extended the life of pumps, it was a direct threat to the company. They wanted their pumps to expire after the warranty so customers had to place new orders. Employees were told if they discussed the CSV with customers, they would be immediately fired.

Cary and Karen became experts in the water pumping industry and began to win over new customers. Sales doubled every year. As their business became well-known, competitors did everything they could to discredit their products. At the same time, praise from industry experts viewed the CSV as a great solution to many water pumping needs. Today, Cary and Karen have a loyal following of customers and distributors worldwide, generating several million in sales revenue.

Cary offers the following tips to new inventors.

- When you come up with a new invention, don't quit your day job. It takes time for a new product to generate enough income to replace your old job.
- Make your invention streamlined and simple in terms of ease of use and manufacturability.
- Start marketing early and find out where comparable products are currently selling rather than trying to open new markets.

To learn more about Cycle Stop Vales, visit www.cyclestopvalves.com.

PART ONE – INVENTION ROADMAP

The secret of getting ahead is getting started. The secret of getting started is breaking your complex overwhelming tasks into small manageable tasks, and then starting on the first one.

Mark Twain

Chapter 1:
World of Opportunity

The patent system added the fuel of interest to the fire of genius.

Abraham Lincoln

As the products roll down the assembly line, the inspector tests the current batch. At the end of the line, products and documentation slide into the packaging. As one, they are placed neatly into the shipping box. The box is taped, weighed, and positioned onto the pallet.

From simple novelties to high tech gadgets, ideas are turned into products on a daily basis. Perhaps your creativity will make a difference in my life and the lives of millions of people.

A win-win situation exists when you help others and at the same time are rewarded for your efforts. When you focus on ways to best serve people, you're compensated for your labors.

An invention doesn't have to be a breakthrough medical device, fire prevention tool, or technological masterpiece. A wonderful and profitable invention may save a person 30 minutes of housework, eliminate the drudgery of a repetitive task, or provide entertainment.

Possibly the only reason your invention is not moving forward is your lack of knowledge to get into the market. You had the passion to create your invention and filed for a patent. Now you are stuck or uncertain how to proceed. No problem. Help is here. By reading this book, your thinking will change from, "How do I do this?" to "Wow! I now know how to capitalize on the many opportunities waiting for me!"

Opportunities to Sell Your Patent

Your patent has value just waiting to be unlocked. In this book, you'll learn how to sell your patent to a company for a lump sum payout or license for royalties. You'll also discover how to develop your invention into a product and then manufacture, market, and sell it.

The following are ways to sell or license a patent:

1. **Sell or License to a Company (Product)** – You sell or license your patent to a company who develops the invention into a product. The company markets the product to consumers, businesses, or government. You are compensated with a lump sum payment, fixed payments spread out over time, or royalties. The company may also buy your patent as a way to block their competitors.

2. **Sell or License to a Company (Remedy)** – A company's product is infringing on your patent. As a remedy, the company pays you as a lump sum amount or enters into a license agreement and pays you royalties for each product they sell.

3. **Sell or License to a Company (In-House)** – You sell or license your patent to a company for their internal use. Your invention might be a new machine, device, or part, to help a company's production line run faster, more efficient, or more cost effective.

4. **Sell or License to a Company (Joint Venture)** – You and another inventor combine your inventions together. You bundle the intellectual property to form a more appealing solution to a company. You partner together or one inventor sub-licenses from the other.

5. **Sell via an Auction** – The interest in offering patents via the auction block continues to grow. Just like any other type of auction, the auctioneer brokers a deal between sellers and buyers. Selling patents at auctions has generated millions of dollars.

6. **Sell to an Aggregator** – There are companies who accumulate patents to form invention portfolios. You sell your patent to them. Then, they look for opportunities to license or sell a bundle of patents to a company who wants to create a new product line or to defend against competition.

7. **Sell to a Troll** – There are companies whose business model is to buy patents for the purpose of suing large companies for infringement. These companies are known as patent trolls (derogatory term) because many see them as a negative influence in the market. You can sell your patent to them for a lump sum payout.

8. **Sell through a Patent Broker** – A patent broker facilitates transactions between patent owners and buyers. When you list your patent for sale, the broker finds buyers and helps with the deal. Buyers can be product companies, patent aggregators, or trolls.

When you turn your patent into a product there are tons of opportunities waiting for you. With a finished product, you sell direct to customers or through distributors, sales reps, and retailers. The following are options available to you:

9. **Advertising Specialty** – Maybe you've seen the pens, calculators, flash drives, and unique products with a company logo? Advertising specialty is a $19 billion industry. Your product as a promotional item is given away by companies to lure prospects and to thank existing customers. This is an opportunity to sell hundreds or thousands of units at a time.

10. **Amazon** – Selling your product on Amazon.com gives you instant credibility and direct access to millions of shoppers in one place. When customers place an order with Amazon, you receive an email notification, and then you ship direct to the customer.

11. **Auctions** – With stiff competition from Amazon, eBay is changing its business model. eBay wants to emphasize more new products for sale via non-bid "Buy it Now" transactions and eBay Stores. With millions of web visitors per month, eBay and other auction websites position your product in front of a large audience.

12. **Brokers and Agents** – Product brokers and agents have established relationships with retailers and distribution channels. For a commission or flat fee, they put together a deal on your behalf.

13. **Carts and Kiosks** – You've likely seen people selling products and services from carts and kiosks. They sell at shopping malls, airports, zoos, theme parks, train stations, sporting events, and elsewhere. With annual retail sales of $12 billion they are a viable distribution channel for your new product.

14. **Catalogs** – Selling products through catalogs accounted for over $400 billion last year. Catalogs sell products via print and online giving your invention a huge audience and big opportunity.

15. **Consignment Shops** – For a new unproven product, some retailers are willing to sell on consignment as a test. With consignment, you are not paid until a product is sold to a consumer. Consignment shops carry an assortment of products or specialize in certain categories such as automotive, clothing, furniture, gifts, and sporting goods.

16. **Direct Mail** – Even with the internet, direct mail still works. While email often ends up trapped in spam filters, direct mail puts physical product information directly into the home and business.

17. **Distributors and Wholesalers** – You supply the product and the distributor / wholesaler takes inventory, sells to customers (retailers or end-users), and ships the product.

18. **Fairs** – There are nationwide opportunities to sell arts and crafts products at fairs. If you like the free-wheeling gypsy lifestyle, you can take your product on the road and sell from town to town year round. You have to consider the travel costs to determine if this is a good opportunity.

19. **Government** – As we know, our government spends plenty of money. Federal, state, and local agencies procure all kinds of products to function on a daily basis. Your product could be included in a NASA mission, on a Navy voyage, or in government offices across the country.

20. **Home-Based Businesses** – There are about 35 million home-based businesses in the United States with over $300 billion in revenue. Many are looking for new and unique products to sell via their webstores and mail order.

21. **Infomercials** – If your product is low priced and easily demonstratable, then selling via infomercials may be your ticket. Some companies charge up-front fees, while others absorb all development and marketing costs and give you a percentage of sales.

22. **Network Marketing** – Also known as multi-level marketing or affiliate marketing, some operations are legitimate while others are illegal pyramid schemes. Network marketers organize around a product line and then recruit independent members who work on a commission. You can create your own network marketing business centered around your product line, or attract existing networks to take on your product.

23. **Original Equipment Manufacturer (OEM)** – As a supplier, you create and sell your product to a company who combines it with their branded product or system. This joint venture model is common in the computer industry. For example, a computer sold by Hewlett-Packard may include a hard drive from IBM, motherboard from Intel, and mouse from Logitech.

24. **Private Label** – Many retailers buy products from suppliers and sell as their own brand. Examples include Kirkland brand sold by Costco, Target Brands, and Sam's at Walmart. As a private label supplier, you sell large qualities without the big marketing and sales costs.

25. **Retailers** – Selling the right product at the right price to retailers can generate thousands of sales for you per month. Retailers include convenience stores, department stores, drug stores, specialty stores, supermarkets, and mass merchandisers.

26. **Retail (yours)** – Rent retail space and sell your products direct. This is how Radio Shack and The Body Shop got started. You can also acquire complimentary products to offer your customers a complete product line.

27. **Showrooms** – Showrooms are wholesale marketplaces where representatives sell your products to retail buyers. Major showroom marketplaces are located in Atlanta, Chicago, Dallas, Las Vegas, Los Angeles, and New York.

28. **Sales Reps** – Independent sales representatives sell your product on commission. They meet with retailers, distributors, and go to trade shows.

29. **Special Interest Groups** – There's a group for just about every interest. There are groups for cars, quilts, investing, etc. Sell your product directly to these groups. Sometimes the group has a gift shop, sellers table, or webstore.

30. **Swap Meets** – This might be a humble starting point for your product but it can pan out. The company Clothestime started in a California swap meet and later created their own retail chain with over 500 stores.

31. **Tele-Marketing** – Although not popular today, they still exist. Tele-marketing companies take on your product, train their salespeople, and sell products over the phone.

32. **Trade shows** – Trade shows enable you to meet and sell directly to customers, distributors, and retail buyers. If your product needs to be seen in order to be understood, then it's important to exhibit at trade shows.

33. **TV Shopping** – With millions of dollars per minute transacting on QVC, HSN, and others, this is a great opportunity if you have the right product.

34. **Webstore (yours)** – Creating a website for your product is a basic requirement. Sell your product online with a shopping cart and at the same time refer people to retailers carrying your product.

35. **Webstore (others)** – There are countless webstores selling products to customers around the world. Webstores operate as either retailers or facilitators. As a retailer, the webstore buys your inventory and ships to customers. Webstores as facilitators generate sales on a commission and pass the order to you.

As you can see from the above list, there are many opportunities available for your invention. In the next chapter you'll learn the roadmap to turn your patent into prosperity.

Chapter 2:
Invention Roadmap

All you need is the plan, the road map, and the courage to press on to your destination.

Earl Nightingale

Topics in this Chapter:

- The Market-Step™ Process from Idea to Market
- Protect Your Idea
- Market Research and Evaluation
- Patent Review
- Decision
- Sell or License Path
- Self-Market Path
- How Long Does It Take?
- Product Evolution

Suppose you took a trip driving across the country. You anticipate beautiful scenery, historical sites, and wide open landscapes.

Assume you didn't have a roadmap. You would likely take wrong turns, backtrack, and zigzag your way across the country, assuming you even make it.

The same is true with inventing. Without a roadmap, you'll likely waste plenty of time and money. Having a clear roadmap helps you navigate and capitalize on the many opportunities that lie ahead.

I've created the **Market-Step™** process to take you step-by-step to sell your patent. As you follow the roadmap, there are a series of procedures, examples, and exercises.

There are two main paths to take. Each path starts the same, but there is a fork in the road where you need to make a decision. The Market-Step process consists of the following two paths.

The diagram below outlines the main steps to move from idea to market success. Use this roadmap as a navigational tool to guide and monitor your progress.

The Market-Step™ Process Diagram

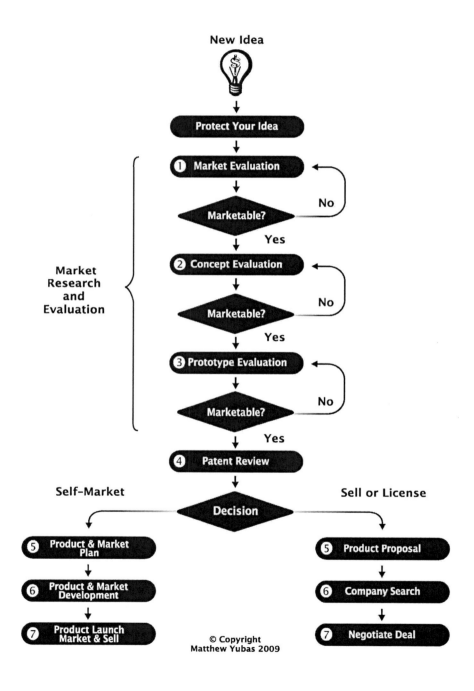

© Copyright
Matthew Yubas 2009

The Market-Step™ Process Steps from Idea to Market

Self-Market	Sell or License to a Company
1. Market Evaluation	1. Market Evaluation
2. Concept Evaluation	2. Concept Evaluation
3. Prototype Evaluation	3. Prototype Evaluation
4. Patent Decision	4. Patent Filing
5. Product and Market Planning	5. Product Proposal Document
6. Product and Marketing Development	6. Company Search and Contact
7. Product Launch and Generate Sales	7. Negotiate a Deal

Protect Your Idea

When you have an idea, you need to protect it. The first line of defense is to set the date of conception. Start by documenting your idea in an inventor's logbook, but don't file a patent until you evaluate its marketability. Another tool to protect your idea is a non-disclosure agreement (NDA). For a sample NDA, see Appendix G, Non-Disclosure Agreement.

Market Research and Evaluation

❑ **Step 1: Market Evaluation**

Start the **Market-Step** process by evaluating the marketability of your invention. With a quick evaluation of the market, you screen out bad ideas before wasting time and money. Your invention is marketable when it solves a problem, meets a need or want, overcomes competition (products and patents), and generates a profit.

❑ **Step 2: Concept Evaluation**

The second step of the **Market-Step** process is to determine if people like your invention concept. A concept evaluation is an easy-to-use survey method you can create yourself. The results provide you with valuable feedback so you have a better feel whether to proceed with your invention. In addition, a concept evaluation allows people an opportunity to provide helpful suggestions and advice.

❑ **Step 3: Prototype Evaluation**

The third step is to create a prototype and have an evaluation. A prototype can be a physical model, detailed drawing, or animation. With a prototype, you obtain opinions to make sure you're on the right track. In addition, a prototype evaluation helps you uncover any necessary feature changes before moving onto the next stage.

Marketable? After each of the first three steps, you need to review the evaluation results to determine if your invention is marketable. If results are encouraging, advance to the next step. If results are mixed, you might need to go back and revise your idea and re-test. If results are discouraging, revise the invention or cancel the project entirely to save yourself time and money and move on to your next idea.

Patent Review

❑ **Step 4: Patent Filing (Sell or License), Patent Review (Self-Market)**

If you intend to sell or license your invention to a company, you need to review existing patents. If your invention is patentable, then file for a patent. Start with a Provisional Patent Application for a year of protection while you test the market.

To self-market, a patent is not required. However, a patent can serve as a competitive advantage and valuable business asset. You need to review existing patents to make sure your product does not cause an infringement.

If you were granted a Utility Patent, make sure you pay the maintenance fees to keep the patent enforced. There are three sets of maintenance fees. The first is due at three years and six months from the grant date, then at seven years and six months, and finally at eleven years and six months. Failure to pay any maintenance fee will result in your patent being abandoned (you lose all rights).

Decision

Do you prefer to sell or license your invention to a company? Otherwise, do you prefer to market yourself? To help you make a proper decision, see Chapter 3, Decision to Market, License, or Sell.

Sell or License Path

If you decide to sell or license to a company for royalties, your path is the following:

❑ **Step 5: Product Proposal**

Companies need to understand your invention from a business perspective. If you leave it up to the company to figure out your invention, you're much more likely to be rejected. Before approaching a company, summarize the market need, invention benefits, competitive advantages, and profit potential into a Product Proposal document.

❑ **Step 6: Company Search and Contact**

Search for companies who make, market, and sell products that are comparable with your invention. Then find a prime contact in the marketing department to pitch your invention. If there's a fit, send a cover letter and Product Proposal for consideration. By not performing a proper search strategy, you waste time and money, and increase the chance of rejection.

❑ **Step 7: Negotiate a Deal**

If the company likes your invention, discuss the terms, create and sign an agreement, and earn royalties or a lump sum payout. There is a particular process to follow when a company wants to negotiate. Using specific tactics can earn you a better deal with a bigger payoff.

Self-Market Path

If you decide to self-market, your path is the following:

❑ **Step 5: Product and Market Plan**

Once it's determined your invention is marketable, the next step is to create a simple plan. You need to plan your product's design and marketing before starting development. Having a thought-out plan increases the chance of a successful product.

To self-market, you need money for research, development, manufacturing, marketing, and startup expenses. To entice investors, write a business plan to inform them about the opportunity your invention presents.

❑ **Step 6: Product and Market Development**

By developing a product with the needs of the customer in mind, you can't go wrong. The first step to develop your invention is to hire an engineer or designer. At the same time, your marketing plans begin to take shape.

Thinking about marketing early on is important. You don't want a finished product sitting in a warehouse collecting dust while you come up with marketing ideas. Manufacturing can be outsourced or you can set up your own production process.

❑ **Step 7: Product Launch and Generate Sales**

The launch phase is the most exciting part of your journey. You are finalizing the product, packaging, marketing, and distribution. On the day of the launch you announce product availability. Thereafter, your focus is primarily on marketing, sales, and customer support.

How Long Does It Take?

How long will it take you to make money from your patent? To self-market, it can easily take a minimum of six months to plan, develop, and launch your product. When selling or licensing, it can take at least a minimum of three to six months to prepare, search for companies, negotiate, and sign a deal.

While cutting down on development time is always desirable, it should *not* be done by skipping important steps. For example, during the Development Step, while engineers are developing the product, you can work on advertising and promotional activities.

Product Evolution

To turn an idea into a product that you market, it's common to create, test, obtain feedback, make improvements, and repeat the process.

Products evolve through the following stages:

- Prototype
- Alpha
- Beta
- Commercial Release

Prototypes are important during early market research and market tests. You'll convert your idea into a prototype so people can evaluate it visually. The prototype is a general working model with basic product features.

After the prototype stage, the first product version is an "alpha" product. The alpha product has basic functionality and is able to perform rudimentary tasks. It doesn't yet have fancy features, materials, or colors. It's just the basic product, suitable for internal testing and learning the development process.

As development advances, the next version is a "beta" product. The beta product has enough of the key features and functions to provide a reasonable customer experience. The objective is to gather valuable feedback from potential customers before you go into production. Since making changes during production is expensive, you want to uncover any mistakes during the beta stage.

With knowledge from beta testing, make any changes to create the commercial product – a fully functional, tested, and packaged product ready to launch, market, and sell.

Is it best to self-market or license your invention to a company? Is it better to receive royalties or a lump sum payout? In the next chapter, uncover the direction for your invention.

Chapter 3:
Decision to Market, License, or Sell

Don't let adverse facts stand in the way of a good decision.

Colin Powell

Topics in this Chapter:

- Self-Marketing vs. Licensing Example
- Do You Prefer to License Your Patent?
- Do You Prefer to Sell Your Patent?
- Do you Prefer to Self-Market?
- Decision

Important: Sometimes when you try to license or sell your invention to companies, they are not interested. To understand if a market exists for your invention, companies might want to see a positive track record of sales. Therefore, you have to manufacture, market, and generate sales on your own. Once you sell perhaps 1,000 to 5,000 units, you can either continue to market on your own, or go back to companies and negotiate a deal from a better position.

At this point, you have a patent or have filed a patent application. You're likely wondering what to do next. In general, options for you include:

- **License your patent to a company for royalties** – If you license to a company you can earn passive income (sit back and collect) without the burden of manufacturing and marketing a product yourself.

- **Sell (assign) your patent for a payout** – When you sell a patent to a company, you take the money and give up all further rights to the invention. As a result, by taking a one-time payout, you lose the chance of future earnings if the product is a huge success.

- **Self-market** – By venturing on your own, there's the excitement of running your own business and an opportunity for large rewards. At the same time, you have business expenses and the responsibility of generating a positive cash flow.

Self-Marketing vs. Licensing Example

Here is a sample financial comparison of self-marketing versus licensing:

Background

- Unit costs to manufacture and package = $25
- Number of units sold = 20,000
- Product Sales = $2,000,000

Licensing Royalty

Assumption: Royalty = 5% of Net Product Sales

Royalty   = Royalty percentage x Net Product Sales
= 5% x $2,000,000
= $100,000

Self-Marketing Profit

Assumptions: Startup expenses = $50,000
Operational, Marketing, and Sales expenses = $150,000

Gross Profit   = Product Sales – (Unit cost x Units sold)
= $2,000,000 – ($25 x 20,000)
= $2,000,000 – $500,000
= $1,500,000

Net Profit   = Gross Profit – Expenses
= $1,500,000 – ($50,000 + $150,000)
= $1,500,000 – $200,000
= $1,300,000

In this example, the self-marketer earned $1,300,000 versus $100,000 by licensing. The self-marketer made more money, but only after risking his or her own money (and perhaps an investor's money) and putting in many hours per week.

An advantage to the self-marketer is the business can be sold and proceeds invested to generate future cash flows. On the other hand, the licensor (inventor) may make less, but has more free time to work on other ideas. As you were reading this scenario, did you see yourself as the self-marketer or licensor?

Do You Prefer to License Your Patent?

To understand whether licensing is better for you, select either "**Yes**" or "**No**" for the following questions:

Licensing Decision		
1. Do you have a patent, or is your patent attorney confident your invention is patentable?	Yes	No
2. Do you want to license your patented invention to a company for royalties?	Yes	No
3. Do you want to retain ownership rights to your patent for the duration of its life?	Yes	No
4. Can you present information showing the invention offers a market opportunity and can earn a profit for the company?	Yes	No
5. Are you willing to search for companies, present your invention, and negotiate the terms of a contract or use an agent/consultant to do this for you?	Yes	No

- How many of above questions did you answer Yes? _____

Do You Prefer to Sell Your Patent?

To understand whether selling your patent to a company is better for you, select either "**Yes**" or "**No**" for the following questions:

Selling Decision		
1. Do you have a patent, or is your patent attorney confident your invention is patentable?	Yes	No
2. Do you want to sell (assign) your patented invention to a company for a lump sum or payments over time?	Yes	No
3. Are you willing to give up all rights to your invention once it's assigned to a company?	Yes	No
4. Can you present information showing the invention offers a market opportunity and can earn a profit for the company?	Yes	No
5. Are you willing to search for companies, present your invention, and negotiate the terms of a contract or use an agent/consultant to do this for you?	Yes	No

- How many of above questions did you answer Yes? ____

Do you Prefer to Self-Market?

To determine if self-marketing is better for you, select either "Yes" or "No" for the following questions:

Self-Marketing Decision		
1. Do you want to build a business around your invention?	Yes	No
2. Do you have or can you raise money to cover business expenses?	Yes	No
3. Are you skilled at business planning (or can find someone who is)?	Yes	No
4. If you're working, do you have spare time to build your business on the side?	Yes	No
5. If you're working and want to quit your job, do you have reserves to pay your living expenses and business expenses for at least six months?	Yes	No
6. Can you find mentors to advise you in business matters?	Yes	No
7. Do you have a good knowledge of the industry related to your invention?	Yes	No

- How many of above questions did you answer Yes? ____

Decision

Now it's time to see if a certain path is best for you. Of the three sets of questions above, which section had the most Yes answers?

- ❑ License your patent to a company for royalties.
- ❑ Sell your patent for a lump sum payment.
- ❑ Self-Market

If you're still not sure which path to take, don't worry you are fine for now. As you continue to read and learn, see which option is best for you. If you're hesitant, seek coaching and opinions from people who have been through the process.

If you have chosen a direction, it's still a good idea to learn about the other paths. In some cases, the person who wants to self-market, later decides to license to a company. In other cases, people with the initial intent to license, found self-marketing the best path.

Chapter 4:
Product Failure and Success

Entrepreneurs are risk-takers, willing to roll the dice with their money or reputations on the line in support of an idea or enterprise. They willingly assume responsibility for the success or failure of a venture and are answerable for all its facets.

Victor Kiam

Topics in this Chapter:

- What is a Product?
- Why Do Products Fail?
- Why Do Products Succeed?

What is a Product?

This book identifies a Product as "any tangible or intangible product or service." Tangible products are physical objects, such as a new type of hammer, toaster, or electronic device. An intangible product is something you can't hold in your hands; things like software, web sites, and publishing content.

Why Do Products Fail?

It's often said that we don't intentionally plan for failure; we just fail to plan. We all believe we're doing the best we can to improve the chances for product success. The following are some of the key reasons for product failures in the marketplace.

- Not protecting your idea
- Not following a roadmap from idea to product launch
- Not determining marketability for new ideas
- Obtaining a patent before determining marketability
- Not understanding the buying process of the customer
- Designing a product without performing a patent search for potential infringement

- Designing a product without considering costs, pricing, and manufacturability
- Not considering the competition when marketing your product
- Personal goals override company goals
- Trying to do it all yourself

While companies may blame the economy for product failure, failure is more likely the result of misjudging the customer, poor understanding of the market, and inefficient management of the business.

Why Do Products Succeed?

What factors determine product success? In addition to avoiding the above pitfalls, it's important to know that successful products:

- Solve a problem or satisfy a need or want
- Are easy to use with clear instructions
- Have great packaging (for consumer retail products)
- Have a stylish design
- Are available where the target market shops
- Are priced according to market conditions
- Offer a risk-free guarantee

To create a new product, the company (or you):

- Begins the new idea process by identifying problems, needs, and wants
- Uses a process to screen new ideas
- Has sufficient funding in place for development, marketing, and sales
- Has one person who maintains the product vision and manages the project
- Has a fun and exciting work environment

Keep in mind, a technically superior product does not always win in the market. The customer may make a purchase decision based on practical functionality, style, packaging, clear documentation, or even courteous customer service.

If you have yet to make a prototype, continue to the next chapter to learn about prototyping. If you have a prototype and received positive feedback, go to Chapter 8 to see how to sell or license your invention.

Chapter 5:
Market Research

Marketing is not an event, but a process . . . It has a beginning, a middle, but never an end, for it is a process. You improve it, perfect it, change it, even pause it. But you never stop it completely.

Jay Conrad Levinson

Topics in this Chapter:

- Primary and Secondary Market Research
- Determine Your Industry
- Market Research Sources
- Focus on Your Invention's Benefits
- Your Invention Must Have Competitive Advantages
- What's the Profit Potential?

Whether you intend to sell, license, or bring your invention to the market yourself, market data forms the foundation to success. Market data gives you and your invention credibility. Instead of just telling others how great your invention is, show them market data validating a need in the market and how your solution is the best.

Primary and Secondary Market Research

There are two types of market research: primary and secondary. Primary research is gathering information using surveys, one-on-one interviews, and focus groups. Secondary research is data found through magazines, newspapers, trade journals, or the internet. It's best when you acquire market data from both primary and secondary sources.

Primary research provides you with specific data related to your product. For example, if you need to determine the appropriate set of product features and functions, then on-on-one interviews and focus groups allows you to gather options and suggestions. In addition, you can ask questions about pricing and willingness to buy.

In-person interviews are best, but you can conduct surveys online when large numbers of data are needed. There are web-based survey tools in which you set up questions. When ready, you email a link to your participants. Participants click the link and answer the questions. At the conclusion, the survey tool provides you with a summary of the answers. Popular survey tools include Survey Monkey (www.surveymonkey.com) and Zoomerang (www.zoomerang.com). These tools are free for basic use and charge a fee for larger projects.

Secondary research helps to back your claims using known experts or sources. For example, you have a new medical device invention. To back your claims of effectiveness, you find a study published in the New England Journal of Medicine explaining how a particular ailment can be effectively treated. In fact, your invention provides the same treatment method confirmed in the study. As a result, with credible sources to back your claims, it's easier to obtain licensing deals, funding from investors, and selling to your customers.

Determine Your Industry

The first step of market research is to determine which segment of the market your invention belongs in. Segments include:

- Apparel
- Audio / Video
- Automotive
- Beauty / Makeup / Hair / Personal
- Books
- Business Supplies
- Collectibles
- Computer Hardware
- Computer Software
- Diet and Nutrition
- Entertainment
- Games and Hobbies
- Health and Fitness
- Housewares / Small Kitchen Appliances
- Jewelry
- Personal Development
- Sporting Equipment
- Tools

Next, research the following aspects of your invention: the needs and wants of potential customers, market trends, market size, competitors, and pricing. As a guide, answer these questions:

- Who is the best customer for my product? (target market)
- How many people are likely to buy my product? (approximate numbers)
- Where do they shop?
- How much do they typically spend for my type of product?
- How can I gain their attention?
- Who is my competition and how can I surpass them?
- What is the size of the market, and is it growing?
- What trends are likely to reduce or boost sales?
- Are there any regulations relevant to my product?

Market Research Sources

The Internet is a great place to begin your market research. The following are helpful websites for market research:

- Google (www.google.com)
- United States Census Bureau (www.census.gov)
- United States Patent and Trademark Office (www.uspto.gov)
- Webster's Online (www.webdir.net)
- Wikipedia (www.wikipedia.org)
- Yahoo (www.yahoo.com)

With a search engine, use keywords such as "market trends," "market size," and "competition" along with your product type. For example, use search terms ["toy robot" "market trends"]. As a result, the search engine presents links to news and company pages. Read as much as you can to learn about market dynamics.

In addition, you can find a wealth of market research in specialized reference books. Although these cost anywhere from $50 to $200, many market research journals and books are free to view at a public or university library. Look in the library's business, social science, or reference sections. Be prepared to read them on site because they cannot be checked out.

The following are some of my favorite books for market research:

- **Industry Surveys** (Standard & Poor's) commentary of industry drivers, trends, and key businesses

- **Industry Handbook** (Dun & Bradstreet) commentary of industry drivers and trends

- **Industry Norms & Key Business Ratios** (Dun & Bradstreet) industry ratios of assets, liabilities, sales, and profit

- **US Market Trends & Forecasts** (Gale Group) market segments, market value, market share, and growth rate

- **Market Share Reporter** (Gale Group) market segments, market value, and market share

- **US Industry & Trade Outlook** (McGraw-Hill) detailed commentary of market segments

The library is likely to have free computer database search tools such as InfoTrac, ProQuest, New York Times Archive, or ABI/Inform. These databases allow you to search through a wide variety of newspapers, professional publications, academic journals, and trade magazines, not normally found on the Internet.

While there's plenty of free information available, there are also detailed market reports you may buy online. These reports often provide valuable information including market size, future trends, market drivers for success, and key players. Major market research companies consist of Gartner (www.gartner.com), Forrester (www.forrester.com), and IDC (www.idc.com).

Tip: Many public libraries provide vast amounts of information over the Internet. You may even be able to access database services from your home computer for free through your public library. Login with your library card number and a personal identification number to gain access to dozens of normally costly databases.

Focus on Your Invention's Benefits

People buy products based on benefits. So ask yourself, what are the benefits of your invention? What problems does it solve? What needs and wants does it satisfy?

You might say, "Wait a minute! When I buy a car, I want a V8 engine, and that's a feature."

Well, let's look a little closer at your want. Why do you want a V8 engine? You may want a car with performance. You may want a car to pull a heavy load, such as a boat. In addition, you may like having power when you need it. So, in fact, the benefits you want are quickness, power, and peace of mind. You believe V8 engines provide these benefits. At least, that's the message from the car manufacturers. (At the same time, there are cars with a V6 engine with the same capabilities, cost less, and produce better gas mileage.)

The point is, you need to look at your invention from a benefits point of view. If your invention does not offer any benefits, or you don't communicate those benefits, it's more difficult to license or sell.

Here are examples of benefit statements I've used for different inventions:

- Quick and Easy Set up and Cleanup
- Saves Installation Time by 45%
- Prepares a Healthy Meal in Half the Time
- Saves Lives and Prevents Injuries Due To Unattended Cooking Fires
- Reduces 30% of the Germs Spread by Sneezing
- Reduces Labor Costs by up to Three People
- Teaches and Adds Hours of Fun and Entertainment

Benefits for Consumer Products

Consumers seek products to remedy problems and satisfy needs and wants. Consumer benefits deal with emotionally driven personal motivators. Motivators include money, love, safety, recognition, acceptance, pleasure, and pain.

Benefits consumers seek include:

- **Make Money** – We seek to make money to provide for basic survival, to gain love and recognition, and to use for pleasure. We work hard, educate ourselves, join clubs, and take on entrepreneurial adventures.

- **Save Money** – We like to save money so we have more of what money can do for us. We buy insulation for our homes to lower energy costs, buy fluorescent bulbs instead of incandescent, and buy fuel-efficient cars.

- **Save Time** – Time is our most precious commodity. Some people trade off between time and money. Time moves on, so we try to make the most of it. We buy organizers, dishwashers, and frozen dinners.

- **Safety, Health, and Peace of Mind** – We want to stay healthy, so we buy fitness products, follow diet programs, and buy vitamins. For safety concerns, we outfit our homes, cars, and offices with alarm systems, take self-defense classes, and some buy guns.

- **Recognition and Acceptance** – We like feeling special and accepted. We join clubs, strive to win awards, and seek prestige in the things we buy.

- **Pleasure, Comfort, and Love** – Of course, we're motivated by pleasure. Why else would we eat ice cream and chocolate? We seek simple escapes like eating sweets, or more elaborate ones like taking a vacation to reduce stress. We buy clothes, perfume, lipstick, expensive cars, and many other things to look attractive for the intention of finding love.

Benefits for Business Products

Benefits are different for business products versus consumer products. Businesses seek to remedy problems mainly related to revenue, costs, and customers. Business benefits revolve around the bottom line – money. Your invention can be successful if it helps a business generate higher revenue or saves money. In addition, businesses buy products and services to help comply with government regulations.

Business benefits sought are:

- **Higher Revenue and Higher Margins** – Businesses must generate revenue to survive. They'll invest in new products, marketing campaigns, websites, and sales training programs.

- **Lower Costs and Higher Efficiency** – Businesses need to cut costs and increase efficiency to produce profits. Examples of products they'll invest in include automated equipment, computer software, and energy-efficient systems.

- **Customer Retention** – Businesses know it's easier to retain a customer than acquire a new one. Examples of products desired include customer relationship software, survey programs, and gifts.

Benefits and Features	
Check off the benefits your product idea provides and name the associated features.	

Benefits (For Business)	Features
❑ Higher Revenue, Margins	
❑ Lower Costs	
❑ Higher Efficiency	
❑ Higher Customer Retention	
Benefits (For Consumer)	**Features**
❑ Make Money	
❑ Save Money	
❑ Save Time	
❑ Safety, Health, Peace of Mind	
❑ Recognition, Acceptance	
❑ Pleasure, Comfort, Love	

Your Invention Must Have Competitive Advantages

Not only must your invention have benefits, but those benefits must be better than those offered by existing similar products. So, if your invention offers ease of use, it must be easier to use than the competition's product. For example, the CD offers advantages over the audio cassette including better sound quality, quicker access to music tracks, has a longer shelf-life, etc.

I suggest your invention offer at least two or more competitive advantages. The more advantages the better. If your invention has only one market advantage and another product comes along with the same one, then there is no longer an advantage.

Competitive Advantages	
Check off the competitive advantages your invention provides and name the associated features or functions.	
Advantage	**Features**
❑ Easier to use	
❑ Faster	
❑ More fun	
❑ More efficient	
❑ Longer lasting	
❑ Better quality	
❑ Saves more time	
❑ More stylish	
❑ Makes more money	
❑ Saves more money	
❑ Less expensive, better value	
❑ More safety	
❑ More pleasure	
❑ Other:	

What's the Profit Potential?

Companies want to know the profit potential of your invention. Potential means we don't know the exact future amount, but we provide estimates.

In general, the larger the company, the larger the profit potential needed. For example, when talking with global giant Proctor & Gamble, the licensing manager said they are looking for new products with earnings potential of at least $100 million per year.

As a way to determine profit potential, you'll need to estimate revenue potential and the cost of goods sold.

Revenue Potential

Two ingredients determine revenue potential: selling price and the number of products sold. If you have not determined an appropriate retail price yet, for now, use the average or typical price the competition is charging.

Keep in mind the selling price, from a manufacturer's point of view, is the wholesale price. So, if the retail price is $40 and the retail discount is 50%, then the selling price for profit potential calculations is $20. If a manufacturer sells direct, then the selling price is the retail price.

To estimate the total number of units sold, first you'll need to obtain industry data. There's a good reference book called *Market Share Reporter*, available in many libraries. This book contains data covering several industries.

If any competitors are public companies, look at their annual reports. If the reports do not discuss how many units they sold, but provide product revenue, then take the product revenue and divide it by the selling price. Where the market share of this product is known, you can determine the total units sold in the industry. For example, if product revenue is $2 million, selling price is $20, and market share is 10%, the result is a total of 1 million units sold in the market:

Total Market Size = (Product Revenue / Selling Price) / Market Share
= ($2,000,000 / $20) / .10
= 1,000,000

Another resource for sales estimates is retailers. Talk to store managers and salespeople to uncover if they have estimates of unit sales per year. Many are open to talk if you respect their time by keeping the conversation short.

If your product type is tracked by a trade organization, they may have sales estimates for the industry broken down into market segments related to your invention. To find a trade organization, perform an internet search using keywords ["product type" and industry], or ["product type" and "trade show"].

Once you find the total units sold in the market, you'll need to estimate the number of unit sales. One method is to survey people and compare your invention with similar products they currently use. The survey must describe your invention and ask if they would switch from their product to yours if it were available. Summarize the surveys to determine the percentage of people who would switch. Then, to estimate sales, multiple total market size by the percentage of survey responses who would switch.

For example, if a total of 1 million flashlights are sold in a year, and 10% of survey respondents indicate they would buy your new product, then the unit sales forecast is 100,000 units. If the selling price is $20, a manufacture could realize $2 million in revenue.

Revenue Potential	
Total units sold in the market	1,000,000
x Percentage of interested purchasers	10%
= Sales forecast	100,000
x Selling Price	$ 20
= Revenue Potential	$ 2,000,000

Cost of Goods Sold

Producing your invention has costs including parts, labor, and packaging. One way to learn the cost is to talk to a contract manufacturer and ask for a quote to produce quantities related to the sales forecast (i.e. 100,000 units). The quote should include parts and labor. The quantity to ask for should be similar to the sales forecast. To provide a quote they'll either need a list of parts or to look at your drawings. For more about contacting manufacturers, see Chapter 14, Product Planning.

If you can't find a manufacturer to provide a quote, you can look up the costs yourself. First, create a list of parts. Then look through parts catalogs and contact them for the cost of each component in the quantities related to your sales forecast. To determine assembly costs, you'll need to obtain and estimate from a manufacturing engineer.

An accountant who specializes in the industry related to your invention, may be able to provide a cost of goods estimate.

Let's use an example to estimate a cost of goods. The parts, labor, and packaging for the finished product costs $5.00 each for a quantity of 100,000 units.

Cost of Goods Sold	
Each Part	Cost
Solar cell	2.50
Rechargeable battery	1.00
Switch	0.10
Case	0.40
Assembly	0.50
Packaging	0.50
Total Unit Cost	$ 5.00

Profit Potential

With estimates of revenue and cost of goods sold, you can calculate profit potential. For example, let's assume a company can sell 100,000 units a year at a selling price of $20. The resulting revenue is $2 million. Since each product costs $5, the cost of goods from selling 100,000 units is $500,000. Therefore, the profit potential is $1,500,000.

Formulas for determining profit potential are:

- Revenue = Number of Units Sold x Selling Price
- Cost of Goods = Number of Units Sold x Unit Cost
- Gross Profit = Revenue - Cost of Goods Sold

Profit Potential	
Revenue	Year
Units Sold	100,000
Selling Price	$20
Total	$ 2,000,000
Cost of Goods	$(500,000)
Gross Profit	$ 1,500,000

It's also helpful to explain how you arrived at the numbers by showing survey results, industry statistics, and/or government reports.

To help you perform the financial calculations, the above formulas are available as fill-in-the-blank Microsoft Excel spreadsheets in the *Templates* package at my website (www.ProductCoach.com).

PART TWO –
PROTOTYPE DEVELOPMENT

Hide not your talents, they for use were made. What's a sundial in the shade?
Benjamin Franklin

Chapter 6:
Create a Prototype

The whole of science is nothing more than a refinement of everyday thinking.
Albert Einstein

Topics in this Chapter:

- Prototype Development and Evaluation Flowchart
- Goals for Your Prototype
- User Scenarios
- Prototype Requirements
- Prototype Development

Note: If you have not created a working prototype, please read this chapter. If you have a prototype, feel free to skim this chapter to see if you missed anything, and then move to the next section.

A prototype helps you confirm functionality, obtain comments, and generate excitement. Prototype development often requires multiple steps where you create a prototype, gather feedback, make modifications, and then ask for additional responses.

The prototype process is:

Turn your idea into a prototype
1. Uncover user scenarios
2. Create prototype requirements
3. Develop a prototype

Validate your prototype
4. Create an interview plan
5. Recruit people to interview
6. Conduct the interview
7. Summarize the feedback

If you're creating a prototype yourself, perform activities one through seven in consecutive order. If two or more people are involved, you can save time by working in tandem. One person or team can perform activities one through three, while the other works on activities four and five. When the prototype is ready, complete activities six and seven together.

Prototype Development and Evaluation Flowchart

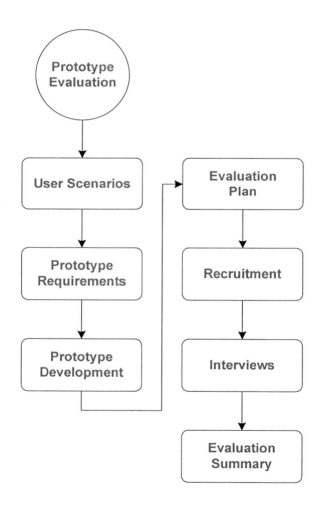

TURN YOUR IDEA INTO A PROTOTYPE

You need feedback on both the visual and functional aspects of your prototype. For example, a new cell phone is evaluated for how it operates as well as its design appeal. Since a cell phone is required to function according to industry standards, it must be tested and certified by engineers. At the same time, cell phones need an appealing look and feel.

The key steps for you to creating a successful prototype involve:

- Stating your prototype goals
- Developing user scenarios
- Writing prototype requirements
- Sketching a design
- Searching for a designer (or designing it yourself)
- Searching for a prototype maker, engineer, or manufacturer

Goals for Your Prototype

It's important to be clear on why you're building a prototype. For example, if the primary objective is to test if the invention works, then, you won't necessarily care what the prototype looks like, as long as it functions properly. On the other hand, if the prototype needs to impress investors or interest companies for licensing, it must look clean, concise, and stylish (rather than a plain black box).

Prototype Goals
Select the goals for your prototype (✓):   ❑ Determine if the idea functions as imagined   ❑ Have users evaluate the look and feel   ❑ Have users evaluate the functionality   ❑ Interest investors   ❑ Interest companies for selling or licensing   ❑ Other:

User Scenarios

User Scenarios are an important way to improve the success of your prototype by simply observing people using a product. You want your finished product to fit with the way someone would normally use your type of product. People are more likely to adopt a simple and familiar solution. If a product is not user-friendly, customers either return the product or do not use it at all.

For example, if you're creating a replacement to a CD player and most people are accustomed to power and play buttons on the left side, you should use a similar arrangement. An exception is if your product strategy is style rather than traditional practicality. For a high-end stereo equipment maker such as Bang and Olufsen, style is a key selling point.

To start, observe and interview people as they perform tasks with a product comparable to your invention. This gives you insight on how people might use your product.

User Scenarios

Use the following template to record your observations of people using a product similar to yours.

Install
What are the steps someone goes through to install or assemble the product when they first receive it?

Turn on and Use
What steps does someone go through to turn on, start, or use the product?

Turn off
What steps does someone use to turn off, put away, uninstall, or disassemble the product?

Tools
What specific tools are needed to install, assemble, use, uninstall, or disassemble the product?

After observing and interviewing at least ten people, summarize the results. You might be surprised how some use your prototype differently than expected or intended. These insights are very useful and can lead to new features, or, possibly, spin-off products and accessories.

These observations help ensure your product is familiar enough to increase the probability of product acceptance. A good strategy is to design your invention with the generally accepted look and feel of a known product and then integrate your innovation to add value and uniqueness. This improves your chance for success in the market.

Prototype Requirements

Before visiting a prototype maker, it's important to specify what you want built. Listing your requirements for the prototype saves time and money, and improves the quality.

The first step is to translate your idea into guidelines a designer can understand. To explain your idea, write a Prototype Requirements document.

Prototype Requirements are a detailed description of how your prototype should look, feel, and function. Prototype Requirements, along with drawings and diagrams, provide clarity and increases the chance a designer creates the prototype as you intended, rather than trying to read your mind. Prototype Requirements are typically written with a word processor and can be as short as one or two pages.

A Prototype Requirements document describes:

- Features
- Functionality
- Appearance
- Performance levels
- Quality and reliability levels
- User's environment
- Packaging and labeling needs
- Certification and regulation specifications
- Cost levels
- Forecast of units to manufacture
- Timeline for shipment

Sources of requirements come from:

- **Customer problems, needs, and wants** – Derived from surveys, interviews, and market trends.
- **Customer price sensitivity** – Derived from surveys and interviews to determine the quality of the parts used.
- **Competitive advantages** – Derived from competitive research to determine what features and functionality can overcome the competition.
- **Innovation** – Derived from your imagination.

I suggest creating a Prototype Requirements document with the following steps:

- List each of the customer's problems, needs, and wants.
- Describe the features and functions for each problem, need, and want.
- Modify and enhance features and functions based on your innovation, pricing, quality, style, positioning, and product life.
- Prioritize the list based on saleable features and functions customers are willing buy.
- Write the list of features and functions into the language of a requirements document (see below).
- Select the highest priority requirements based on saleable features, complexity, budget, and timing.
- Include drawings and pictures for clarification.

The requirements document must be clear and straightforward. For instance, "The product shall have the ability to …" or "The product must operate under the following conditions: …" Use bulleted or numbered lists and group similar parameters.

An example of requirements includes:

- Overall dimensions must be 3.25" long, 1.5" wide, and 1.25" thick.
- The outer casing must be made of a clear plastic.
- There must be four pushbutton switches located on the base and labeled: Off, High, Medium, and Low.
- The prototype must not crack or break apart when dropped onto a concrete floor from a height of three feet.

Prototype Development

There are a number of prototype methods for turning your idea into a visual or functional model. Prototype development typically goes through a number of cycles. So start with an inexpensive model for quick feedback to see if you're heading in the right direction.

If your product is a physical object and you want to evaluate visual appeal, start with a foam, wood, or clay model. Then, as you gather more feedback, create a plastic model. Keep evolving the prototype until you receive good responses from at least 80% of the evaluators.

Finding a Prototype Maker

If you do not have the technical know-how to make a prototype, contact a mechanical engineer, industrial engineer, electronic engineer, software engineer, programmer, or prototype company (depending on your product type). It's best to find an engineer who uses leading computer aided design (CAD) software such as SolidWorks or Pro/ENGINEER. If you created drawings using Google SketchUp, the engineer will likely convert the drawings into their preferred CAD software format.

To find a prototype maker, talk to business and technical contacts in your community for recommendations. Another resource is local inventor groups. Search the Internet using the term ["inventor groups"]. In addition, search for a prototype company using the Yellow Pages under the heading of Prototype or Product Developing. Search the Internet using terms ["your product type" and "prototype maker"] or ["your product type" and "designer"]. An example of a good engineering and prototype company is Product Development Resource (www.newpdr.com).

For an inexpensive place to start, contact local university engineering departments and ask if they design and build prototypes. Do not disclose the idea at first; rather, inquire if they'd be willing to help with designs and prototypes.

Another place to find technical talent is through local chapters of major organizations such as:

- Institute of Electronic and Electrical Engineers (www.ieee.org)
- American Electronics Association (www.aeanet.org)
- American Society of Mechanical Engineers (www.asme.org)
- Society of Manufacturing Engineers (www.sme.org)
- Software and Information Industry Association (www.siia.net)

Steps to Create a Prototype

There are two approaches in working with companies to build a physical prototype. One is to work with an engineer who creates a computer aided design (CAD) model. Then, take the CAD files to a prototype maker who builds the physical prototype.

The other method is to work with a company with both engineering and prototype capabilities. This is usually the better way to proceed.

The following are the general steps to create a prototype:

- Search for an industrial designer, engineer, or prototype company who has experience designing your type of product.

- Have them sign a non-disclosure agreement (see Appendix G for a sample).

- Provide your Prototype Requirements and sketches and request a price quote. When they give you the quote, don't be afraid to ask questions and clarify anything you don't understand. Often a deposit of 50% is required to begin the project.

- Typically, the first design step is to create a 3D Concept Model. The Concept Model is the overall shape and look of the prototype. You are able to view on the computer a three-dimensional image with the ability to rotate and move parts around on the screen. Discuss any changes you would like with the engineer.

- Once you approve the Concept Design, the next step is an Engineering Design. An Engineering Design is the detailed design of all parts, mechanisms, and assemblies. The engineer specifies the exact dimensions, materials, and colors. You can view the Engineering Design just as you did the Concept Design but this 3D CAD image is more detailed. Ask the designer to print an "actual size" drawing so you have a better feel of the actual size and shape of your prototype.

- Once you approve the Engineering Design, the next step is a physical prototype. If the prototype is made of plastic, the company typically emails the CAD files to a rapid prototype maker. CAD files are converted to stereolithography (STL) files. STL files contain the x, y, and z coordinates to describe the object. The rapid prototype maker produces the parts and ships them back to your designer. The designer assembles the parts and possibly sands and paints to meet your requirements.

Note: If your prototype is produced on a computerized milling machine, then a computer-aided manufacturing (CAM) design file is needed. A CAM file contains the x, y, and z coordinates to shape your prototype.

You don't need to know everything about the technology behind the prototype process, but it's good to be informed. The following section explains prototyping in more detail.

Physical Objects

A physical prototype is needed to evaluate a product's mechanical functionality and visual appeal. Examples include toys, tools, jewelry, and appliances.

Physical prototypes are created by hand tools, machine tools, and rapid prototyping techniques. They're made by either removing material (e.g., drilling), or adding material (e.g., pouring a mold).

You create a physical prototype by simply shaping an object by hand with tools (e.g., sawing, grinding, drilling, and milling). Start with a block of foam, wood, plastic, or metal and remove material until it acquires the desired look and feel.

An elaborate method for shaping an object involves using a computer-controlled milling machine. Known as Computer Numerical Control (CNC), the machine automatically shapes an object based on a computer-aided design or set of instructions. Use CNC when you need high accuracy for parts such as gears. A prototype project created by CNC can take two to three weeks, depending on its complexity.

If your prototype is metal, you have a number of options. A metal prototype may be made by casting, compacting, forging, or extrusion. The best method depends on the design and materials.

Making a Simple Mold

You can make simple molds using clay, silicon, and resin:

- Shape your object in clay and let it harden.
- Suspend the clay object in a container with string or place it on a support.
- Pour liquid silicon into the container to cover half of the object. Let the first half of the silicon harden. (Curing time varies but can be two to four hours.)
- Pour in additional silicon until the second half is covered. Let the second half of silicon harden.
- You now have two halves of a mold. Open the mold and remove the original clay object.
- Put the empty two halves of the silicon mold together and wrap it with rubber bands.
- Cut a small hole at the top and pour plastic resin into the mold. When the resin hardens, you have a prototype.

Rapid Prototyping Technologies

Before advances in computers and materials, a complex prototype could take weeks or months to build. Today, the most technically advanced method to create a prototype is known as Rapid Prototyping (RP). With an RP machine, a prototype can be produced in a matter of hours.

RP was invented in 1988 with the introduction of Stereolithography by 3D Systems of Valencia, California. Rapid Prototyping machines literally create an object out of liquid resin, powder, or sheets of laminated paper. Costs for this process depend on the size and complexity of the object. A small prototype can start at $250, but costs increase for size, complexity, and painting or silk screening.

In general, RP is useful for showing a model to a focus group or trade representative. It also provides an engineering proof of concept. The selection of one method over another depends on your need for ruggedness, flexibility, or just the look and feel.

The following are the leading methods used in Rapid Prototyping:

- **Stereolithography Apparatus** (SLA) – This is a very popular method to create prototypes. The process is based on the use of a photopolymer liquid resin that solidifies when exposed to ultraviolet light. A software program transfers the designer's 3D CAD model into an electronic file for stereolithography machines ("STL" format), composing the information into thin cross-sections or layers. A laser then traces each layer onto the surface of a vat of photopolymer resin, building the part in repeated layers until a solid replica of the original CAD model is completed. SLA is one of the least expensive rapid prototyping methods and can be produced quickly. See 3D Systems for more about SLA (www.3dsystems.com).

- **Selective Laser Sintering** (SLS) – This method creates a solid 3D object, layer by layer, from plastic, metal, or ceramic powders by "sintering" (combine with heat), using a carbon-dioxide laser. The versatility of SLS technology allows for a broader range of advanced rapid prototyping and manufacturing applications. SLS costs more than SLA, but is stronger, more durable, heat resistant, and chemical resistant.

- **Fused Deposition Modeling** (FDM) – This method creates successive cross-sections of a 3D object from the bottom on up. Similar to a hot glue gun, plastic is extruded through the tip of the FDM machine. The FDM head moves along both the x- and y-axis across a foundation and deposits a layer of material. (Imagine making a drip castle on the beach.) This process continues until all layers of the part are completed. FDM is durable and produces a smooth surface like SLA. See Stratasys for more about FDM (www.stratasys.com).

- **Laminated Object Manufacturing** (LOM) – This method creates a 3D object from layers of special paper with a polyethylene coating on the backside. Paper is fed through the machine with the aid of small rollers. As the paper passes through, steam is used to heat the paper's coating so each new layer adheres to the previous one. A carbon-dioxide laser then traces, or etches, the outline of the cross-sectional pattern into the top layer of paper. Once the laser has finished etching the pattern, it burns a border into the paper containing the etched pattern. This enables the part to stay intact as each new layer is created. Since LOM parts are made from paper, humidity and temperature affect the structure. Therefore, request lacquer be added as a protective measure. Overall, LOM is very useful for creating large parts quickly, but not as accurate as SLA.

- **3D Printing** – This method creates a 3D object using a powder material. A type of ink-jet printing head selectively deposits, or prints, a binder fluid to fuse powder in designated areas layer by layer. For each layer, the platform is lowered, powder is added and leveled, and the process repeated. Typical layer thickness is on the order of 0.1 mm. This process is very fast, and produces parts with a slightly grainy surface. The finished part can be filled and coated with special types of resin, urethane, glue, or wax to improve its strength and durability. For more information about 3D Printing, see Z Corporation (www.zcorp.com).

Instead of a physical model, prototypes can also be demonstrated through computer animation. Animation methods are especially useful as an alternative to creating complex and expensive physical prototypes. Animation software uses your 3D CAD designs to create virtual prototypes. Instead of handing someone an object to examine, you provide a DVD or email links to your website to view the prototype online.

Electronic Devices

Electronic prototypes are used to test the functionality of your electronic invention. They don't have to look pretty; they just need to function according to specifications.

An electronic engineer can design a circuit on paper or with a computer design tool. Once the design is created, electronic parts are laid out and connected to form a circuit. Here are the major methods for assembling an electronic prototype:

- **Breadboards** – A board with rows and columns of connections allowing circuits to be designed and tested. They're best for simple designs of low-frequency analog or digital circuits.

- **Wirewrap** – A method of making circuit connections by wrapping wire from the metal lead of one part to another. This is a quick and easy method to create reliable connections.

- **Perfboards** – A fiberglass board with a grid of pre-drilled holes to house electronic parts. The electronic parts are placed onto the board with their metal leads fed through the holes. The leads are either soldered or twisted together with other parts. The connections are not always reliable but may be fine for a small project.

- **Printed circuit boards** – A method of making circuit connections by etching a copper diagram on a fiberglass board. This method uses chemicals to form the printed circuit board (PCB). Holes are drilled along the copper lines to place the electronic parts. The parts are positioned on the board and soldered in place. This method is more costly and used as a refining step after a breadboard, wirewrap, or perfboard prototype.

Start with a breadboard or wirewrap prototype to prove the function of the circuit design. Certain high-frequency circuits do not work well on a breadboard. Therefore, you need to build the prototype from a printed circuit board.

You can also design and demonstrate an electronic prototype with simulated circuit design software. The software helps you layout the design and test it with simulated inputs and outputs. This method might provide enough information for evaluators to offer feedback. Once you've proven a design works, develop a circuit and continue testing it under various conditions similar to the final product.

Software Products and Websites

There are two primary reasons to prototype software and websites. One is to evaluate visual appeal and the other is to test functionality. The visual element is what users see and interact with (e.g., clicking buttons, choosing items from a list). The functional element is how the software works behind the scenes (e.g., database processing, bill paying).

Two prototyping methods capture the visual aspect of software and websites: paper sketches and screens. Paper sketches are best for early designs for feedback on content and where objects are placed. Interactive screens work best for mature prototypes.

Paper sketches are simply sheets of paper with handwritten objects to show the interface to potential users. Arrange sketches on several pages so they mimic the way a user would normally interact with the software or website. Paper sketches give evaluators the sense the design is not set and may be easily changed. This allows them to offer creative solutions.

Keep in mind, using screen layouts, evaluators tend to respond as if the design is less likely to change. As a result, they tend to offer not as much feedback.

As the design matures, create screen designs using visual tools such as Microsoft VisualBasic or Adobe Dreamweaver. These tools allow visual objects to be created and quickly placed on-screen for evaluation.

The functional evaluation of software and websites is performed in steps. The first step involves drawing flowcharts, diagrams, or outlines to show the work process. This is done on a whiteboard, paper, or computer using Word, Excel, or other organizing software. Source code is developed in tandem with the visual elements. Test cases are created to examine the results of various scenarios.

Chapter 7:
Get Feedback on Your Prototype

A tool is but the extension of a man's hand, and a machine is but a complex tool. And he that invents a machine augments the power of a man and the well-being of mankind.

Henry Beecher

Topics in this Chapter:

- Prototype Interview Plan
- Recruit Attendees
- Conduct Interviews
- Feedback Survey
- Prototype Summary

With a prototype in hand, it's time to gather feedback. You'll want to make sure your prototype solves a problem or satisfies a need or want, and does it better than comparable products in the market. Feedback lets you know what potential customers look for when buying your type of product. At this point, you need to validate features and functionality, uncover possible product shortcomings, and discover areas for improvement.

In addition, you want to learn what motivates customer purchases. This information helps you with product and later with marketing strategies.

To obtain feedback, the best method is interviewing people either individually or in a small group. Keep in mind an interview is not necessarily a one-time event. You may conduct an interview, refine the prototype, and then perform another series of interviews for fine-tuning. Your interviews can be conducted as formal focus groups or with relatively informal individual or small groups.

A focus group interview typically involves a script designed in advance by a professional researcher. The focus group interview, conducted by a professional moderator, takes place behind a one-way mirror so you may observe the dynamics. Focus groups are also videotaped for later analysis.

In the past, when I conducted focus groups, I took my engineers to watch. Many times, focus group members would use the prototype differently than as intended. The engineer said something like, "They are using the prototype wrong." In reality, people sometimes prefer to use products differently than as intended. The key is to design products the way people currently perform a task.

You can perform the interviewing yourself or hire a marketing consultant or agency to create a plan, recruit attendees, and lead the discussion. An agency might charge as much as five to ten thousand dollars to organize and conduct a focus group.

To gather feedback, use the following steps:

- Create an interview plan
- Recruit candidates
- Conduct interviews
- Summarize the feedback

Prototype Interview Plan

To guide the process of obtaining prototype feedback, start by creating a simple plan. A *prototype interview plan* outlines your: Goals, objectives, who you want to interview, your budget, questions to ask, and how you'll conduct the meetings. The entire plan can be as short as one or two pages. Use the following template as a guide.

Recruit Attendees

Recruit people who have some experience with the type of product you're creating. For example, if your product is a new gardening tool, recruit people who use gardening tools as either hobbyists or professionals, depending on your target market.

Recruit from a variety of sources. Consider using people who have previously participated in one of your surveys. Tap those who currently use a product you hope to replace or improve. Some of these people might be part of a special interest group with meetings which focus on your product type. Visit these groups to ask if they are open to evaluating your product at a later time.

Prototype Interview Plan

Goals and Objectives

Type of feedback you seek (e.g., ease of use, functionality, industrial design, does your idea solve a problem).

Participant Profile

Profile of participants you want to evaluate your prototype (e.g., age, income level, job title).

Participant Experience

Level of experience an evaluator should have (e.g., uses similar product daily for at least five years).

Group Size

Number of groups and size of each (e.g., one-on-one, six groups of five people each).

Recruitment

Methods and places you'll look for people (e.g., user groups, club members, unions).

Budget

The amount you can spend for interviewing (e.g., costs of meeting room, travel, interviewee compensation such as cash or free lunch).

Meetings

The meeting place and duration of each meeting (e.g., office conference room for two hours).

Materials

Materials needed (e.g., prototypes, audio recorder, video recorder, white board, paper, pencils, refreshments).

Questions

The questions you'll ask (e.g., What's important when choosing this type of product?).

If your idea is a common household product, talk with friends, relatives, neighbors, and other associates. Attend trade shows or conferences to talk with buyers and sellers. If recruiting is difficult, use a marketing company specializing in interviews or focus groups, to recruit for you. They usually have a database of people available for product interviews.

How many people should be interviewed? Typically, a minimum sample size of 30 is preferred. In general, the greater and more diverse the people you talk with, the better. Recruit from each of your possible market segments to discover which segment is most interested.

Determine an incentive for luring someone to the meeting. People generally want something in return for their time. Often a cash incentive is effective, but lunch, dinner, or snacks also work. Before you officially start recruiting, ask what would persuade them to participate.

I've held successful focus groups over lunchtime in which people willingly accepted a sandwich, drink, and cookies, in return for providing feedback.

If you suspect your discussions may give away secrets, ask people to sign a non-disclosure agreement (NDA). The NDA provides limited protection against people disclosing confidential information to others or building your invention themselves. You can find NDA forms on the Internet or you use the sample in Appendix G. Ask an attorney to review an NDA to make sure it suits your needs.

Conduct Interviews

To prepare for interviews, you need to develop questions with the intention to collect useful feedback. Ask both general questions related to their needs and wants, and questions specifically about your prototype.

Be open to negative feedback. Do not argue or try to defend yourself. If evaluators don't like your prototype, ask for the underlying reasons.

You may interview people one-on-one or in small groups. In a group setting, some people unintentionally dominate and suppress others. Make sure everyone is heard by requesting feedback from those who have not had a chance to contribute.

The meeting place can be a conference room, home, or outdoors. The environment should be comfortable and in a place where your product type is normally used. At the beginning of your interview, thank the attendees for participating and ask them to briefly identify themselves. Reinforce you are not selling anything, but conducting research for a new product idea.

It's helpful to document the session with audio or video equipment, so let attendees know they're being recorded and the recordings are for research purposes only.

Tell them the type of product type you are developing. Prior to showing the prototype, ask the following type of questions and record their answers:

- What is your experience with this type of product?
- If there is one thing you wish your current product could do better, what would it be?
- When using the product, is it _____ (fast enough, easy to use, small enough, efficient, cost effective)?
- When using the product, does it _____ (break down often, wear out, leak, crash often, produce the wrong results, or act unreliably)?
- What features and benefits do you look for when choosing this type of product?
- What is more important to you: product quality, functionality, customer service, warranty, or price?
- What would it take for you to switch to a new product?

When asking questions:

- Do not tell them the typical problem your prototype solves, let them tell you *their* problems.
- Do not tell how great your prototype is, let them tell you if it is.
- Do not settle for yes or no answers. Delve into why they answered the way they did.

Next, reveal your prototype. Demonstrate its functions and point out features. Let attendees examine and use it. Ask the following questions:

- How well do you think the invention solves your problem or satisfies your needs and wants?
- Do you think this is an improvement over existing products?
- What do you think are the key advantages this provides over other products?
- How do you like the colors, shapes, functions, etc.?
- What is the maximum you would spend on the finished product?

Note: Don't ask, "What's a fair price?" Pricing is difficult for most people to determine. Asking for the "maximum price" is often a more effective way to uncover pricing.

Watching someone use your prototype provides valuable information. Have evaluators perform a task scenario and see how well they do it. For example, if your product is a new gardening tool to prune flowers, ask them to perform this task and notice if they operated the tool with ease and comfort as intended.

Prototype Evaluation Survey Sample

Your opinions are very much appreciated. Please answer the following questions.

1. Do you have a need or want related to the product type mentioned?
   ❑ Always ❑ Most of the time ❑ Sometimes ❑ Rarely ❑ Never

2. How well do you think the finished product will meet your needs?
   ❑ Excellent ❑ Very Good ❑ Somewhat ❑ Poor ❑ Not at all

3. If this product was available, and the price was reasonable, would you likely make a purchase for yourself or as a gift? You are not under any obligation to do so.
   ❑ Definitely ❑ Very likely ❑ Somewhat ❑ Unlikely ❑ Not at all

4. If available, would you recommend this product to someone else?
   ❑ Definitely ❑ Very likely ❑ Somewhat ❑ Unlikely ❑ Not at all

What do you like about the product?

What do you dislike about the product?

Please provide some suggestions for improvement:

Thank you for your time!

Feedback Survey

At the end of the interview, ask attendees to fill out a brief survey. Remember to reinforce the fact their feedback is valuable and kept private. The answers you receive help shape your product. In addition, the information provides a foundation for your marketing activities.

If a majority of people you talk with are satisfied with their existing product, and your product idea offers no significant advantages, you probably want to re-evaluate your invention. On the other hand, you may uncover a significant percentage of people who are either dissatisfied with their current product or are looking for something better. If this is the case, you are on to something exciting.

Prototype Feedback Results

At the end of each meeting, summarize the discussions and surveys.

Summary

Demographics of people surveyed:

Problems, needs, and wants solved by your prototype:

What they liked about the prototype:

What they did not like about the prototype:

How the prototype was used differently than expected:

Suggestions given:

Scores

Number of people surveyed:

Number of surveys with top scores:

Percentage of surveys with top scores:

Prototype Summary

Prototype development is an important step in the invention process. A prototype helps you prove functionality, gather feedback, and generate excitement.

Before you create a prototype, it's important to specify what you want built. To have a meeting-of-the-minds with a prototype maker, create a Prototype Requirements document. This document helps you save time and money, and improves quality.

To find a company to build your prototype, talk to business and technical contacts in your community for recommendations. In addition, use an internet search engine with terms ["your product type" and "prototype maker"] or ["your product type" and "manufacturer "].

Contact companies and ask if they have experience building prototypes related to your invention. Send them your requirements and ask for a quote on the cost to produce a prototype. It's also a good idea to ask them to sign a non-disclosure agreement before you send the requirements. Of the quotes within your budget, ask to meet the designer and tour the facility.

Select the company who you think is easiest to work with and has the required expertise. Negotiate the price and time to finish the prototype. When the prototype is made, make sure it conforms to your requirements before you sign off and pay the invoice. If there are flaws, ask to have them corrected.

If you plan to self-market your invention, prototype feedback helps you determine the proper features and functionality before moving into the manufacturing stage. Any changes during production are very costly, so you need to uncover any shortcomings early with your prototype.

When you intend to sell or license your invention, work out all the bugs before showing your prototype to a company. By gathering feedback from potential end-users and then making refinements, you reduce the chance of being rejected by a company.

In the next chapter, learn the profitable process to sell or license your invention. Even if you have your mind set on self-marketing, the next chapter shows you tips and tricks to market research, contacting companies, legal terms, and negotiating.

PART THREE –
SELL OR LICENSE FOR ROYALTIES

That's an amazing invention, but who would ever want to use one of them?

President Rutherford Hayes
(Referring to the telephone invented by Alexander Graham Bell)

Chapter 8:
How to Sell or License Your Patent

I find out what the world needs, then I proceed to invent. My main purpose in life is to make money so that I can afford to go on creating more inventions.

Thomas Edison

Topics in this Chapter:

- Licensing Definition
- Selling Definition
- Sell Your Patent at Auction
- Sell to a Patent Aggregator
- Sell Through a Patent Broker, Not a Submission Company
- Why You Shouldn't Advertise an Invention for Sale or License
- Patent Value
- The 7-Step Process
- What Do Companies Want?

Selling or licensing involves an exchange of intellectual property for compensation. Intellectual property to sell or license can take the form of patents, trademarks, copyrights, or trade secrets.

Licensing Definition

What is licensing as it relates to inventions? Licensing is giving a company permission to manufacture, distribute, and sell a product based on your patent. In exchange, you'll receive payments, known as royalties. When licensing, you are essentially "renting" your intellectual property. You are the **licensor** and the company is the **licensee**. The legal document to provide a company the rights to license your invention is a License Agreement.

Selling Definition

Selling an invention is legally defined as an "assignment." You assign your intellectual property to a company in exchange for compensation. The compensation can be a lump sum payment or a series of payments (monthly or quarterly over a fixed number of years). In the United States, assignment of a patent is governed by statute, 35 U.S.C. § 261.

The legal documents involved in selling your patent are a "Patent Purchase Agreement" and "Assignment Agreement." The Patent Purchase Agreement covers the business and legal terms including the parties involved, the patent being assigned, purchase price, and payment details. Once the Patent Purchase Agreement is signed and monies are paid, then an Assignment Agreement is signed to transfer of rights from the inventor to the buyer.

The Assignment Agreement must be filed with the Patent Office within three months of signing. Keep in mind, once you sell the invention, you no longer have any rights to the intellectual property.

As an illustration, think of the process of selling your car. You draft a document that says you are selling your used 2009 Ford Truck to John Smith for $10,000 (purchase agreement). When Mr. Smith gives you the money and you hand over the keys, you then sign over the Vehicle Title (assignment).

If you have the choice between a lump sum and a series of payments (such as a monthly payment for two years), compare the total series of payments to a safe investment such as a Certificate of Deposit. If the lump sum, when invested, pays more than the total series of payments, then take the lump sum. (Be sure to check with a financial advisor for the tax consequences related to your tax bracket.) In general, it's better to receive a lump sum payment in case the company files for bankruptcy or has other litigation issues. If a series of payments are preferred, ask to establish an escrow account (third party to hold and distribute the payments).

Sell Your Patent at Auction

Auctions offer a venue to sell your patent outright. Certain companies specialize in auctioning intellectual property. Patents often sell for $100,000 to $1 million but also as little as $10,000.

Ocean Tomo (www.oceantomo.com) operates an auction to sell patents, trademarks, and internet domain names. They charge $1,000 to list patents for auction. When a patent is sold, Ocean Tomo receives a 15% commission from the seller and 10% from the buyer. Ocean Tomo focuses on high-technology patents in the areas of computers, electronics, telecommunications, and information systems.

IpAuctions, Inc. (www.ipauctions.com) auctions patents, trademarks, copyrights, databases, software, and internet domain names. They charge $250 to list patents for auction. When a sale is made, their commission ranges from 7.5% to 20% for the seller. There is no buyer's fee.

I have not personally participated in a patent auction, but if this looks like an option for you, contact these companies for more information.

Sell to a Patent Aggregator

A patent aggregator is a company that buys or develops several patents to use at a later time. The company accumulates patents for the purpose of:

- Creating a portfolio of technology for internal use (turn into products or processes, and to create competitive advantages).
- Creating a portfolio of technology to sell or license.
- Enforcing through lawsuits (does not create products).

A number of large international organizations pool their patents into patent holding companies for internal development and commercialization. They develop their own inventions and buy patents from outside inventors and entrepreneurs. Over time, patents that are not part of their core business, are sold or licensed.

Another type of aggregator does not develop their patents into products, but rather looks for companies infringing on their patents and sues for damages. They develop their own inventions as well as buy patents from companies, entrepreneurs, and inventors. Some view this type of patent aggregator (nicknamed "patent troll") as a negative influence on the market. A notable case regarding email technology involved NTP, Inc. (the aggregator) versus Research in Motion (RIM, maker of BlackBerry mobile phones). After six years, the case settled out of court with RIM paying NTP over $612 million.

In some instances, if an inventor's patent is being infringed and can't afford a legal defense, a patent aggregator buys the patent for a lump sum, or an amount plus a percentage of any winnings from litigation.

An example of a large patent aggregator is Intellectual Ventures (www.intellectualventures.com). The company was founded by Nathan Myhrvold, the former Chief Technology Officer of Microsoft Corporation.

To see if your patent is attractive to a patent aggregator, find companies by searching the web with the keywords "patent troll," "patent aggregator," "patent dealer," or "patent holding company."

Sell Through a Patent Broker, *Not* a Submission Company

Be aware of the invention help companies that claim they will submit your invention into the industry. These companies are only interested in the fees they charge you. First, they charge a $600 to $1000 fee for a "market study." The market study they perform is worthless. Then they tell you the market results were positive and you should move forward. To take the next step, they charge an additional $10,000 to $15,000. These invention companies take your money and you'll receive nothing in return.

A better solution is to sell your patented invention through a patent broker. A patent broker brings sellers and buyers together. Many patent brokers focus on technology-based inventions. Tynax (www.tynax.com) and iPotential (www.ipotential.com) are examples of patent brokers. To give you an idea of the large scale of activity, iPotential has transacted over $265 million worth of patents from 2003 to 2008.

A patent holder lists an invention for sale on a broker's website (most offer a free listing). According to Tynax CEO, David Smith, "We profile the buyer's areas of interest, and then our system matches their needs with listings available. We email the buyer with an alert that a new listing is available matching their needs. We also post the listing in the buyer's console. The buyer does not see the patent numbers at this stage, but is revealed after an agreement is made with the buyer and the seller."

Tynax helps the inventor present to a buyer and negotiate terms. David Smith continues, "Patent brokers charge anywhere between 20% - 40% of the total price. Tynax charges 25%. Tynax represents either the buyer or the seller, as we believe we cannot effectively represent both sides in a single transaction."

To find a patent broker suitable for your invention, use the search terms "patent broker," "patent exchange," and "technology scouting companies."

Why You Shouldn't Advertise an Invention for Sale or License

In June, 2009, I performed a survey to understand if listing an invention for sale on an invention website is worthwhile. There were 23 people who said they listed their invention for sale on an invention website, and six people on their own website. As a result, no one was able to sell or license their invention. I'm not surprised.

Product companies, for the most part, are not searching inventor websites looking for new inventions. People within these companies are busy doing their day-to-day work. When they venture out looking for new ideas and trends, they do so within their industry.

For example, a power tool maker researches new ideas by attending power tool trade shows and conventions. They also spend time reading power tool magazines and websites. They are not likely to visit invention websites.

To sell or license your invention, you need to directly contact the companies who manufacture and market your type of product. For the power tool example, you would contact Skil, Bosch, Black & Decker, and others. Don't wait for companies to contact you, be proactive.

Patent Value

Your patent is valuable to you and to companies interested in acquiring the invention. However, when you want to sell your patent, how do you determine its worth?

While there are a number of methods to estimate the value of a patent, there is no universally agreed-upon valuation process. Attorneys and financial analysts will use a method they are trained and comfortable with.

The more information you gather to back up your assertion of value, the better the chance of receiving the amount you're seeking.

In general:

Patent Value = Economic Value - Legal Risk

Economic Value

To determine Economic Value, current market conditions and future trends are taken into consideration. Methods to determine Economic Value include:

Profit Analysis – A method to determine economic value is from profit earned over the life of the patent. The net present value (NPV) formula is a common method to calculate current value based on future revenue, costs, and expenses.

In more detail:

- **Revenue** – The estimated revenue based on product selling price and forecast of quantities sold.

- **Cost of Goods** – The estimated unit cost of parts, assembly, and packaging. Keep in mind, manufacturing costs per unit are reduced as quantities increase.

- **Development Expense** – The estimated expense of resources to design, develop, and manufacture the product.

- **Marketing and Sales Expense** – The estimated expense of resources to create marketing and sales plans and expenditures of the marketing and sales campaigns.

Return on Investment – When a company estimates a patent is worth a certain value, they want to buy the patent at an amount to generate a return on investment. Return on Investment (ROI) is a measure of financial gain versus the amount invested over a time period. In this case, financial gain is profit over time. The investment includes the cost of the patent, development, marketing, sales, production, administrative, salary, and office expenses.

The following is a simple ROI formula:

$$ROI = \frac{Gain - Investment}{Investment}$$

Every company's return on investment needs are different and vary depending on economic conditions. While one company may require a 10% ROI to proceed, another may seek 25%.

Replacement Product Value – If your invention is intended to replace a product in the market, use current sales trends as a means to estimate your patent's value. For example, the DVD replaced the VCR as the preferred video player. DVD players were introduced in 1996 and outsold VCRs just five years later.

To estimate your patent's value, research the current size and trends of the market and make assumptions of market share captured over the life of the patent.

For example, in the first year a new tool is introduced, the market size is $100 million and the product captures 5% of the market. In year two, market share is

10% of a $110 million market, and so on. To be more convincing, create two set of estimates with conservative and aggressive assumptions of future market size and market share acquired.

You can search for market data with keywords "market size" or "product sales" along with the product type you plan to replace. Another source of data is the reference book "Market Share Reporter" published by Gale Research.

Legal Risk

An interested company reviews your patent in terms of legal risk. The greater the probability of legal risk, the lower the value of a patent. The following are potential legal risks:

- **Circumvent** – Would it be easy for a competing company to design around the patent?

- **Duration** – What are the number of years remaining on a granted patent?

- **Grant** – Has the patent been granted? If not, what is the likelihood of receiving a grant?

- **Infringement** – What is the likelihood of infringement and resulting cost of litigation? Litigation costs can be associated with filing a suit against an infringer, or being the defendant of infringement.

- **Invalidation** – Even though a patent is granted by a patent office, the patent can be challenged in court by a competing company. What is the possibility the patent could be invalidated?

- **Product Liability** – What is the likelihood of being sued for product liability?

To come up with a numerical approximation of the legal risk, there are a number of mathematical equations based on probability functions.

Georgia Pacific Factors

A prominent patent infringement lawsuit of Georgia Pacific Corporation versus United States Plywood Champion Paper, set a precedent on valuing a patent. While not all valuation experts agree the Georgia Pacific case provides the best patent value guidance, the determining factors are used by many attorneys.

The case provided 15 factors to determine a financial award. The 15 factors (later known as the Georgia Pacific Factors) can be grouped into categories of profitability analysis, market factors, technical, and reasonable royalty rates. When selling your patent, an interested company's legal and financial analysts are likely to estimate a value based on the Georgia Pacific Factors. To learn the details of the case, search for "Georgia Pacific Factors."

Economic Uncertainties

There are associated risks due to uncertainties in the future. Companies may seek to reduce the value of your patent by pointing out the unknowns. Reduce uncertainty by obtaining reports or opinions from expert sources related to your product. In general, economic risks for your patent may include:

- **Competition** – The availability of competing products and likely response of the competition to try to design around the patent.
- **Technology** – The probability of new technology on the horizon to obsolete the patent.
- **Regulation** – The probability of government passing legislation banning the manufacture and use of the product category.

Strategic Value

You can increase the perceived value by bringing to a company's attention the additional strategic benefits your patent provides. Value is more than just profit when a patent becomes part of a larger strategic vision. Companies acquire patents to:

- Gain control of a market
- Enter a new market faster
- Fend off competition
- Increase company valuation
- Prevent a patent troll from acquiring the patent
- Bundle to license a total solution to other companies

Contact a Patent Valuation Expert

To help determine patent value, there are valuation experts who can crunch the numbers for you. If you're about to enter into negotiations, it is wise to have a professional valuation performed. The following are valuation resources:

- Accounting experts with Accredited in Business Valuation (ABV) credentials. Search for service providers at the American Institute of Certified Public Accountants website (www.aicpa.org > Consumer Information > Find CPA).
- Licensing Executives Society (www.les.org > Service Directory > search members for "valuation opinions").
- Ocean Tomo (www.oceantomo.com > click on Valuation).

IPscore from EPO

To determine patent value yourself, the European Patent Office offers a free software tool called IPscore. Originally developed by the Danish Patent and Trademark Office to reduce the number of valueless patent applications, IPscore produces charts and diagrams based on a number of assumptions.

To download the free IPscore software and user manual, go to the European Patent Office website (www.epo.org > Search > IPscore). For a direct link to IPscore, visit my website (www.ProductCoach.com) and click on Resource Links. (By the way, one of the computer requirements to running IPscore is having Microsoft Access installed.)

The 7-Step Process

Before approaching a company to license or sell your patent, you'll need to do some homework. Think from the company's point of view. They are flooded with requests and don't have time to perform assessments on every product idea they receive.

When a company takes on an invention, they invest in development, manufacturing, marketing, and sales. Therefore, you must first prove to the company the unique benefits your invention offers. Companies want to see marketability test results, manufacturing cost estimates, and profit potential. In most cases, your product idea must be patented or patent pending before a company even talks with you.

To sell or license your invention, follow these steps:

1. **Market Evaluation** – Perform research to confirm marketability. Search for competition to uncover advantages in your design. Perform a basic patent search (www.google.com/patents) for similar patents. Confirm that your invention offers a number of clear benefits to the end-user. Estimate selling price, expenses and calculate a profit potential. If the research in this step is positive, you may be on to something exciting.

2. **Concept Evaluation** – Create a concept survey and obtain feedback on your product idea. Feedback helps you tailor your invention to the needs and wants of your market. If at least 80% of the people surveyed strongly agree the need exists and your product idea is a useful solution, you are on the right track.

3. **Prototype Evaluation** – Create a working prototype and obtain feedback to confirm the usefulness, benefits, and features. If the prototype is expensive to make, have an artist create detailed drawings or create a video simulation. If at least 80% of the people surveyed strongly agree your prototype is superior to existing solutions, you likely have a marketable invention.

4. **Patent Filing** – File a provisional patent application which allows one year of protection to determine marketability and seek a deal with a company. If you filed a utility or design patent, you can approach companies while you wait for the notice of allowance.

5. **Product Proposal** – Create a Product Proposal document from a business perspective to stimulate the interest of companies. Similar to a sell sheet but more convincing, the Product Proposal offers detailed market data to provide credibility.

6. **Company Search** – Search retail stores and the Internet for names of manufactures who market to the same target customer. Make a personal contact with each company and send an introductory letter and Product Proposal.

7. **Negotiate Deal** – Interested companies evaluate your invention based on product line fit, financial return, manufacturing, and distribution. Prepare and negotiate terms such as royalties, advances, territory, field of use, etc. When you and the company agree to the terms have them create a licensing agreement and review it with an attorney. After any edits are made to the licensing agreement, sign it, carry out the terms, and receive compensation.

What Do Companies Want?

Keep in mind, companies constantly need new products to stay in business. New products increase revenue and profit, provide access to new markets, out-perform their competition, and help retain existing customers.

Companies look for a fit with their product line in terms of functionality, target market, design, quality, and profitability. Your product might not fit one company, but could be perfect for another. In general, companies want a product with the following:

- **Will make a profit** – Companies want profitable products in line with their business. For example, a company such as P&G expects products to produce $100 million, while a small company might be happy with $5 million in revenue.

- **Is patented or patent pending** – Companies want patents to defend against competition. If an invention is not patented and in the public domain, the company does not need you, they can make it themselves.

- **Has an advantage over existing products** – Companies do not want a "me-too" product. Your product idea should have a clear advantage over existing products in the market.

- **Has received positive market tests** – It's best if you can show positive market test results from concept surveys, interviews, focus groups, or sales.

- **Is developed past the idea stage** – Companies do not want just an idea written on a napkin. At a minimum, companies are interested in an invention if it appears feasible based on your prototype.

- **Has synergy with existing products** – Companies want a product related to their expertise in manufacturing, marketing, and sales. For example, a company which sells sporting goods is less likely to be interested in licensing power tools.

- **Is safe for the end-user** – Companies are concerned about product liability lawsuits. Your product must be clearly safe to use. (It also helps if your product is environmentally friendly.)

When a company is interested in your invention, they want to see a prototype. A prototype can be a physical model, detailed CAD drawings, or video simulation.

In some cases, an acceptable prototype is a very detailed artist's illustration. Ask the company what's required. If developing a physical prototype is too expensive, see if they will contribute to the costs.

A company becomes very interested in your invention when they understand the profit potential opportunity. To get executives to salivate over your invention, learn how to create a Product Proposal in the next chapter.

Chapter 9:
The Product Proposal

The single biggest problem in communication is the illusion that it has taken place.
George Bernard Shaw

Topics in this Chapter:

- Product Proposal Format
- Product Proposal Template

There is often a disconnect between inventors and companies. Inventors like to discuss their invention's features, but companies want to know about a product idea from a business perspective. Since companies get flooded with idea submissions, they need to quickly determine if an invention represents a good opportunity.

The Licensing Executives Society performed a survey in 2006 to understand licensing trends. One aspect of the survey looked into why deals fail.

Companies listed the following reasons why licensing deals did not succeed:

- Absence of reliable market data
- Limited resources to analyze the opportunity
- Insufficient internal marketing experience or capacity
- Absence of any useful data on comparable deals
- Market data too expensive to obtain

To introduce your invention to a company, you must first create a document called a **Product Proposal**. A Product Proposal provides information about your invention from a business perspective. Without such information, a company is very likely to reject or simply ignore the invention.

The Product Proposal describes:

- The need in the market.
- How your invention fills the need.
- The benefits offered to the end-user.
- The advantages over other products.
- The target customer.
- How the invention profits the company.

Product Proposal Format

Since companies are very busy, the Product Proposal should be no longer than four pages and be straight to the point. Create a Product Proposal as a Microsoft Word or other word-processor document. If emailing the document to a company, first save the document as a PDF file to secure the contents.

On the cover page provide:

- The product name.
- A list of main benefits.
- A professional quality photo or illustration.
- Contact information.

On the next two to three pages, provide the following information:

- **Product Name** – Your working title or trademarked name.
- **Intellectual Property** – Indicate you have a Patent Pending or Granted Patent (do not supply the patent number *), and if you own a Trademark or Copyright.
- **Product Type** – Name the product type or product category (e.g., housewares, sporting goods, tools, medical device, auto accessory, children's game, software utility).
- **Market Need** – Describe the market need for your invention.
- **Product Description** – Describe how your invention solves a problem or satisfies a need or want, and how it looks, feels, and functions.
- **Development** – Describe the state of development (e.g. prototype, in development, finished product).

- **Benefits** – Describe the benefits derived from using your product (e.g., enhances safety, provides entertainment, saves money, makes money, or saves time).

- **Competition** – Name products offering a solution to the market need.

- **Advantages** – Describe your invention's advantages over the competition.

- **Customer** – Describe the typical customer who would use your product (e.g., age, sex, socio-economic status, education, occupation, and income).

- **Testimonials** – Summarize feedback you have received from surveys, interviews, focus groups, or market tests.

- **Market** – Describe the size of the market and trends related to your product.

- **Financial** – Show likely unit costs, expenses, and profit potential.

- **Developer Bio** – Provide personal background information (e.g., credentials, business experience, and industry familiarity).

Keep in mind, an appealing Product Proposal is backed by real market data (not just guesses). To learn how to gather market information, see Chapter 5, Market Research.

Important: If you have an issued patent, do not provide the patent number unless the company asks for the number. Companies fear being sued for patent infringement. If your invention is very similar to a product the company is selling, or in development, and it is shown a company knew of a patent they were infringing upon, then they can be sued for triple damages.

With a completed Product Proposal, you're ready to contact companies. Please turn to the next chapter to learn how to research, call, and make presentations.

Product Proposal Template

Product Proposal	
After completing your market research, use this template to create your Product Proposal.	
Product Name	
Intellectual Property	
Product Type	
Market Need	
Product Description	
Development	
Benefits	
Competition	
Advantages	
Customers	
Testimonials	
Market	
Financial	
Developer Bio	

Chapter 10:
How to Find and Contact Companies

The bathtub was invented in 1850 and the telephone in 1875. In other words, if you had been living in 1850, you could have sat in the bathtub for 25 years without having to answer the phone.

Bill DeWitt

Topics in this Chapter:

- How to Find Companies
- How to Contact Companies
- Use a Phone Script When Calling Companies
- Companies With Their Own Submission Process
- Presenting Your Invention

How to Find Companies

There might be several companies suitable for your invention. The objective is finding the right company. The first place to research are retailers such as Target, Walmart, CVS, as well as specialty stores. Look for comparable products, then on the packaging note the name of the manufacturer. Make a written list of product names, company names, and company websites.

To search online, use an Internet search engine and enter ["your product type" and manufacturer] as keywords. For example, if your product idea is a new coffee maker, enter ["coffee maker" manufacturer] as keywords. Review the search results for company names. Then go to each company's website to see what they do. Many websites have an "About" page describing the products they offer.

The following Internet resources can help you locate companies. The Internet changes often, so these websites may change.

Product Search
- www.google.com/products
- www.yahoo.com > click "shopping"

Major Retailers
- www.amazon.com
- www.walmart.com
- www.target.com

Business Directories
- www.thomasnet.com
- www.hoovers.com

Trade Shows
- www.tradeshowweek.com
- www.tsnn.com

Tip: Only approach companies who:

- Have product lines in the same category as your invention.
- Sell to the same target market.
- Manufacture products from the same materials and technology your invention uses.

How to Contact Companies

Do not send product information to a company unless you have a direct contact name. Companies are very busy and without a contact name, a company representative is more likely to throw your mailing in the trash.

Use the following process to contact companies:

- For each company on your list, search the internet for a contact person in the Marketing Department related to the product line of your invention type. If it's a small or medium sized company, search for a Director or Vice-President.
- Call the company and ask for the contact person.
- When you connect with the contact person, discuss the benefits of your invention.
- Ask if they buy or license-in new products (if not, then look elsewhere).

- If yes, ask if they have a submission process. Often, companies have legal forms for you to fill out.

- If they ask for product information, send your Product Proposal and a one-page cover letter. The cover letter includes a summary of:
    - The market need.
    - Invention benefits.
    - Any positive feedback and testimonials you've received.
    - Possible fit with their *product line name.*

- Follow-up within a week to make sure they received your information.
- Then follow-up in another week to see how the evaluation is going.

You want to find a contact person in the Marketing Department. The best people to contact are Product Managers, Marketing Managers, Brand Managers, or Category Managers. I worked for several years as a Product Manager. The Product Manager is in charge of the product line and often seeks new ways to generate revenue. Another option is to contact the Sales Department. Often, sales people know the names of decision makers you can contact.

To find the names of people in the Marketing Department, search the internet for company press releases, company directories, exhibitor listings at trade shows, and promotions of people to new positions such as Manager, Director, or Vice-President. In addition, there are networking websites (e.g. www.linkedin.com and www.spoke.com) with profiles of marketing people for a number of companies.

Tip: If you are asked to email your Product Proposal or other information, turn your documents into an Adobe PDF file. You can secure PDF files to prevent someone from copying your pictures and text.

Use a Phone Script When Calling Companies

Before calling a company, it's important to have a prepared script. You want to sound natural, but you also don't want to fumble your words. Using a phone script helps you stay on track. The following sample phone scripts provide guidance in various situations.

When first calling a company:

- If you know the contact name:

  "Hello, could you please connect me to *(contact name)*."

- If you have not found a contact name:

  "Hello, please connect me to the Product Manager for the *(product-type)* product line. "

- If they won't connect you without a name, or ask what the call is regarding:

  "I'm a developer with a new product. It appears to fit with your *(product name)* product line. Do you have someone in the Marketing Department I can briefly talk with?"

Talking to the contact person:

- When first connected to the contact person:

  "Hello, I'm *first and last name*, and I'm an developer with a new product. The benefits are *(state the benefits)*. This fits with your *(product name)* product line. Do you have a process to evaluate new products?" [Make notes of their process.]

- Ask during the conversation:

  "Has your company ever licensed-in or purchased inventions before?" [If not, this company is not a good candidate. Continue the conversation but put the company lower on your priority list.]

- If asked to send information about your invention:

  "Yes, I'll be happy to send you information. Should I mail it to (recite the mailing address listed on their website)? Lastly, is there something I can write on the envelope so the letter doesn't look like junk mail?"

[Send your cover letter and Product Proposal. Often adding "Personal" on the envelope helps route the letter to your contact. Use a mailing method with a tracking system such as USPS Priority Mail, USPS Certified Mail, FedEx, or UPS.]

Tip: If calling companies makes you nervous, practice with companies not on your list. Call the headquarters of some well-known manufacturers and go through the phone script. See how you feel and make corrections to your script until you are comfortable.

Tip: If a company is not interested, always ask for a referral. Then, when calling the next company, mention you were referred by "person's name from company name."

Companies With Their Own Submission Process

During your research, you may see companies with a specific invention submission process listed on their website. It's important to follow their guidelines and not try to go around them. Many companies only accept submissions if you have already filed for a utility or design patent, or provisional patent application.

Usually there is a document for you to sign agreeing the submission is non-confidential. This means the company is under no obligation to keep your invention secret. This doesn't imply the company is trying to steal your idea. Your protection is from your patent filing.

In addition, some companies request you sign a document which states the company is under no obligation to enter into any agreement with you. This implies, by reviewing your invention, the company is not required to offer you a deal.

In addition to the requested documents, submit your Product Proposal so the company can understand the business opportunity your invention provides. If a company says they do not accept additional documents, follow their procedures to avoid rejection.

Here are some examples of companies with an invention submission process:

- The Coleman Company, Inc.
  www.coleman.com/coleman/ColemanCom/inventionsub.asp
- DeWALT Industrial Tool Company
  www.dewalt.com/us/service/company/invention.asp

- Igloo Products Corporation
  www.igloocoolers.com/contact-us/product-idea-submissions/
- Kimberly-Clark
  www.kimberly-clark.com/aboutus/innovating_with_kc.aspx

Presenting Your Invention

If a company shows interest in your invention, ask to meet your contact in person to create a human connection. If meeting face to face is not possible, create a short video. You can post the video on your website, but make sure the webpage is password protected and search engine indexing is disabled ("noindex" HTML tag). If you use YouTube, Google Video, or other video sharing websites, make sure you set the Sharing option to Private to avoid public viewing.

Presenting your invention to a company is not difficult and doesn't require special skills. Prior to a presentation, outline the points you want to discuss. Important points should include:

- The need, want, or problem faced by consumers or businesses related to the invention
- The solutions to the need, want, or problem
- The benefits of your invention
- The fit of your invention with the company's product line
- The competition
- The advantages of your invention over the competition
- The profit potential

At the meeting, before showing your prototype, explain the need in the market. Then describe the best solution to the market need (which just happens to be your invention).

Now unveil your prototype. Describe how the invention benefits the end-user. Then demonstrate the prototype and highlight important features. In addition, describe scenarios in which end-users can make use of your product. Then cover the remaining points in your presentation.

In addition to the invention, your personal character is very important to the company. With the expectation of doing business together for many years, there should be a personality fit.

Therefore, you want to avoid appearing brash, arrogant, or demanding. Present yourself as honest, courteous, and dependable.

At the end of the meeting, ask for their thoughts, next steps to proceed, and when to call or email again. You need to keep the process moving forward. Companies have many ongoing projects and are easily distracted.

When you leave the meeting, write a summary for yourself. Review how well you did and the things you may need to improve. Note your gut feelings whether the people seem trustworthy, organized, and have the ability to produce, market, and sell your product. When you arrive home, email a thank you note to the attendees of the meeting. Include a summary of the points agreed upon, answer any remaining questions, and list next steps.

Chapter 11:
Negotiating a Deal

In business, you don't get what you deserve, you get what you negotiate.

Chester L. Karrass

Topics in this Chapter:

- Submission Follow-up
- When a Company is Interested
- Option Agreement and Letter of Intent
- Researching and Evaluating an Interested Company
- Important Terms of an Agreement
- Negotiating to Reach an Agreement and Getting Paid

Each company has its own method of reviewing invention submissions. The review is based mainly on fit with their product lines, marketability, profit potential, ability to manufacture, and timing.

For example, Kimberly-Clark has a department dedicated to screening new ideas. They review ideas from both a legal and preliminary marketability point of view.

If the invention passes initial screening, the next step is a review by their licensing department. If still interested, the company asks for more information.

Some companies use their legal department as the first step in the review process. If your submission passes their legal requirements, the marketing department or new products committee makes an evaluation.

In some cases, a Product Manager makes the first assessment of an invention. If interested, the Product Manager may then turn the invention over to senior management or a new product team for further evaluation.

Submission Follow-up

After you submit your invention, follow-up with a phone call to your company contact within a week to 10 days. Ask the following questions:

- Have you received my invention submission?
- What's the next step?
- Can I come in and make a presentation?
- When should I follow-up again?

During the call, be courteous and professional. If they tell you to call back on a certain date, be sure to mark your calendar and follow-up.

When a Company is Interested

After a company reviews your invention, they express interest when they:

- Specifically say they are interested.
- Ask to see a prototype.
- Ask you to come in to make a presentation.
- Want to see your market data.

When a company shows interest in your invention, ask if they will sign a non-disclosure agreement (NDA). If they will not sign an NDA, consider another company. If the company prefers to use their NDA, review it with an attorney.

At some point, they want to know what you want regarding compensation. **Make sure you prepare ahead of time to discuss terms such as royalties, advances, etc.**

Use the following steps to prepare, negotiate, and obtain a great deal:

- Ask your company contact questions related to sales, marketing, and development.
- Prepare the terms you want.
- During negotiations, discuss with your company contact the terms you are looking for.
- Follow-up each discussion with an email summarizing the terms discussed and agreed-upon.
- When all terms are agreed-upon, email your contact a summary.

- Ask the company to convert the agreed-upon terms into a legal agreement. *
- Review the agreement with an attorney to make sure the legalese match the terms. For an explanation of a typical license agreement, see Appendix H, License Agreement Explained.
- If the terms in the agreement appear different than what was discussed, call your company contact, point out any discrepancy, and ask to make changes.
- When you are satisfied, sign the agreement.

* If you want to create the agreement, ask your attorney to perform the work. However, at this point, since all the terms are agreed-upon, it should not matter if you or the company creates the agreement.

Option Agreement and Letter of Intent

When a company is interested in your invention, they want to perform detailed research. Research may include appraising the patent's value, legal risks, market demand, competition, and strategic value. To evaluate your invention, this "due diligence" may take several months.

To formalize the process of working together, a Letter of Intent or Option Agreement is often created between the company and inventor. Keep in mind, companies define and use these documents differently, but the following is a general explanation of each.

Option Agreement

An Option Agreement is a contract outlining both the desire to investigate your invention along with the option to license or buy. After the company performs their due diligence, and if everything looks good, the company can "exercise its option," meaning the company is satisfied with the results and wants to license or buy your invention. The Option Agreement includes highlights of a purchase agreement or license agreement such as royalties, advances, and guaranteed minimums.

The Option Agreement includes important obligations of the company and of the inventor, over a period of time. Company obligations may include paying you an Option Fee (non-refundable) plus attorney costs, keeping the invention confidential, and sharing with you the results of their research.

Your obligations, as the inventor, include providing the company with details of the invention and not selling or licensing your invention to other companies.

Letter of Intent

A Letter of Intent (LOI) is usually not a binding contract but rather a "meeting of the minds." Instead of jumping directly into a deal, a LOI is an intermediary step of working together. A LOI can be formed at any stage of discussions. A LOI has no standard format and is typically written in plain English.

One use of a LOI is to indicate the company's desire to research your invention with the intent to license or buy. Another use of a LOI is to summarize the business terms of a deal. Having the terms agreed-upon before the legalese is added, makes it easier to create a license agreement, patent purchase agreement, or assignment agreement.

To Enter or Not Enter into an Initial Agreement

Should you enter into an Option Agreement or Letter of Intent? It depends on the likelihood of the company to enter into a deal, whether other companies are ready to make a deal or not, and long-term benefits from working with the company.

Before agreeing to an Option Agreement or Letter of Intent, discuss the likely terms of a deal assuming the research is positive. For example, you say, "Let's fast-forward in time and assume all your research is positive. The terms I'm looking for are x, y, and z. Is this close to your expectations?" If the company says they can work with those terms, proceed with the Option Agreement or LOI. If their view of the business terms are nowhere near yours, politely decline to continue to work with them.

Since an Option Agreement and Letter of Intent have legal implications, they should both be reviewed with your attorney before signing.

Researching and Evaluating an Interested Company

Let's say a company is interested. The question is, are they a good fit? Fit is important because you hope to work with a company for a number of years. You hope they do a good job developing, marketing, and selling your invention. Similar to dating, you wouldn't want to marry everyone who offers you a marriage proposal.

Research a company using Google or other search engine:

- Has the company been sued, and if so, what were the reasons? [search: "company name" and lawsuit]
- Has the company won any awards for quality, innovation, etc? [search: "company name" and awards]
- Are there good reviews for the company's products? [search: "company name" and reviews]
- Is there any good or bad news about the company? [search: "company name" and "press release"]
- Is the company a public company? If so, you can see detailed information from their annual 10-K reports. Go to Securities and Exchange Commission (www.sec.gov) or use a Google search. [search: "company name" and "10K SEC"], [search: "company name" and "annual report"], and [search: "company name" and "stock"]

Questions to ask your company contact (general):

- Where do they currently market and sell their products?
- Who are their target customers?
- What other products have they licensed and what has been the outcome?

Questions to ask your company contact (related to your invention):

- How many units do they think they can sell the first and second years?
- Do they currently have the technology or skills needed to create your product, or is this something they need to research and develop (which takes a longer time)?
- What would be the approximate product launch date?
- How much do they plan to spend on marketing and sales programs for your product?

Company Evaluation - Research	
Research and evaluate companies to see if they are a fit.	
Company Info	**Notes**
Company name:	
Company website:	
Has the company won any awards?	
What are the reviews of company products?	
Is there any good or bad news about the company?	
Has the company been sued and what were the issues?	
What was the company's revenue and profit the previous year?	
Is the company's revenue and profit increasing or decreasing over the past three years?	

When asking these questions, be polite and patient. You don't want to appear being pushy. At the same time, they should understand the answers to these questions are important for you to make a decision to go forward with the company or not.

For example, an inventor obtained a licensing agreement with a company but never asked how many units they think they can sell. After many months with the invention in development, it came out that the sales forecast was for only about 1,000 units. Displeased, the inventor terminated the deal.

Company Evaluation – Discuss With Your Contact	
Ask your company contact the following questions to see if they are a fit.	
Company	**Notes**
Where does the company market and sell its products?	
Who is the target customer?	
What other products has the company licensed, and what was the outcome?	
Your Invention	
How many units can they sell?	
Do they currently have the technology and skills to create the product?	
If they licensed your invention, what is the approximate product launch date?	
Approximately how much do they plan to spend on marketing and sales programs?	

Important Terms of an Agreement

If a company wants to buy your invention, then you are assigning your intellectual property to them. The intellectual property transferred is typically a patent, but may also include trademarks and copyrights. An assignment agreement lists the intellectual property you are selling, the compensation you expect to receive, and legal clauses. Once the conditions are met, such as you receiving payment, the company fully owns the intellectual property.

If you or a company prefers to license, you are essentially renting your intellectual property to them over a certain time period. So what is a Licensing Agreement? A Licensing Agreement is a contract with certain legal language covering the business transaction and specific terms, including time period, territory, exclusivity, and royalty payment.

Terms of a license agreement generally include (and open to negotiation) the following:

Exclusivity

In most cases, a company wants exclusivity. "Exclusive Rights" means only one company may license your invention within a certain territory, in a certain market, and over a certain time period. If your invention applies to more than one market, you could have separate licensing agreements with different companies who specialize in certain markets and territories.

In terms of negotiating, ask if they want exclusivity or not. Typically they will want exclusivity. When you agree to this, you are giving them something with the implied understanding you hope to receive something in return at a later time.

Royalty

Royalties can be obtained as a percentage of net sales, number of units sold, or by the number of units produced. Royalties are often based on a percentage and rates often range from 2% to 10% of net sales. A common royalty rate is 5%.

If your invention were a process being used to make something, you would receive royalty payments for each unit produced. For example, royalty payments are one cent ($.01) for each metal spring produced by your new high-speed spring fabricator.

To determine a reasonable royalty, books and online databases provide rates for many product categories. Resources for royalty rates include:

- Royalty Source (www.royaltysource.com)
- Royalty Stat (www.royaltystat.com)
- EPM Communications – Royalty Trends Report (www.epmcom.com)

What if your patent is filed but not yet allowed by the patent office, can you still obtain a deal? Yes. In one case, a client received a deal in which he would receive a 5% royalty whether the patent is allowed or not. If the patent is allowed, he would receive a 10% royalty.

Keep in mind, companies do not need a patent to sell a product. Companies prefer a patent to help deter copycats and other competition. Without a patent though, companies can still stay ahead of competition with good marketing, innovation, and customer service. Remember the product WD-40? It didn't have a patent and generated millions of dollars in sales.

Definition of Net Sales

Typically, net sales are specified in a license agreement as *product revenue minus any returns or allowances*. Product revenue is based on the manufacturer's retail price when selling direct to the customer, and wholesale price when selling to a retailer or distributor.

For example, if royalty payments are 5% of net sales, and net sales are $2,000,000, then your royalty payment = $2,000,000 x .05 = $100,000. Allowances are reductions in price usually made when a product is not selling at the higher price points.

Be aware of net sales definitions with deductions for bad debts, marketing expenses, and sales commissions. If these expenses are included, it lowers your royalties. During negotiations, request to exclude any extra expenses used to determine royalties. Stick to the typical definition of net sales as product revenue minus any returns or allowances.

Royalty Payment Schedule

There is a statement indicating when you are paid. At a minimum, your royalty payments should be received quarterly. Quarterly payments are a common practice. Often it is stated you receive a check 30 days after the end of the quarter. As an example, for product sales from January 1 to March 31, you receive a royalty check no later than April 30.

Advance

Advance payments are yours to keep whether or not the company makes or sells the product. Advances may be in the form of cash, stock, stock options, or other types of compensation. There are generally two forms of an advance.

One type of advance is an up-front non-refundable payment to cover future royalties. For example, you receive an advance payment of $25,000 to cover the royalty payments in the first year. As a result, you begin to receive royalty checks when $25,000 in accumulated royalties for product sales are exceeded.

The other form of advance is a **"licensing fee"** paid to you at the time of signing. This is an up-front non-refundable payment to you and is not toward future royalties. This might be used to entice you to sign a deal or to cover your expenses.

The mindset you need is to not be greedy. Whatever you ask for, justify the amount. A good method is to ask for an amount to cover your costs for prototype, patent, and other development expenses.

A good negotiating tactic is to waive an advance and instead have the company pay for all future patents related to this invention and any improvements. This shows you are looking to invest in your invention. Having the company pay for patents for new product improvements and international patents may generate more revenue for you in the long run.

Guaranteed Minimum Annual Royalties (GMAR)

Make sure your agreement has a GMAR. A GMAR is a statement specifying the minimum royalties you receive on a yearly basis. Not all agreements have this provision.

Inventors have told me in the past they unfortunately had a deal without a GMAR. When the company only sold a few hundred units yielding little royalties, the inventor had no way out of the contract.

With a GMAR provision, if product sales are not large enough to generate the minimum royalties, the company can pay you the difference, you can agree to carry the shortfall forward to the following year, or you can terminate the agreement.

A method to determine the GMAR amount is based on expected sales year after year. During early discussions with your company contact, you want to find out expected sales revenue of your product. You use this amount as the basis of GMAR negotiations.

GMAR can be calculated by the sales forecast, multiplied by the wholesale price, and then multiplied by the royalty percentage. For example, the sales forecast is for 100,000 units, with a $25 wholesale price, and a 5% royalty rate. Therefore, the GMAR calculation is: 100,000 units x $25 x 5% = $125,000. This is your starting GMAR value for negotiating. The company might suggest the GMAR to be a percentage of the forecast, such as 80%.

Negotiating is a matter of give and take. If you allow the company one point, ask for another. The amount of a guaranteed annual royalty should increase each year and perhaps level off when product sales begin to peak. Research sales growth rates of comparable products. Usually you can obtain this information from public company annual reports or market studies.

Keep in mind, if a company's sales projections are too low, resulting in low royalties, it might be wise to move on to another company. A low amount can be evaluated against the royalties you were expecting, weighed against sales reports of comparable products, or compared to offers from other companies.

Time Period

Time Period is the duration a company may manufacture, distribute, and sell your product (e.g., one year, five years, life of patent). This is often called the "term of the agreement" meaning the length of time of the agreement. Often a license agreement is for five years and renews automatically for the same period unless a termination is enacted by either party.

Territory

Territory refers to regions of the world where the company may distribute your product (e.g., only United States, only Canada, North America, the entire world). Only grant exclusive rights in a territory if the company is actively marketing and selling in the territory. For example, if the company wants exclusive rights to Europe, this is fine as long as they have a marketing and sales presence in one or more European countries and agree to a minimum royalty guarantee.

Territory can also mean specific distribution channels. For example, if the company only sells through webstores and catalogs, then you would grant those rights to just those distribution channels. This allows you to create a deal with another company who distributes through mass retailers like Walmart and Target.

Do not give exclusive rights of a territory to a company if they do not have a presence in that territory. The license agreement should clearly state in which countries or regions the company could market and sell.

Field of Use

Field of Use specifies the types of markets to sell the invention. Do not give exclusive rights to a company in a field unless they have expertise in that area. The license agreement should clearly state which field of use the company can market and sell.

For example, suppose your invention is an improved tennis ball. Perhaps you discover the new ball is great for tennis and as a pet toy. If a company has a strong presence in the tennis industry, they should be allowed to sell only to the sporting goods stores. For the pet supplies market, you would offer the rights to another company.

In another example, if your invention is a medical device for both consumers and hospitals, a company may only have established marketing and sales in one area. If the company only knows the consumer market, you could give them those rights. You could have a separate deal with a company who markets and sells to hospitals.

Improvements

If you or the company makes modifications or enhancements to your invention, the agreement should state you retain all rights to any changes and receive ownership to any subsequent patents. If the company makes any changes, the agreement should state they disclose to you in writing any changes within 30 days.

If you make changes to the invention, which creates a new product or new field of use, typically the agreement states the company has the right of first refusal. This means when you create a new invention based on the licensed invention, you need to disclose the new invention to the company. The company has the first right to license it from you. If they don't want it, then you can seek another company for a licensing agreement or market the product yourself.

Production Schedule

There should be timelines listed in the agreement. You want to know when the company intends to begin product development. You want to obtain a timeframe of when the company plans to launch the product into the market (e.g. Spring 2010). If they don't meet these timelines, there are clearly stated consequences such as your right to terminate the agreement.

Quality Control

You should have the right to inspect and approve product quality. Ask what their quality guidelines are and who is in charge of quality control. You don't want to be an unreasonable perfectionist, but the product coming off the assembly line should meet your understanding of customer expectations. You would be surprised at how many products are not adequately inspected. With companies cutting costs, sometimes there's not enough quality control people to perform the needed tests.

Accounting Audit

How do you know the company is paying you fairly? There needs to be a provision in the agreement stating you have the right to inspect the accounts. This means an auditor would come in and inspect the business and appropriate royalties you should have received. If an error is made, you receive the difference within 10 days.

To pay for the services of an auditor, one fair way to do this is if the difference is off by 5% or more, the company has to pay the auditor. If the difference is less than 5% then you pay the auditor. This assures the company you won't complain every month and cost the company a bundle in auditing fees.

Termination

Causes for termination of the agreement should be clearly outlined. You want to have the right to terminate the license agreement if the company defaults on any provision including:

- Product is not launched by a certain date or time period
- Company fails to make the minimum royalty payments
- Royalty payments for a quarter are 50% less than the previous quarter
- Company goes bankrupt
- Company is sold or acquired
- Company commits a felony

As a result of termination, any due royalty payments and any property or material you provided, should be mailed to you within 30 days. Since they have no further need for manufacturing your product, negotiate for tooling and molds be turned over to you as well.

Term Sheet Sample	
Prepare ahead of time the terms important to you.	
Item	**Ask For**
❑ Advance: toward royalties	$ 50,000
❑ Advance: licensing fee	$ 10,000
❑ Royalty	6%
❑ Guaranteed minimum	$ 50,000 year one $ 75,000 year two $ 100,000 year three and beyond
❑ Net sales definition	Product sales minus returns, allowances, and discounts
❑ Payment schedule	30 days after each calendar quarter
❑ Territory	Exclusive North America
❑ Field of Use	Exclusive Consumer Housewares
❑ Term of agreement	5 years, renew automatically
❑ Termination	Company breaches on any terms, fails to make minimum payments, goes bankrupt, is acquired or sold, commits a felony, or royalties per quarter are 50% less than the previous quarter.
❑ Improvements	Retain all rights to any improvements and derivative products.
❑ Quality control	Right to inspect product before shipment and then yearly.
❑ Audit	Right to audit books and if royalty difference is greater than 5%, company pays auditor.

❏ Product liability insurance	Paid by company; covers company and myself.
❏ Infringed upon	If my patent is infringed upon, then not required to sue infringer; company can sue.
❏ Infringement	If sued for infringement, company pays for defense.

Additional Legal Clauses

There are additional legal clauses in a typical agreement you should review with your attorney. Important clauses include: Representation and Warranties, Assignment and Transfer, Indemnification, Infringement Lawsuits, Product Liability Insurance, Dispute Resolution, Governing Law, Jurisdiction, Waivers, and Attorney's Fees Provision.

Importantly, if there is a lawsuit claiming your product infringes on a patent, or you determine another product is possibly infringing on your patent, you want the company to cover all legal costs.

You also want to make sure the company acquires product liability insurance so you are covered in the event of a lawsuit. The legal clause would, in essence, state you are indemnified and held harmless against all claims, suits, losses, and damages from any product defects or omissions.

> For more information and examples of terms, see Appendix H, License Agreement Explained.

Negotiating to Reach an Agreement and Getting Paid

You have the right to be compensated for your efforts. Not every business opportunity is a good opportunity. If you feel pressured and uncomfortable with a business deal, it's better to walk away and find another. When in discussions with companies, you should be flexible, polite, patient, positive, and ethical.

Discuss the Terms

Before a licensing agreement or patent purchase agreement is drafted, you should work out the terms with the company. A summary of terms is often called a "Term Sheet" but others might refer to this as a "Letter of Intent." A term sheet is not a contract but rather a document outlining agreed upon elements such as royalties, advances, etc. It saves time to work out the business details before getting the attorneys involved in creating the legal documents.

When negotiating, you need to prepare ahead of time. For a licensing deal, you should have an idea of what royalties, guaranteed minimums, advances, and other terms you *must have* and those you would *like to have*. For example, if the typical royalty is 5% for your product type, you can start by asking for 6% along with a small advance. Perhaps the company is only willing to provide 5%. In exchange of a lower rate, you ask for a larger advance. In this case, you win with the 5% you were originally willing to take, along with a higher advance, and the company feels they won a point by reducing the royalty rate.

Creating and Reviewing the Agreement

When all the terms you and the company contact want to discuss are completed, summarize in a letter and confirm these are correct. Then ask the company to create the license agreement. Since all the terms are agreed-upon, it should not matter if you or the company creates the agreement.

Keep in mind the agreement is a legal contract and you should have an attorney review the agreement on your behalf. Make sure the terms you agreed upon are clearly stated in the agreement.

Sign and Carry Out the Terms

When the agreement is signed, the first step for you and the company is to carry out the terms. For example, you might need to provide the company with detailed engineering CAD files. In doing so, the company provides you with the specified advance payment.

Monitor the progress of product development. It's best the agreement states the company sends you monthly reports during the development phase up to product launch. In addition, let them know you intend to stay in-touch on a monthly basis.

Some companies hire the inventor as a consultant to guide the engineers or marketers. Depending on the going rates, you can ask for an hourly rate such as

$100 per hour, or a rate of $1,000 per day plus expenses. Again, don't be greedy. Ask what they think is a fair rate.

When the product launches, ask your company contact for reports on how marketing and sales are going. Put dates on your calendar as to when you're supposed to receive royalty payments.

Note: If selling your patent, you must notify the Patent Office of the transaction in writing within three months of the date of signing the Assignment Agreement. Mail a cover letter and a copy of the agreement to:

Mail Stop Assignment Services
Director of the U.S. Patent and Trademark Office
P.O. Box 1450
Alexandria, VA 22313-1450

Before you mail the assignment to the Patent Office, make sure you receive your lump sum payment from the company (or for a series of payments you have an escrow account set up).

You Can Do It

Selling and licensing might seem overwhelming. Similar to learning how to ride a bike, you can read about it or watch others, but to really know something you have to experience it. Your comfort with selling and licensing begins when you complete market research, call companies, and engage in discussions. If you need assistance, learn how to hire an agent or consultant in the next chapter.

Chapter 12:
Working With Agents and Consultants

Discovery consists of seeing what everybody has seen and thinking what nobody else has thought.

Jonathan Swift

Topics in this Chapter:

- Let Someone Else Find Companies for You
- Where to Find Agents to Sell or License Your Invention

Let Someone Else Find Companies for You

Do you like selling, making presentations, and negotiating contracts? If you answered "Yes," then contact companies directly. If you answered "No," then use a Consultant or an Agent.

An Agent, also referred to as a Product Rep, is a broker between you and companies looking for new ideas. The Agent has industry contacts and knows how to pitch an idea. They search for companies which manufacture products similar to yours, and deliver a presentation to the company representatives.

Typically an Agent does not take an up-front fee but only a piece of the deal, often between 25% and 50%. Since they only make money if a deal is made, they are very selective about the inventions and inventors taken on as clients. Once you decide to work with an Agent, you sign an agreement to work with them exclusively.

The alternate option is to work with a Consultant. Similar to an Agent, Consultants find companies and negotiate terms on your behalf. The major difference is a Consultant works on a fee basis. In addition, some consultants may want a piece of the deal, but many are fee only.

If you decide to work with an Agent, use the following steps:

- Search for Agents (see the next section).
- Discuss with Agents how they work and which industries they target.
- Both you and the Agent sign a non-disclosure agreement to cover confidential issues, such as marketing strategies and financial arrangements.
- Send the Agent your Product Proposal.
- If the Agent likes the Product Proposal, discuss terms for working together.
- Review, negotiate, and sign the Agent's Representative Agreement.
- Send the Agent a prototype they can use for presentations.
- The Agent searches for business opportunities.
- The Agent negotiates on your behalf to obtain the best deal.
- The company generates an Agreement you review and sign.
- You and the company carry out the terms of the Agreement.

Some points concerning working with Agents:

- The Agent's Representative Agreement covers the Agent's responsibilities, your responsibilities, payment terms (usually 25% to 50%), a disclaimer clause, and a termination clause.
- Discuss allowable expenses the Agent may charge. Most Agent expenses should be their burden as the cost of doing their business.
- The terms of working together should be detailed in the Agent's Representative Agreement.
- The Agent's Representative Agreement should specify the Agent only receives payment as a result of generating revenue for you.

Where to Find Agents to Sell or License Your Invention

So if using an Agent seems appealing, where do you find one? Here are some options:

- Use an Internet search engine with ["your product type" and "product representative"] as keywords. For example, using Google, enter [screwdrivers "product representative"] as keywords.
- Call manufacturers in your industry and ask if they use Agents or can they recommend one.

- Search industry trade show directories and look for Agents or Product Reps listed as speakers or exhibitors.
- Call other inventors and ask for Agent recommendations.
- Go to Licensing Executives Society (www.les.org).
- Go to International Licensing Industry Merchandisers' Association (www.licensing.org).

For information and examples of licensing terms, see Appendix H, License Agreement Explained.

PART FOUR – SELF-MARKET, DEVELOPMENT, PRODUCTION, AND LAUNCH

Obstacles cannot crush me. Every obstacle yields to stern resolve. He who is fixed to a star does not change his mind.

Leonardo da Vinci

Chapter 13:
Market Planning

In marketing I've seen only one strategy that can't miss -- and that is to market to your best customers first, your best prospects second and the rest of the world last.

John Romero

Topics in this Chapter:

- Product Planning Flowchart
- Market Planning
- Your Future Customer
- Product Positioning
- Pricing for Profit
- Marketing Communications Plan
- Plan with a Launch Checklist

While you might be tempted to go out and start manufacturing right away, please be patient and go through the very necessary planning stage. Planning saves you time in the long run and helps prevent costly mistakes.

Planning involves completely thinking through product marketing and development details from start to finish. This is a key step to taking your invention and turning it into a product. Detailed planning can seem arduous, but clear plans lead to greater product quality and shorter development time. The closer you are to producing your product, the more costly changes become. Therefore, it's best to uncover any remaining issues now before full development begins.

If you need to present a formal product plan to an investor, banker, or partner, see Appendix C, The Market-Step Product Plan. Even if you don't need a formal plan, put your thoughts on paper anyway.

At this point, focus on:

Market Planning (Ch. 13)

1. Selecting a target market
2. Positioning in the mind of the customer
3. Determining a price
4. Planning marketing communications
5. Creating a launch checklist

Product Planning (Ch. 14)

6. Creating product requirements
7. Reviewing regulations and certifications
8. Creating a manufacturing plan
9. Creating a project plan
10. Setting a budget

If you're completing the planning stage yourself, perform activities one through ten in sequence. If you have two or more people, you can save time by working in tandem. One person or team can take on Market Planning and the other Product Planning.

Product Planning Flowchart

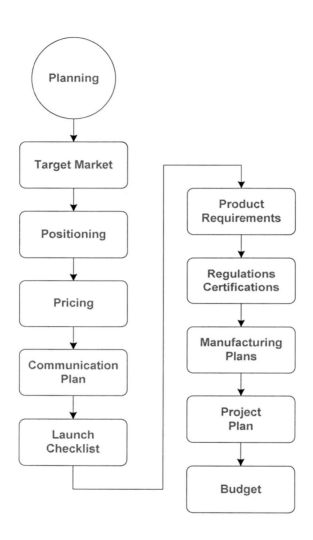

Market Planning

Think of all the aspects of marketing in terms of building a house. The foundation of marketing is an understanding of the problems, needs, and wants of the customer (#1 in the diagram).

What benefits do your future customers seek? What information are they looking for? Why can't they solve their problems with what's currently available in the market? What are the customer's characteristics? What is their buying process? Who are the decision makers? Who influences the customer's buying process?

4. Communications

Advertising, Brochures, Direct Mail, Flyers, Publicity, Trade Shows, Web

3. Strategies

Positioning, Pricing, Target Market, Product Line, Branding, Packaging, Distribution

2. Market Environment

Competition, Market Trends, Market Size, Opportunities, Threats, Success Factors

1. Customer

Problems, Needs, Wants, Demographics, Psychographics, Buying Behavior, Influencers, Decision Makers

After you understand the customer, the next step is to review the Market Environment (#2). This is an evaluation of competition, market trends, size of the market, opportunities, threats, and market drivers of success.

Once you have a grasp of the customer and market environment, develop the strategies and tactics. Strategies (#3) include selecting a target market, positioning, pricing, product features, branding, packaging, and distribution. From the strategies, flow the Marketing Communications tactics (#4) such as advertising, direct mail, publicity, website, and others methods to generate awareness, prospect leads, and sales.

Your Future Customer

When you launch your product, you won't have the budget to market to everyone in the world. Therefore you need to be clear on who is most likely to buy your product.

The most suitable customer is known as your target market. Having an understanding of your target market allows you to create a better product, create more effective marketing, and earn a higher profit.

To help identify your target market:

- Review any interviews and surveys to look for characteristics of people who were most interested in your invention.
- Brainstorm a list of potential groups (people or companies) who would benefit most from your product.
- View websites and packaging of comparable and competitive products to uncover the type of customers they target.
- Talk to retailers and distributors to understand who buys comparable or competitive products.
- If your invention replaces an existing product type, review the characteristics of the current users.

Brainstorm Potential Groups

Ask yourself "What types of people (or companies) have the greatest need or want for my product?" If your product benefit is a time saver, then who will save the most time by using your product? If your product benefit is a money saver, then who will save the most money by using it? If your product benefit is entertainment, then who will most appreciate the fun and pleasure delivered by your product?

For example, if your idea is a new type of screwdriver, then think about who currently uses them. You might conclude screwdrivers are primarily used by Auto Mechanics, Carpenters, and Homeowners over the age of 65. This is a good start.

If potential groups of end-users of your product idea are not obvious, use the Internet for research. For example, use a search engine such as Google and enter keywords ["screwdriver" and "customers"] or ["screwdriver" and "market segment"]. Search results might include various articles, press releases, and product information. Review the information and look for different types of people and businesses mentioned as users. They're your potential future customers.

Customers of Comparable Products

Who are the current buyers of comparable and competitive products? Target customers are usually identified in competitive marketing literature, websites, or on their product box.

For example, a toy's packaging might indicate it's for children ages 6 to 10. A brochure for a computer product might note the product is intended for Information Technology Managers, road warriors, and home office users. The website of a medical product might show images of seniors and discuss health issues. These are all key indicators of a target market.

Talk to Retailers

Another approach to uncover potential customers involves talking with retailers and distributors who sell products similar to yours. Talk to sales people, managers, and purchasing people.

For example, go into a Home Depot and speak to workers in the hardware department. Let them know you're working on a new type of screwdriver. Then, mention you're curious to know who buys similar types of screwdrivers. The people they mention are your potential target market.

Replacement Technology

If your product uses new technology, review the characteristics of people who already use a product you're hoping to replace. As an example, if you had developed the DVD player, you might have targeted people who owned a CD, LaserDisc player, or VCR. If you'd developed the first word processor, you might have sought people who used a typewriter.

From your research, which groups of people or businesses can benefit most from your invention?

Customer Groups
Name at least three groups who might benefit from using your product: Group 1: _____ Group 2: _____ Group 3: _____

Once you've identified potential customer segments, study their characteristics. For example, a new screwdriver might be best used by Auto Mechanics who are predominately male, age between 18–45, and trade school educated.

Please review the sample customer profile and then enter the characteristics of three groups of your potential customers. Be as detailed and specific as possible. For additional information, see Appendix B, Select Your Target Market.

Customer Profile Sample		
	1	2	3
Group Name:	Auto Mechanics	Carpenters	Homeowners 65+
Personal			
Age range:	18–45	18–45	65–75
Education:	trade school	trade school	college
Family size:			
Income:			
Location:	all	all	all
Nationality:			
Occupation:	auto mechanics	carpenters	all
Race:			
Religion:			
Sex:	M	M	all
Social class:			
Business			
Industry:	auto repair	new homes	
Location:	all	all	
Size:	small	all	
Type: *	service	service	

* Manufacturer, Distributor, Retailer, Government, Service Provider

Customer Profile

Enter three groups of potential customers and their demographics.

	1	2	3
Group Name:			
Personal			
Age range:			
Education:			
Family size:			
Income:			
Location:			
Nationality:			
Occupation:			
Race:			
Religion:			
Sex:			
Social class:			
Business			
Industry:			
Location:			
Size:			
Type: *			

* Manufacturer, Distributor, Retailer, Government, Service Provider

Once you've identified your target market, research the issues they face related to your product. Understanding your customer helps you design your product to their exacting needs.

What benefits and features will they pay for? What benefits and features might they consider unimportant? You might uncover features and functions your customer simply does not want. In addition, understanding your customer provides guidance to creating your marketing strategies and tactics.

Customer Desires

Get into the mind of your future customer. Think about their needs, desires, and buying process.

What problems, pains, needs, or wants does your target market have?

What is their compelling reason to buy your product?

What is their selection criteria (important features, functions, and benefits)?

What questions will your target market likely have when considering your product?

Important Product Characteristics	
From research and interviews, use the list below to check off the customers' important criteria when selecting your product, and provide details.	
Characteristic	Details
❏ Color	
❏ Customer service	
❏ Dependability	
❏ Documentation	
❏ Durability	
❏ Ease of installation	
❏ Ease of use	
❏ Materials	
❏ Packaging	
❏ Place of purchase	
❏ Price	
❏ Sound	
❏ Speed	
❏ Style	
❏ Value	
❏ Visual appeal	
❏ Warranty	
❏ Other:	

Product Positioning

Positioning is a powerful concept. Positioning tells people what your product does and how well it does it. With all of the noise in the market, your product needs to stand out amid the competition. Your product needs to have a clear identity.

People want to understand how your product compares to the competition (comparable solutions). Is your product more expensive or less expensive? Does it offer the best value? Is it the market leader, the most dependable, the most convenient, the easiest to use, the most comfortable, and so on?

For example, when it comes to cars, Volvo is synonymous with safety. Their advertising focuses on safety, which reinforces this positioning. In addition, Volvo is positioned as more expensive to complement the perceptions of quality and safety.

Over ten years ago, Hertz was number one and Avis was a distant second in the car rental market. Then, Avis came right out and said in its advertisements, "We're Number 2. We Try Harder." As a result, people figured Avis would make every possible effort to give its customers good deals and great service. Whether Avis really does try harder is not known, nor does it matter. The positioning worked.

Positioning helps customers identify with your product and is a means for setting product expectations. Positioning provides a foundation for all communications including advertising, press releases, packaging, and the product name itself.

Just stating the product has a certain position is not enough. If you position your product as reliable and it falls apart, you lose credibility and customers. You can say you're the best product, but you need to back it up with quality and service. In other words, the product must perform as stated.

A way to determine positioning involves charting all the competing products in the market. For example, a chart of "price" versus "product capabilities" shows relative value of competing products. Create a chart with selling price with a range of low to high on the x-axis. Then, use capability (features and benefit) range from less to more on the y-axis. For each competitor, note the selling price and estimate capabilities. With the products plotted on the chart, look for openings to provide value and stand out from the competition.

The following sample chart looks at three products in the market (Product A, B, and C) in terms of price and capability.

The observations are:

- Compared to Product A, New Product is the same price but has more capabilities.
- Compared to Product B, New Product is less expensive and has more capabilities.
- Compared to Product C, New Product is less expensive for the same capabilities.
- Overall, from this chart, New Product offers the best value in terms of price and capability.

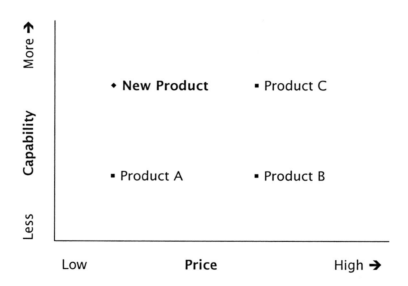

Sample Positioning of Competitors

Your task is to chart the position of your direct competitors and comparable products (including products vying for the same retail shelf space) in terms of price and capabilities customers want. Look for opportunities in the market to serve your customers with greater value. Keep in mind capabilities may include better customer service, ease of use, or greater product availability. For more information, see Appendix A, Investigate Your Competition.

Pricing for Profit

Pricing is one of the most difficult product decisions to make. There's no magic formula for perfect pricing, but I'll offer some guidance to narrow your price within a range.

Your retail price should fall somewhere between the highest amount customers are willing to pay and an amount to cover your product costs, expenses, and profit margin. In general, most retail products are priced +/- 20% to the average competitor price for a particular product class. How your product compares to the competition influences whether your price should be above or below the average.

Setting a Price Point
$$$ The Upper Limit The most customers are willing to pay
$$ Middle Average competitive price (+/- 20%)
$ The Lower Limit Product costs, expenses, and profit margin

Upper Price Limit

The highest your product can be priced is based on what customers are willing to pay. Gather pricing feedback from potential customers (interviews and surveys), distributors and retailers (interviews). Describe the market need, the product's benefits, and advantages. Then ask, "What do you consider the maximum price for this product?" The typical amount they tell you is the upper limit. In addition, read Internet blogs and discussions to see what people are saying about price for your product type.

If your product is a specialty item containing rare materials or superior sophistication, then set a high price. In addition, if you have a unique, sought after product and there are no competitors, price it very high in the beginning. You can drop your price later as needed to meet the competition. For example, years ago a software program manipulated graphic images in record time. No other product like it existed and the company charged $500 and generated large profits. Eventually, other products came along and did the same thing for much less. The company then lowered their price.

If your product is for business end-users, keep in mind they are usually less price sensitive than consumers. Businesses conclude quality products lead to increased productivity, and therefore are cost effective. If you can quantify the fact your product saves money, makes money, or saves time, then a business becomes very interested.

The amount you may charge depends on the value customers derive. Let's assume your product saves two hours of labor every workday, which translates into a $5,000 savings per year. In this case, the customer may be happy to spend $1,000 to receive five times the cost savings.

Middle Price Point

If customers perceive your product as high quality with advantages over the competition, go ahead and set your price above the average or typical competitive price. You can also charge higher prices (perhaps up to 20% more) if you can provide faster service, a better money-back guarantee, and better customer support. To obtain the higher price, your marketing must communicate the product and service offers the benefits and advantages.

If your marketing budget is higher than the competition's, this is another basis to set a price higher than the average or typical competitive price. If, for example, you run television, radio, and magazine advertising, while the competition does not, your costs are greater, but you have a greater chance of reaching and influencing more people.

Lower Price Limit

The lowest possible selling price must be at a point where you can still generate a profit. The lowest price you can charge, on average, depends on product unit costs, expenses, and profit goals. If you sell through a distributor, then remember to determine your profit based on the distributor's price, not the retail price. Here's how to calculate profit:

- Gross Profit = (Selling Price x Units sold) – (Unit cost x Units sold)
- Net Profit = Gross Profit – Expenses

Use a spreadsheet to calculate profit using various selling prices, number of units you can sell, and expenses. If you're not sure about your numbers, talk to an accountant or product specialist for guidance.

For more financial information, see Appendix D, Product Math. In addition, there are time-saving Invention Templates with financial calculations for pricing and profit. Learn how you can benefit from using the Invention Templates at my website (www.ProductCoach.com).

Shopping Styles

Another pricing consideration is how your typical buyer shops. Roper Starch, a market research company, conducted a worldwide survey of 40,000 people and concluded shoppers come in four styles. For the most part, buyers are either:

- **Innovators** – 21% buy the latest innovative product. Innovators want the latest gadget and pay almost any price. If your product is cutting edge, cool, and creative, then innovators want your product. Set a high price when you launch your product.

- **Deal Makers** – 29% love the buying process itself. Deal Makers research, compare prices, and look for value. If your product offers a good solution at a competitive price, you can win many sales. To win over the Deal Makers, set your retail price within 10% to 20% of the average competitive price depending on the advantages and quality of your product.

- **Price Seekers** – 27% indicate price is the most important consideration. Price Seekers want the lowest price because they only want a basic product to get the job done. They often buy generic non-brands or wait for sales. You can make a profit with the lowest price if you keep costs and expenses to a minimum.

- **Brand Loyalists** – 23% buy mostly name brands. Brand Loyalists want a name brand they can trust. They are willing to pay higher prices with the expectation of quality. If there are no brand name competitors for your type of product, you can capture these people with professional-looking brochures and nice packaging, emphasizing quality in your messages. In this case, set a higher-than-average competitive price to attract brand loyalists. If brand names exist in your market, either build a brand name based on plenty of marketing, or lower your price to appeal to Deal Makers and Price Seekers.

Your product won't appeal to everyone, so think about which group of shoppers your product best attracts, and set the price accordingly.

Quantity Discounts

People expect a price break when buying in quantity. Discounts vary depending on industry norms, competition, and profit potential.

A quantity discount pricing structure to consider is the ratio of 1:2:5. For example, a quantity of 10 receives a 5% discount, 20 items a 10% discount, and 50 items a 15% discount. The quantity level can be any sequence of 1:2:5. For example, if it's normal to purchase one item, the quantity discounts are then for 5, 10, 20, 50, 100, 200, and 500 items (5:1:2:5:1:2:5). When you create a discount program, be sure at the highest discount, there is still room for profit.

Consumables

A product can be a combination of product plus a consumable element. For example, ink jet printers from HP and Epson are relatively inexpensive. The real money is the consumable ink cartridges. Each cartridge sells for about 10% to 20% of the printer's selling price. Another example is selling a razor as the base product, and then selling blades as the consumable. A pricing strategy for a product plus a consumable involves offering the base product at an inexpensive price, and then making most of the profit with a high-priced consumable. The key is to design your product so your consumables are compatible with only your product.

You might try offering your consumables on a subscription basis. For example, the water-dispensing machine is low priced or free, along with an agreement to buy a certain volume of bottled water monthly. This provides recurring revenue you can count on as long as you maintain quality products and service.

Pricing Considerations

Other pricing considerations include seasonal market demands. On Valentine's Day, the price of roses increases. Notice if you're able to raise prices or if you need to lower prices during certain times of the year. Track consumer reactions as you raise or lower prices. Does a price change affect sales volume and therefore overall revenue? Play with prices to see if total sales revenue increase.

If you're not sure about the right price, advertise your product with different prices in three magazines. See which brings in more revenue.

New competitors regularly appear with lower prices and new features. Stay ahead by listening closely to your customers and offering new features. Competitors with an inferior product might be going after a different market segment, allowing you to maintain your price. If they offer a similar quality product and service, you might need to drop your price. It depends on the total value offered to the customer.

You can lower your price and remain profitable by lowering your costs. Cut costs by buying larger quantities of supplies at a discount, finding cheaper or more efficient labor, and using less expensive packaging. You might find customers don't really need the high quality you offer. In this case, cut costs by using less-expensive product materials.

Marketing Communications Plan

Communications inform, influence, and encourage. Though sometimes thought of as just advertising and promotion, a communications plan is the use of all possible mediums to make future customers aware of your business and product. A well-executed communications plan raises awareness, produces sales leads, generates interest, and motivates purchases.

Any transaction between sellers and buyers begins with awareness of your product. Marketing you can use to generate awareness includes:

- Advertising
- Blog posts
- Direct mail
- Direct email
- Free samples
- Magazine articles
- Newsletters
- Personal networking
- Product reviews
- Press releases
- Social media (MySpace, Facebook, Twitter, YouTube)
- Speaking appearances
- Trade shows

Awareness stimulates buyers, motivating them to seek more information about your product. Buyers investigate your product further by:

- Calling you
- Sending you email
- Returning a direct mail postcard
- Searching for product reviews or discussions
- Talking to existing customers
- Talking to opinion leaders
- Visiting a retailer
- Visiting your website

The Buyer diagram below summarizes marketing programs available to create awareness and influence the customer's buying process.

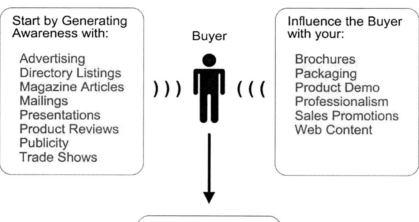

You can influence purchasing decisions from the onset with attractive brochures, packaging, etc. If buyers are interested, they'll investigate your product, weigh its pros and cons, and then make a purchase decision.

You first have to convince customers your product is the solution to their needs. Since people can be skeptical, provide testimonials from satisfied customers, beta testers, or product reviewers. Show lab test results, certifications, awards, or survey results.

Influence a buyer's investigation by:

- Creating a product package designed to stand out and educate with clear benefit statements
- Having a website to educate, inform, and offer time-oriented specials
- Including a risk-free money-back satisfaction guarantee
- Offering free samples, free trial periods, low introductory special price, or free shipping
- Providing excellent customer service with prompt and accurate information

Talk to retailers, distributors, and marketing consultants to find out which communications methods have successfully generated sales for your type of product. Study how competitors market and sell their products. If they're successful, model a similar approach.

You're always better off using an integrated approach rather than putting all your money into one tactic. Using all the marketing tactics at your disposal – e.g., press releases, trade shows, and advertising – will give potential customers opportunities to learn about you from multiple sources.

Marketing Communication Tools

Check off the marketing communication tools other companies have used for your type of product (✓):

❑ Articles	❑ Free Samples	❑ Seminars
❑ Billboards	❑ Internet Banner Ads	❑ Social Networking
❑ Blogs	❑ Magazine Ads	❑ Speeches
❑ Brochures	❑ Newsletters	❑ Sponsorships
❑ Business Card	❑ Newspaper Ads	❑ Statement Stuffer
❑ Catalogs	❑ Packaging	❑ Technical Papers
❑ Contests	❑ Podcasts	❑ Television Ads
❑ Coupons	❑ Posters	❑ Trade Shows
❑ Datasheet	❑ Presentations	❑ Video Posts
❑ Direct Email	❑ Press Kits	❑ Websites
❑ Direct Mail	❑ Product Launch Kits	❑ White Papers
❑ Directory Lists	❑ Product Reviews	❑ Yellow Pages
❑ Flyers	❑ Radio Ads	

Your marketing communications plan does not have to be complicated. For example, a simple, yet effective, communications plan to launch a product could involve:

- Submitting a product for trade magazine reviews
- Placing advertisements in trade magazines
- Issuing a press release when the product is available
- Purchasing a list of names from trade magazines and sending direct mail to the subscribers, and then following-up responses with a telephone call
- Buying search engine keywords to drive traffic to your website

As a way to start, submit articles and press releases to relevant trade magazines. Not only is this a relatively inexpensive, but people tend to believe news and articles before they'll believe advertising. If you are not sure where to begin, look at the marketing programs used by successful competitors.

Even if your product sells in a retail store, marketing is required to generate awareness and interest. Discuss with the retailer how you can work together to increase revenue.

Fishing Product Scenario

Let's say your product is a fishing lure. To generate awareness, you rent a list of names from a fishing magazine. You send a postcard to all the people on the list. You have a great offer while boasting the benefits of your lure. The postcard directs people to local retailers who sell fishing equipment. The customer walks into the retailer, shows the postcard to a store person, and is directed to the fishing lure section. Your fishing lure package has a benefit message of catching more fish and offers a money-back guarantee. The customer compares the price to the competition and your product looks like the best value. The customer makes a purchase.

Inside the package, you include information about how the customer can visit your website to receive free fishing tips and special deals for additional fishing lures. On your website, there is a form to enter a name and email address. With the customer's information, you periodically email information about future specials, fishing tips, as well as new product announcements.

Plan with a Launch Checklist

A Launch Checklist is a handy tool for planning and organizing. The launch checklist is a list of all the tasks needed for launching your product in the market. I suggest creating a Launch Checklist as soon as you decide to bring your invention to market.

The term "launch" means the product is produced, available for shipping, and you're ready to receive sales orders. The launch date is often called first customer ship (FCS) or general availability (GA). Visualize your product shipped out the door to the customer, and then think about all the items needed to produce product sales. Include every major item you need to accomplish before launch. This launch checklist keeps you focused and frees your mind to work creatively.

Product Launch Checklist Sample

When the following items are completed, the product is ready to launch.

Product
- ❑ The product is designed
- ❑ The product receives industry certification
- ❑ The product is produced
- ❑ The product passes testing
- ❑ Packaging and shipping containers are completed and received

Documentation
- ❑ User manual is written and edited
- ❑ Online help is tested and verified

Marketing
- ❑ Beta product is sent to product review magazines (two months before launch)
- ❑ Advertising appears on launch date (check lead times)
- ❑ Brochures are produced (printed and electronic files)
- ❑ Direct mailers are designed, mailing list selected (printed)
- ❑ Press Release is written and contacts identified (send on launch date)
- ❑ Product Launch Kit is written (electronic files)
- ❑ Website contains product information, contact information, a sales lead form, and press release
- ❑ A product launch party is scheduled

Sales and Support
- ❑ Distributor agreements are in place
- ❑ Sales and customer service people are trained
- ❑ Customer relationship database is ready
- ❑ Sales letter is written and edited
- ❑ The 800 telephone number is operational

Post-Launch
- ❑ Track sales leads (amount and source)
- ❑ Track sales revenue (amount and source)

Some items such as print advertising have long lead times. For example, if you want an advertisement to appear in a magazine at the same time you launch your product, you might have to submit your ad materials three months before launch date. Review the lead times for each task to make sure they are ready for the launch. For magazine advertising, see the publisher's media kit for details.

For more details about creating a marketing plan, see Appendix C, The Market-Step Product Plan. Please see the next chapter to begin planning for product development.

Chapter 14:
Product Planning

A tool is but the extension of a man's hand, and a machine is but a complex tool. And he that invents a machine augments the power of a man and the well-being of mankind.

Henry Ward Beecher

Topics in this Chapter:

- Product Requirements
- Regulations and Certifications
- Infringement Search and Freedom to Operate
- Manufacturing Your Product
- Project Plan
- Budget Setting
- Tips to Making Your Product More Marketable

The objective of this chapter is to plan the development and manufacture of your invention. The basis of product development is a detailed understanding of your future customer and competition. In addition, pricing and positioning dictate the quality and materials used to create your product. Before you design the product, you should have pricing (retail, wholesale, and manufacturing costs) figured out.

Product Requirements

One of the keys to successful development is to determine Product Requirements. A Product Requirements document lists what you want your product to have and do. Write the Product Requirements from the customer's perspective.

Written requirements help define the scope, direction, and focus of what you need to develop. Product Requirements, along with drawings, diagrams, and photographs provide further clarification to designers and manufacturers.

A Product Requirements document dramatically increases your chances a designer and manufacturer will create the product as you intended, rather than trying to read your mind. This document is simple to create with your word processor and can be as little as one or two pages.

A Product Requirements document includes:

- Features
- Functionality
- Appearance
- Performance levels
- Quality and reliability levels
- User's environment
- Packaging and labeling needs
- Certification and regulation specifications
- Cost constraints

If you created your prototype requirements as discussed in the *Create a Prototype* chapter, expand the document with lessons learned from prototype feedback, new design ideas, and any new functionality required to pass regulations and certifications.

Product Requirements Sample — Tabletop Electric Fan

1. The fan must operate at 120 volts, 60 Hz, 0.5 amps.
2. The electric motor must have a life of 10,000 hours.
3. Input voltage regulation must tolerate plus or minus 12 volts.
4. The fan speed is variable at high, medium, and low.
5. High speed must be at 180 revolutions per minute.
6. Medium speed must be at 90 revolutions per minute.
7. Low speed must be at 60 revolutions per minute.
8. There must be four pushbutton switches located on the base and labeled: Off, High, Medium, and Low.
9. There must be a pushbutton switch next to the fan assembly and labeled as Oscillation
10. The fan must oscillate over 90 degrees at a rate of once per ten seconds.
11. The fan must have three blades: each blade 12 inches in diameter and made of ABS white plastic.
12. The blade must be enclosed in a coated aluminum cage.
13. The fan must operate in an environment with temperatures ranging from 32 to 125 degrees Fahrenheit, and humidity from 20% to 100%.
14. The fan must last for at least five years.
15. The fan must pass UL certification.
16. Total parts costs cannot exceed $8.
17. Shipment must begin May 1, 2010.
18. There must be 15,000 fans produced for the first ship date.
19. There must be 15,000 fans produced each month for the following year.

Create Product Requirements with the following steps:

- List each of the customer's problems, needs, and wants.
- Describe a feature or function for each problem, need, and want.
- Modify and enhance the features and functions based on your innovation, positioning, pricing, quality, style, and product life.
- If you plan to sell through retailers and distributors, find out if they have specific requirements (materials, quality, safety).
- Contact a test lab (see next section) to determine if there are any safety requirements for your type of product.
- Prioritize the list according to features and functions customers are willing to buy.
- Write the list of features and functions into the language of a Product Requirements document such as "The product must have ..." or "The product must perform at the following level ..."
- Select the highest priority requirements to produce a product quickly and within your budget. If you have a time constraint, eliminate the nice to have features and functions.
- Include any drawings or diagrams for clarification.

Regulations and Certifications

Your product might require certification or need to conform to certain regulations. If so, make sure to look into this early because certifications and regulations may involve long lead times and expense.

Even if it is not required, certification can provide a competitive advantage and offer peace of mind for potential customers. For example, two power tools are offered for sale. Their prices are about the same and they offer similar features. One proudly displays a safety certification seal of approval. In this case, buyers are more likely to purchase the certified product.

Some certifications are organized within an industry and are not government-based. For example, Microsoft has certification programs to inform customers certain independent software products conform to Microsoft standards. Microsoft has designated official labs to perform tests for a fee. Once your product passes, you can announce these positive results in a press release and add a certification logo to your product box and website.

Occasionally, customers require certification before buying your product. For example, a prospective customer was interested in using my wireless modem to transmit oil-processing data. The catch is they could only use products certified in hazardous environments. After some research, I discovered the testing process would cost $10,000 and take two months to complete. In addition, the product would need modifications to pass the test. As a result, I decided it was not worth the cost of the certification and modification as compared to product sales.

To uncover certification guidelines for your product type, contact the following certification organizations:

- **UL** – Underwriters Laboratories Inc. (www.ul.com) is an independent, not-for-profit product safety testing and certification organization. They offer services to help companies achieve certification acceptance for their products in the United States whether it's an electrical device, a programmable system, or a company's quality process. A UL mark for an electrical device, such as a lamp, is not required by law but offers peace of mind to the consumer.

- **CSA** – Canadian Standards Association (www.csa.ca) is a not-for-profit, membership-based association serving business, industry, government, and consumers. They test many products for compliance to national and international standards, and issue the CSA mark. The United States Occupational Safety and Health Administration (OSHA) recognizes CSA as a "Nationally Recognized Testing Laboratory" for products sold in the United States.

- **CE** – The CE mark (www.cemarking.net) is a mandatory European marking for certain product groups. It indicates conformity with essential health and safety requirements set out in European Directives. The letters "CE" stand for Conformité Européenne, French for "European Conformity." The CE mark must be placed on products sold in Europe (e.g., medical devices, machinery, industrial installations, toys, electrical equipment, electronics, domestic appliances, pressure equipment, personal protective equipment, recreational craft, refrigerators, etc.). CE marking does not apply to cosmetics, chemicals, pharmaceuticals, and foodstuffs.

For specific guidance, contact a local UL, CSA, or CE test lab listed on their websites or found in the Yellow Pages under "Laboratories – Testing."

To have your product certified:

- Contact a test lab and ask for guidance.
- Describe your product and ask for a price quote to test your product.
- Send your product to the lab.
- The lab performs tests and issues you a pass or fail report.
- If your product fails the test, make changes and send a new product to the lab.
- If a regulating agency oversees your product type, submit a "passed" test report to them. The regulatory agency reviews the report and issues a certification. [This process can take months, so check to see how the timing affects your launch schedule.]
- Place the certification mark on your product, packaging, website, brochure, and other communications.

For example, a wireless device in the United States must pass Federal Communications Commission (FCC) testing before use in the public airwaves. First, an independent test lab checks wireless devices for harmful emissions. If the device conforms to FCC standards, the lab issues a report indicating the product conforms to emission standards. The FCC reviews the device and report to finalize approval. The FCC process can take approximately three months from the first test until final approval.

Patent Infringement Search and Freedom to Operate

Before you manufacture your invention, make sure the design does not infringe on any active patents. Even if your invention is granted a patent, it does not give you the right to make and sell your invention. A patent only gives you the right to exclude others from making your invention.

An infringement search only requires the review of currently active patents (i.e., typically the last 20 years). To summarize the differences between a patentability search and infringement search, the following guide outlines the time period and parts of a patent to review.

Patent Search Guide		
	Search Time Period	Examine
Patentability Search	Search all patents dated as far back as to when a particular technology began.	Review an entire patent to determine if your invention is unique compared to any previous patent.
Infringement Search	Search all active patents, which go back 20 years for utility patents, or 14 years for design and plant patents.	Review the Claims section of a patent to determine if it includes all the aspects of your invention.

An infringement search (also called a "product clearance" or "patent clearance") should be left to a trained patent attorney. At the same time, to improve thoroughness and perhaps reduce attorney fees, perform a preliminary search and make a list of patents close to your invention. You can begin your search with a list of patents found in the patentability search (if you filed for a patent), and continue looking through recently granted patents.

Currently, the United States Patent and Trademark Office (USPTO) provides a free patent search (www.uspto.gov). There are alternative websites for patent searching, such as Google Patents (www.google.com/patents), but the USPTO website is your best source. In addition, some university and public libraries (known as Patent and Trademark Depository Libraries) offer free patent search on special computers. They regularly receive archives of new patents on DVD and can provide you with search assistance.

If you think you'll market your product in Europe, search the European Patent Office website, which also includes Japanese patents (www.epo.org). In the event you plan to introduce your product in Canada, search the Canadian Intellectual Property Office website (www.cipo.ic.gc.ca).

What to Look For

A United States Patent includes the Patent Number, Inventor, Date of Patent, Classifications, References, Abstract, Background, Summary, Drawings, Description of Drawings, and Claims.

First, look at the drawings and read the Abstract. The Abstract is a short overview of the patent. If the description of the invention mentioned in the

Abstract is similar to yours, log the Patent Number, Patent Name, Class, and Date of Patent using the template provided in this section or create your own.

The section of a patent examined for infringement is the Claims section. Claims are specific attributes that make a particular patent unique.

You're best off retaining a patent attorney to provide a written opinion concerning possible infringement. With a legal opinion from an attorney, you attain a "freedom to operate." Freedom to operate (FTO) gives you the confidence to sell your product without infringing on the intellectual property of others.

Patent Search Methods

To keep a patent search simple, I'll focus on methods to search the USPTO website, but these techniques could be applied to other patent databases. Websites often change, so actual procedures might differ among databases. Here are the steps for quickly searching patents:

- Make a list of commonly used words pertaining to the function or description of your invention. These are known as keywords. You'll use the keywords to perform a search. From the USPTO homepage, click on Patents, then Search Patents, and then Quick Search. Type a keyword or keyword phrase where it says **Query Term 1** and click the Search button. For example, in **Query Term 1** enter "locking mechanism" and in **Field 1** keep the setting "All Fields" and click the Search button.

USPTO Quick Search

This is a representation of the Quick Search screen at the USPTO website.

Query Term 1: [   ]   in Field 1: [All Fields   ▼]

Term 2: [   ]   in Field 2: [All Fields   ▼]

Select Years

[1976 to Present (full-text) ▼]   [Search]

- If there's a match, you'll be presented with a list of found patents. If you receive over a hundred patents, go back and enter more specific keywords (e.g., "seatbelt locking mechanism"). If you receive only a few patents, go back and enter more general keywords.

- The list includes the Patent Number and Title links. Click on the Patent Number link to display the patent. Read the Abstract and the Claims. If the patent appears similar to your invention, log the patent number, name, classification, and date. In addition, look at the drawings to get a better feel for similarity or not. While viewing a patent, click on the Images link to display the complete patent along with drawings.

- The patent system is organized into classifications and subclassifications. Your patent is filed within a certain classification. You can narrow your patent search to the related classification and subclass. In Query Term 1 enter a classification number and in Field 1 click on the menu list for "Current US Classification" and then click the Search button.

- You'll receive a list of patents based on the classification and subclass you entered. Again, click on the Patent Number link and read the Abstract and Claims. If the patent appears similar to your invention, log the patent number, name, class, and date.

Here's a template to help you track your patent search.

Patent Search Log			
Patent Number	Patent Name	Patent Class/Subclass	Date of Patent

Patents That Match Your Invention

If you uncover any patent comparable as your invention, it does not necessarily mean the game is over. There might be enough innovation in your design to avoid infringement. Some patent attorneys are trained to modify aspects of your invention to avoid infringement. If any patent looks close to yours, discuss it with a patent attorney.

Manufacturing Your Product

Manufacturing involves turning your design into a finished product. While it's possible to manufacture the product yourself, I recommend you outsource production to a contract manufacturer. Outsourcing the manufacturing process allows you to better concentrate on design and marketing. Later, if you decide to manufacture yourself, you will have learned from the outsourcing experience.

Finding Manufacturers

To outsource manufacturing, look for contract manufacturers specializing in your product type. Use a search engine, such as Google, and keywords ["your product type" and "contract manufacturing"].

In addition, look in the Yellow Pages for manufacturers under the following headings:

- Assembly and Fabricating
- Electronic Parts Assemblers
- Manufacturing – Contract
- Plastics Fabricators

Getting your product made outside the United States results in a significant cost reduction. Generally, products made in Mexico cost 70% of those made in the United States, while products made in Asia cost 30% of those made in the United States. There are shipping charges and the potential for long shipping delays that you must consider. If this is your first time, I suggest starting with a local manufacturer.

Don't be intimidated if you're starting out small. Some manufacturers work on small production items. Look for advertising messages such as "No job too small" or "Short runs our specialty" or other indicators a manufacturer is willing to work with inventors and start-up entrepreneurs.

Manufacturers want to see the following items to provide a quote to produce your product:

- Drawings and diagrams of each part with exact dimensions and specifications
- Drawings of how parts physically interact (e.g., exploded view diagram, assembly drawing, or system flowchart)
- Bill of materials (details of all parts)
- Product Requirements

The general steps a manufacturer takes to produce your product include:

- Reviewing plans and drawings
- Ordering parts and materials
- Designing and setting up an assembly line
- Performing production of parts and assemblies
- Performing inspection of parts and assemblies
- Performing quality acceptance testing
- Monitoring quality yields and improving processes
- Packing and shipping the product

If your product has plastic parts, you will need a mold produced. The typical mold process for mass-produced plastic parts is injection molding. This method involves a liquefied plastic injected into an aluminum or steel block. Molds can easily cost $10,000 and up. As products are produced, the mold wears out and parts become less exact. Therefore, the larger the quantity of products produced, the greater need for durability of a mold. The greater the durability, the higher the mold cost.

For example, most small run molds are made of aluminum, while a large run of 100,000 or more often use a steel mold. When requesting a price quote, ask for the life of the mold (number of parts produced).

Design Engineering

Some manufacturers have engineers on staff to produce CAD drawings, but I recommend hiring an engineer on your own. The engineer acts on your behalf as a liaison to the manufacturer to handle technical issues as they may arise.

Look in the Yellow Pages for designers and engineers under the following headings:

- Designers – Industrial
- Engineers – Electronic
- Engineers – Mechanical
- Product Designers

Interview engineers and designers to discover if they have experience with your product type. Check references and credentials. Before discussing your product, ask them to sign your non-disclosure agreement. Then provide your Product Requirements and request a price quote to produce the CAD files. If need be, ask if they interact with a manufacturer and work with you as the product is produced.

Tip: While still in the planning stage, design your product with manufacturing in mind. This means simplifying the design by using the fewest number of parts and as many similar parts as possible. For example, if your product uses screws, have all screws the same type and the same size. This seems obvious, but products exist with a mix of Philips and slot screws. Since parts are purchased in quantity, you save money by using as many similar parts as possible. The lower the number of parts often leads to less expensive assembly costs. Another way to reduce costs is by designing parts to snap or screw together during assembly rather than needing fasteners or tools.

Project Plan

To help organize product development, create a project plan. A project plan is a list of activities and timeline of your entire product development. Creating a project plan helps provide clarity, flesh out assumptions, and uncover technical and practical details. In addition, project plans generally lead to faster project completion, greater product quality, and a closer alignment of product functionality to customer needs.

Your project plan does not have to be elaborate. The methods I suggest allow you to create a streamlined and simple project. A few pages may suffice, depending on the complexity of the product.

Keep in mind, if you intend to outsource product development, all aspects of the product need to be described so the designer has a complete understanding of the product.

Create a project plan with the following outline:

- Product Description
- Goals and Objectives
- Possible Issues
- Deadlines
- Tasks

Tasks make up the bulk of a project plan. For your project plan, create a list of tasks with the following guidelines:

- **Identify activities** – Visualize, brainstorm, and perform research to determine all possible major and minor development activities for completing the product. Talk to people who have created your product type before, reverse engineer similar products, review patents, and talk with designers, engineers, and product consultants.

- **Identify tasks** – For each major and minor activity, list the individual tasks to be completed.

- **Group similar tasks together** – To speed up development time, groups similar tasks together.

- **Order tasks** – Some tasks need to be completed before another task can start. Order tasks within each group.

- **Estimate time to complete** – Estimate the time to perform each task in terms of hours, days, weeks, or months.

- **Determine total time** – Summarize time needed to complete the entire project. Keep in mind some tasks cannot be started until a previous task is completed. To shorten project time, look for tasks to work on at the same time.

- **Find resources** – If you're working on the project with others, assign people or companies to each task. More people doesn't always guarantee shorter project time. Microsoft's Bill Gates had been known to understaff projects to create an entrepreneurial atmosphere and minimize costs.

Another way to create a project plan is to flowchart key activities. First visualize the entire process. Then, with a piece of paper or software, draw activities and see what items come first, next, and which are missing.

In the following project plan example, a list of tasks and timelines are shown. Tasks are grouped by Product Planning, Manufacturing, Product Artwork, Packaging, User Documentation, and Distribution.

In the Time column, "d" represents days and "w" represents weeks. Time in this example is for work performed during weekdays and not over weekends.

For complicated projects, I recommend Microsoft Project to organize and track your project. It allows you to list each task, set a start date, estimate duration, set task precedence, and assign resources. The application automatically generates Gantt charts, PERT diagrams, and more as needed.

A Gantt chart is a graphic display of tasks to help you see the relationships and timelines of all the tasks. A Project Evaluation and Review Technique (PERT) diagram is another graphical method to help organize tasks.

Check the Microsoft website for more information on Microsoft Project. Overall, create a project plan with whichever method is easiest for you to organize tasks and monitor progress.

Sample Project Plan			
TASK	Start	Time	Finish
PRODUCT PLANNING			
Create product requirements and manufacturing plans	Jun 1	10d	Jun 14
Present Product Requirements to engineer	Jun 15	1d	Jun 15
Engineer to provide up to three CAD prototypes	Jun 16	10d	Jun 29
Approve one prototype	Jun 30	1d	Jun 30
Engineer works on detailed design	Jul 1	2w	Jul 17
Approve final design	Jul 18	1d	Jul 18
Engineer creates test requirements	Jul 20	6d	Jul 27
MANUFACTURING			
Manufacturer runs production	Jul 28	2w	Aug 10
Product ships to distribution center	Aug 11	3d	Aug 15
PRODUCT ARTWORK			
Artist to create product artwork	Jul 6	1w	Jul 14
PACKAGING			
Packaging requirements planning	Jun 30	8d	Jul 11
Packaging company creates a prototype and cost estimates	Jul 12	1w	Jul 18
Approve one package prototype	Jul 19	1d	Jul 19
Artist to create packaging artwork	Jul 20	5d	Jul 26
Packaging company runs production	Jul 27	5d	Aug 2
Packaging shipped to product manufacturer	Aug 3	1d	Aug 3
USER DOCUMENTATION			
User Manual first draft	Jul 3	2w	Jul 14
User Manual photo shots	Jul 17	1d	Jul 17
User Manual edits	Jul 18	3d	Jul 20
User Manual final review	Jul 21	3d	Jul 25
User Manual formatting	Jul 26	5d	Aug 1
User Manual printing and shipment	Aug 2	1w	Aug 8
DISTRIBUTION			
Receive product and packaging	Aug 16	2d	Aug 17
Product Availability	Aug 18	1d	Aug 18

Budget Setting

We only have a certain amount of money to spend on development, marketing, and sales. Different product types, different competitive environments, and various stages of growth in the market dictate the amount of money needed and how it should be allocated.

For a budget example, cell phones are highly technical, very competitive, and the market is still growing. As a result, development and advertising costs are high. In contrast, standard flashlights have been around a long time, have only a few parts, and have a mature market. Therefore, development costs are minimal and the budget emphasis is on marketing.

The following is a guideline for allocating money from initial idea to product launch. For example, let's say you have $10,000 to spend. Using the given allocation percentages, you would plan to spend $1,000 (10%) on market research, $6,000 (60%) on product development, $500 (5%) on packaging, and $2,500 (25%) on marketing communications.

Budget Allocation Guideline	
Product Area	**Allocation**
Market Research	10%
Development and Production	60%
Packaging	5%
Marketing Communications	25%

On the other hand, if you plan to raise money, investors want to know how much you need. To determine the amount, review your project plan, assigning a dollar amount to each task in terms of the cost of labor, overhead, and materials. For typical financial allocations used in your product industry, examine the book *Industry Norms & Key Business Ratios* by Dun & Bradstreet. Financial information on assets, liabilities, sales, and profit are broken down by industry. You can usually find this book in the reference or social science section of a public or university library. I also recommend discussing development and marketing costs with an accountant experienced with your product type.

Your Budget		
How much money can you budget to develop and market your product? Allocate the total amount across the following product areas.		
Product Area	**Allocation %**	**Amount $**
Market Research		
Development and Production		
Packaging		
Marketing Communications		

Tips to Making Your Product More Marketable

As you develop your product there are a number of things to keep in mind. Consider the customer, costs, marketing, and distribution:

- **End-user** –Make sure that product benefits and features reflect customer problems, needs, and wants.

- **Purchaser** – Sometimes the purchaser and end-user are different people. For example, if your product is made for a baby, the purchaser might be the grandmother buying a gift. Therefore, think of who might make the purchase and what appeals to those people. For more about buyer behavior, see Chapter 15, How Your Customer Thinks.

- **Costs** – Think of ways to keep product costs down. Look for ways to minimize parts, minimize assembly steps, and minimize packaging.

- **Demonstrable** – Customers make decisions on how a product appeals visually. Make sure the product can be easily demonstrated in actual use that can be seen on video.

- **Retailer** – Retailers think in terms of a dollar amount per shelf space. The more space a product takes up, the more the product should be worth. Make sure your product is sized to fit with comparable products sitting on a shelf or hanging from a rack.

- **Installation** – Make the product easy to install, set up, and use. If tools are required, try to minimize the number of tools, steps, and parts.

Excellent! You have completed the Product Planning stage. Now, take these plans and turn your invention into a real product by following the strategies in the upcoming chapters.

In addition to product planning, it's time to start thinking about funding and setting up a business entity. For information about funding, see Appendix E, Funding Your Idea. For tips on starting a new business, see Appendix F, Business Startup.

Chapter 15:
How Your Customer Thinks

There is only one boss. The customer. And he can fire everybody in the company from the chairman on down, simply by spending his money somewhere else.

Sam Walton, Founder of Walmart

Topics in this Chapter:

- Customer Problems, Needs, and Wants
- The Many Faces of a Customer
- I've Got to Have It First
- Know the Customer's Buying Process

Knowing your customer provides valuable insight about how to make your product more attractive and sellable. There are four points to consider:

- Customers buy when they want to solve a problem or when they want to satisfy a need or want
- Customers do not buy alone, they're influenced by other people
- Customers buy according to their personality
- Customers follow a process before they buy

Customer Problems, Needs, and Wants

When you go to a doctor, what happens? After reading countless magazines, you're called into the examination room. A nurse asks some questions and takes your vital signs. Then the doctor comes in, looks at the chart, and asks questions. Where does it hurt? How long have you had that? Does it hurt when you move?

The doctor is attempting to isolate the problem to offer a solution. How would you feel if your doctor just handed you pills without asking any questions? The point is you need to understand your customer's problems before creating a solution (your product). Typically, problems center on a lack of money, love, health, esteem, recognition, or satisfaction.

The Many Faces of a Customer

Let's explore how a customer goes about making a purchase. There's usually more than one person involved in the buying decision process. For example, a child's toy may have as many as four people involved. A child's friend (first person) starts the process by convincing the child (second person) he needs a certain toy. The child advances the buying process by telling a parent (third person) he needs a certain toy. The child is the user of the toy, the parent is the buyer, and another adult (fourth person) may be involved in making the final decision. In the end, the child, the child's friend, and the parents are all involved in the buying process.

How does the buying process affect you, the developer? Your product needs to appeal to all the people involved in the buying process. For example, to appeal to the child and child's friend, the toy may need to be red and make a lot of noise. To appeal to the parents, it must be safe, easy to assemble, and reasonably priced.

For a business, who is involved in the buying process? Whereas consumers mostly involve friends, family, and product reviews, business customers act differently. Each business has a chain-of-command for evaluating purchases. Your product has to appeal to each person and department involved.

For example, a product must appeal to the Information Technology Manager based on technical merit. The Purchasing Manager must like the warranty and terms. At the same time, the Chief Financial Officer is looking for a favorable return on investment.

The roles generally played by people in the buying process are:

- **Initiator** – The person(s) who gets things started. This may be the neighbor with the new car or an analyst who discovers a flaw in a business process.

- **Influencer** – The person(s) who advocates making the purchase. It may be a crying child, a parent, or a boss.

- **Decider** – The person(s) who makes the final purchase decision. This could be the Initiator, the purchasing department, or a spouse.

- **Buyer** – The person who hands over the cash, check, or credit card. The Buyer and Decider may be the same person or different people.

- **User** – The actual user(s) of the product.

I've Got to Have It First

Do you have a friend or family member who is always first to have the latest gadget? I had an uncle who was this way. I remember he had the first digital watch. He paid hundreds of dollars for it back in the 1970s. Its only function was to tell the time with its four bright red numbers. Today, a $10 Casio watch performs a series of magic tricks in comparison to the first digital watch.

Another example is the microwave oven. Microwave ovens provide time savings and convenient cooking. People who liked the latest gadgets bought them right away. They accepted the microwave's benefits and trusted the safety. Risk-adverse people waited years. They worried about the possible effects of radiation, could not justify the price, or saw no reason to switch their cooking method. Most of us occupy the middle ground.

The authors of *Crossing the Chasm* (Geoffrey Moore) and *The Diffusion of Innovation* (Everett Rogers) explain how different types of people have different comfort levels for trying and buying new products. Studies have proven this concept especially as it pertains to technology-based products.

When a new product becomes available, the length of time people wait to make a purchase is based on their personality type. This is important for product developers to know. When a new product is introduced, it's first purchased by an **Innovator**, then an **Early Adopter, Early Majority, Late Majority**, and last but not least, the **Laggards**:

- **Innovator** – Innovators love new gadgets for the sake of technology and style rather than their role in solving particular problems. They are visionaries, risk-takers, and global thinkers. They are roughly 5% of your market.

- **Early Adopter** – Early Adopters are risk-takers and role models who test the waters ahead of most people in their peer group. They try an innovation and offer opinions on their experience. They are roughly 15% of your market.

- **Early Majority** – Early Majority are practical and somewhat conservative. They want value and require proof your product does the job. They are roughly 35% of your market.

- **Late Majority** – Being cautious and skeptical, Late Majority weigh pros and cons, and still sometimes need peer pressure to make a purchase decision. They are roughly 35% of your market.

- **Laggards** – Laggards are late to change and sometimes suspicious. They take a long time to make a decision. They are roughly 10% of your market.

There's nothing wrong with being any of these personality type categories. In fact, we may be an Early Adopter in some instances and a Late Majority in others. It depends on our comfort level for a particular product type.

How do these different personality types affect you as a product developer? There's good news and bad news. The good news is there are always Innovators, those people who buy anything if the product is innovative and confers some prestige to its owner. They've got to have your product and pay almost anything to acquire it. The bad news is this can give you false hope. When Innovators snap up your product, you might believe you'll become a millionaire in no time. The truth is the rest of the market does not buy like the Innovators. The rest of the market is more skeptical. They need to see real results, they want form and function, and they want reasonable prices

The solution to selling to different personality types is two-fold. When you first market your product, the Innovator marketing message focuses on innovation, uniqueness, and the exclusivity of owning your product. You then need to persuade Innovators and Early Adopters to evangelize for you. Get their testimonials, have them to speak for you, and ask them to spread the word. Since they are role models, others take their advice and buy your product.

Secondly, take the early revenue and plow it back into the business. To attract the rest of the market, communicate with testimonials and benefit-oriented marketing messages. Use advertising and promotion to create awareness, generate interest, and stimulate product purchase.

Know the Customer's Buying Process

We all go through a buying process. What differs is the time it takes to make a purchase decision. For example, buying a car is more involved and takes longer than buying an inexpensive product such as chewing gum.

First, we recognize a problem, need, or want. Then we search for information and sift through the facts. We evaluate the alternatives and make a purchase. If we are looking for chewing gum, the process can take 30 seconds. A car purchase can take up to 30 days.

The following outlines the general buying process:

- **Problem Recognition** – We realize we need to make a change. Problem recognition comes about from self-realization, brought to our attention by others, or from marketing messages. For example, you discover the soles of your shoes are worn out after you just stepped in a puddle (self-realization). Or, perhaps your neighbor just purchased a new car and you feel like keeping up with the Joneses (external).

- **Information Search** – After we've realized a problem, are in pain, or have a need or want, it's time to search for solutions. Some people read consumer magazines and gather information over the Internet. Some people go to a retail store, look at a few products, and ask a salesperson for help.

- **Evaluation of Alternatives** – In our mind, we hold beliefs about how a product should function, look, and benefit us. We have some beliefs based on brand recognition from the bombardment of marketing. From these perceptions and others such as price, packaging, and availability, we narrow our selection to a few choices.

- **Purchase Decision** – Product selection may take minutes, hours, or even months. Just before making a decision, the customer is often influenced by comments and suggestions by Influencers and Decision Makers. This could be from a friend, family member, salesperson, or comments read on the Internet. In addition, there could be last-minute decisions after weighing price versus benefits.

- **Post-purchase** – Once the purchase is made, relief follows because a solution has been found. Sometimes buyer's remorse sets in and we wonder if we made the right decision.

How does the customer buying process affect us as product developers? We need to understand the buying process for our type of product. In the problem recognition phase, we need to know what types of problems people are experiencing. We need to know the sources our customers pay attention to when gathering information. Do they read *Consumer Reports*, follow the advice of a famous athlete, or listen predominately to Mom?

We need to make sure customers are aware of our product when they begin their search. When they evaluate us, we have already anticipated, through market research, their problems, pains, needs, and wants. Therefore, customers view our product as a viable solution.

We know word-of-mouth advertising is effective, so we make sure to offer a quality product and excellent service. Finally, we solve post-purchase buyer's remorse by including a thank-you letter with the product, sending a thank-you letter, or making a follow-up telephone call congratulating them for making the right purchase decision.

What if people don't realize they have a problem? Many people are busy going about their daily lives. They might not realize they have a problem that's related to your product or don't understand the severity of the problem. In any case, marketing is needed to bring the problem to the surface. There was a famous TV commercial for dandruff shampoo. In the commercial, a man was going about his day with a smile on his face until a friend pointed out dandruff flakes on his shoulders. He suddenly became upset because he had an important date with an attractive woman. Not to worry, the friend came to the rescue with *Head & Shoulders* shampoo. After using the shampoo, the man was shown confident and secure with his female companion. The lesson learned is that marketing is needed to disrupt daily patterns, point out problems, and offer solutions. More about marketing is found in upcoming chapters.

During the entire development process, examine your product from the customer's point of view. The best way to collect information about your customers is to interact with them.

Chapter 16:
Product Development

If the automobile had followed the same development cycle as the computer, a Rolls-Royce would today cost $100, get one million miles to the gallon, and explode once a year, killing everyone inside.

Robert X. Cringely

Topics in this Chapter:

- Development Flowchart
- Convert Requirements into Specifications
- Bill of Materials
- Test Cases
- User Documentation
- Patent Marking
- Product Production Steps
- Manufacturing Tips

Your product comes to life in stages. It starts as a concept in your mind. Then, it comes into form as a prototype. After planning, your idea matures into an alpha product, beta product, and finally a commercially available product.

This step of the **Market-Step** process covers product development. Even if you turn all development and manufacturing over to a company, you should read this chapter to be familiar with the behind-the-scenes engineering activities. The development steps are:

Product Development (Ch. 16)

1. Convert requirements into specifications
2. Create a bill of materials
3. Write a test plan
4. Write user documentation
5. Initiate production

Beta Test (Ch. 17)

6. Plan a beta test
7. Recruit beta testers
8. Distribute to beta testers
9. Obtain beta feedback

Marketing Development (Ch. 18)

10. Develop a marketing brand and theme
11. Select a product name
12. Create packaging

If you're completing Development by yourself, complete activities one through twelve in order. If you have two or more people, you may save time by working in tandem. A person or team can develop the product, while another person or team can conduct the beta test, and others can develop marketing programs.

If you are skilled in design and manufacturing, great. If not, use the information here to guide your work with designers, engineers, and contract manufacturers.

Development Flowchart

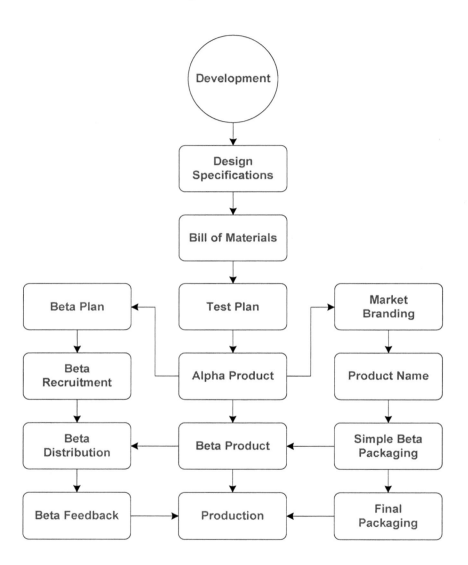

Convert Requirements into Specifications

In the previous planning stage you created a Product Requirements document. Now, you need to examine each requirement and create specifications. Specifications are the details of each feature and function of your product. If you hire an engineer, ask him or her to create specifications for you.

Your specifications may include details about:

- Capacity
- Color
- Energy: Voltage, Current, Power
- Environment: Temperature, Humidity, Pressure
- Function
- Input, Output
- Materials
- Movement: Direction, Speed, Rate
- Reliability, Stress, Strain, Duty cycles
- Resolution
- Shape
- Size: Length, Width, Height, Area, Diameter
- Time
- Tolerance
- Weight

In addition to specifying component characteristics, specifications can include details for accepted standards. For example, the product requirements state: "This product must operate in compliance to IEEE 802.11 standards." Therefore, the specification outlines the details of IEEE 802.11.

The purpose of industry standards are for safety and/or to provide engineers with easier integration of parts and systems. Standards exist for software, electronics, clothing, food, etc., and are maintained by independent organizations and the government.

For more information about standards, visit the National Institute of Standards (www.nist.gov) and the International Organization for Standardization (www.iso.org).

In addition to specifications of each component, you must also specify how components interact. Again, if you are using an engineer, they should work out the product specifications for you.

For example, a motor interacts with a circuit board via a cable and connectors. In this case, you need specifications for the cable length, number of leads, material, voltage levels, etc. Some mechanical products have gears that mesh, so you need to specify how two gears interact in terms of angle, number of teeth interacting, lubrication needed, and the like.

Specifications – Components

Create specifications for each component of your product, using this template as a guide.

Component Name: _____.
List specifications applicable for this component:

Component Name: _____.
List specifications applicable for this component:

Component Name: _____.
List specifications applicable for this component:

Specifications – Interface

Create specifications for the components' interface, using this template as a guide.

Component Names: _____ | _____.
List specifications applicable to the interface between these components:

Component Names: _____ | _____.
List specifications applicable to the interface between these components:

Component Names: _____ | _____.
List specifications applicable to the interface between these components:

Make or Buy

Instead of developing new components for your product, purchase as many as possible. The decision to make or buy comes down to time and cost. If components are hard to find or very expensive, you might have to create them yourself. If you buy a component, you can use it as is, or modify it to suit the overall design of your product.

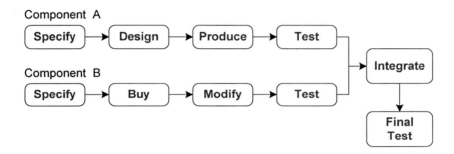

The Make or Buy diagram shows it's possible your product may include some components you design ("Component A") as well as those you buy ("Component B").

Let's use the tabletop electric fan as an example. For each component, we'll determine whether to make or buy it:

- **Fan blade** – Innovative cooling properties, derived from a unique blade design, constitute a major selling point of this fan. You've specified the dimensions, curvature, flexibility, durability, and materials of the blade, then search parts catalogs to discover nothing like it exists. Therefore, design and produce it yourself.

- **Fan cover** – The fan cover is an important safety component. You search catalogs and find many types of covers to work with your design. You call manufacturers to receive a few samples to test.

- **Motor** – The electric motor has been around for years and is now a standard item. You search and find a reliable brand conforming to your specifications.

- **Electrical controls and pushbutton switches** – You specify a circuit to control the variable high, medium, and low speeds. The electronic parts are standard and readily available. You hire an electrical engineer to design a circuit board.

- **Fan Housing** – The fan housing is specific to your innovation and therefore you design it yourself. You give the requirements and specifications to an industrial designer who creates a computer-aided design.

Bill of Materials

Manufacturers want to know all of the parts of your product and packaging. A standard method of tracking parts is known as a Bill of Materials. Bill of Materials is often abbreviated as BOM (pronounced "bomb"). Provide a basic Bill of Materials to obtain a price quote from a manufacturer. If you're hiring an engineer, ask him or her to create a BOM for you. When production begins, your engineer or manufacturer creates a complete BOM with a list of product components and its parts, drawings, documentation, packaging, and shipping material. The following is a sample bill of materials.

A typical BOM has sequential ID numbers, level numbers indicating assemblies and corresponding sub-assemblies, part description, quantity, and part number. Purchased parts come with a part number. If you're designing the part yourself, create a part number using a simple scheme. Always check with the manufacturer first to find out their preferred format. Create a Bill of Materials using a wordprocessor, spreadsheet, or material requirements planning software.

Bill of Materials				
ID	Level	Description	Quantity	Part Number
1	1	Brass plate	1	XYZ 67-89-01
2	2	Philips bolt 3" brass	4	XYZ 123-4567
3	2	Hex Nuts #2 brass	4	XYZ 123-8901
4	2	Washers #2 brass	4	XYZ 123-2345

Test Cases

Testing validates design. You're checking to make sure components and the whole product conform to your requirements, specifications, and regulations. In general, a test plan is written to include specific test cases to examine every aspect of your product.

Test cases exercise the entire product and its components under varying conditions for non-conformance. If you're not skilled at developing test plans, hire a test lab, test engineer, or quality assurance person to write a test plan.

If you use a contract manufacturer, either provide test plans or review the manufacturer's test plans. On the other hand, you can provide product requirements and specifications to the manufacturer who develops test plans for you. Check with the manufacturer about the cost of this service. Make sure you discuss test plans before signing the contract. Test plans must be in place before production begins.

For testing assistance, talk to your engineer or look in the Yellow Pages under Test Lab or Quality Assurance. Search the Internet for organizations with local chapters whose members you may contact. Quality Assurance organizations include:

- American Society for Quality (www.asq.org)
- Association for Quality and Participation (www.aqp.org)
- Association for Manufacturing Excellence (www.ame.org)
- Society for Software Quality (www.ssq.org)

User Documentation

Your customers need instructions about installing, setting up, and using your product. Good documentation often creates a competitive advantage. Your documentation may include step-by-step installation guides, user manuals, and online help. Since clear and concise documentation is important, seek the advice of a technical writer. Search the Internet for technical writers or the Yellow Pages under Writing Services or Technical Manual Preparation.

Before contacting a writer, prepare a detailed description of your needs. When interviewing writers, find out if they have experience with your product type. Once you hire someone, ask the writer to create a style guide to ensure consistency of all your documentation. Then, provide as much content for each document as possible and let the writer edit and fill in the gaps.

To lower product costs, reduce the amount of printed documentation. Your customers need basic instructions such as a Quick Start Guide to install or set up the product. Detailed documentation can be made available on a CD or as a download from the Internet.

Documentation Tips:

- As a guide, look at similar products to see how they created their documentation.
- Try to use as many pictures and illustrations as possible.
- Get feedback on your documentation from your prototype and beta testers.

Patent Marking

You want to put the world on notice your product is covered by a patent. In legal terms, patent marking is displaying your patent number on your product.

When you receive a notice of allowance and pay the issue fee, the patent is officially yours. Make sure you add the patent number to your physical product. If you are working with a development company, make sure you notify them about your patent number. For proper patent marking, use "Patent" or "Pat." followed by the patent number. For example, "Patent 9,999,999" provides proper notice.

Patent marking is not required by law to sell a product. To sue for patent infringement and collect damages, the potential infringer must be given notice. Patent marking on a product is a proper method to give notice.

If you believe a product in the market is infringing on your patent, give notice by mailing the infringer a letter stating their product is infringing on your patent. In some cases, if someone knowingly infringes, the patent owner can receive up to three times the amount of actual damages. Whether someone intentionally infringes or not, they are still liable for damages.

When it's not suitable for placing a patent marking directly on the product, add patent marking to an attached tag or label. If it's not suitable for patent marking on the product, tag, or label, then place the patent marking on the package or associated literature.

If you submitted a provisional patent application, or filed for a patent and have yet to receive a patent number, mark the product and packaging with "Patent Pending." At the same time, make sure there is enough open space on the product for later marking the granted patent number.

Product Production Steps

Some products have a combination of plastics, motors, and electronics. A product such as the tabletop electric fan has several different components and materials. There's the plastic fan blade and housing, the metal blade cover, motor, and electrical circuit.

In this case, you'd want a manufacturer who can produce the plastics, metals, and circuits. Some manufacturers perform all of these in-house and some sub-contract to specialty manufacturers.

For example, a manufacturer who produces only electronic circuit boards, outsources plastics and metal fabrication. The plastics and metal parts are produced and delivered to the primary manufacturer who integrates them with the electronic controls.

In this scenario, you only have to deal with the primary manufacturer, who coordinates separate component production behind the scenes. If your product consists of electronics and plastic parts, have an electronics company as your primary manufacturer.

Before approaching a manufacturer:

- Review the accuracy of your product requirements, specifications, and project plan.
- Create lists, drawings, diagrams, and flowcharts to provide details of the product features and functions.
- Create a Bill of Materials of all the parts used in the beta product.
- Determine production quantities in terms of an alpha, beta, and full production over the first year. Quantities for an alpha might be as few as five, while twenty to fifty units for beta.

To hire a company to manufacture your product, use the following steps:

- Search for manufacturers who produce your product type. Talk to a sales representative about having a product manufactured. Ask for references and follow-up to see if customers were satisfied. Inquire as to how they keep your product confidential.

- Tour manufacturers and look at cleanliness, organization, and quality control.

- Request a price quote by providing requirements, CAD drawings, Bill of Materials, production volume, and deadlines.

- Review quotes for more than just the lowest price. Consider the timeline, ease of working with the manufacturer, and reputation. Ask for detailed explanations of any part of the quote you're not clear on.

- When you've chosen the manufacturer, they'll probably ask you to sign the quote to indicate acceptance. In addition, they'll also request a deposit.

- Upon a deposit, the manufacturer begins planning and ordering parts.

- At the same time, begin working on your packaging. Since packaging design can easily take a month, make sure completion coincides with the start of manufacturing. When packaging is complete, have it shipped to the product manufacturer. (Some manufactures can sub-contract packaging for you.)

- When all parts and materials are in place, the manufacturer begins production. Parts are assembled, tested, and placed into the packaging.

- As the first products are coming off the production line, be there (or have your agent) monitor, inspect, and make sure they conform to your requirements. If production is in another state or country, have the "first article" shipped to you before full production begins. Look for parts out of alignment, cracks, incorrectly printed artwork, and overall proper function.

Manufacturing Tips

- Typically, manufacturers do not start production until they have all parts and packaging for the initial run in their inventory.

- You can request certain parts to come from a particular vendor, or allow the manufacturer to use their vendor of choice. Compare product quality and cost.

- Manufacturers prefer to run a production line continuously until the volume specified in your contract is completed. If they start and then stop for a period of time, there are setup charges to retool the line.

- For testing, you can provide test instructions and equipment or allow the manufacturer to do it. You are charged for parts and labor if the manufacturer has to build special test equipment.

- Provide any products or parts which interact with your product for testing. For example, if you're producing candleholders, provide the manufacturer with the matching candles.

Before you go into production, you might consider another round of customer testing. To learn the benefits and process to Beta Test your product, please turn to the next chapter.

Chapter 17:
Beta Test Your Product

Discovery consists of seeing what everybody has seen, and thinking what nobody else has thought.

Jonathan Swift

Topics in this Chapter:

- Beta Test Plan
- Beta Recruitment
- Beta Feedback
- From Beta to Final Development

A beta test involves trying out your nearly completed product in real situations through representative customers. The beta product has many of the final product's features and functions, but lacks finishing touches.

Do you need to do a beta test? Imagine spending thousands of dollars on manufacturing and then discovering product defects. A beta test helps expose any design flaws before final production. In addition, a beta test is a final verification that your product meets your future customer's needs.

A beta test program can last from weeks to months, depending on your product's complexity and the amount of feedback you want. To determine duration, think about how much time it would take you to fully evaluate your product, then multiply the amount by three to five times! The beta process often takes longer than you anticipate.

In order to clarify the process to the beta testers, you need to create a beta test agreement. This agreement includes a non-disclosure of confidential information clause, liability limits, product limitations, feedback requirements, duration, and any incentives you offer.

The agreement informs beta testers they are not to discuss the beta test with anyone and not post public messages on the Internet. The agreement must inform beta testers of possible bugs, defects, and errors may occur and you are not held responsible for problems it may cause. Ask an attorney to create a beta test agreement.

As an option, search for beta test agreement templates on the Internet as a starting point, make changes, and then have an attorney review the document.

The steps to conduct a beta test are:

- Create a beta test plan
- Create a beta test agreement
- Design the beta product with the key features and functions you want to test
- Recruit beta candidates
- Send qualified candidates a beta test agreement
- Produce your beta product
- Distribute your beta product
- Call or email beta customers at the outset to encourage product usage
- Call or email beta customers weekly with prepared questions to gather feedback
- At the conclusion, send beta customers a thank-you letter and ask them to fill out a final survey
- Summarize all feedback
- Make adjustments to your product as needed

Beta Test Plan

To start, I suggest creating a beta test plan stating your goals, objectives, timeline, recruitment, and questions you want answered. Create a beta test plan using the following Beta Test Plan Sample as a guide.

Beta Recruitment

You need to recruit beta testers as early as possible. Be prepared to spend at least a month to find and recruit qualified candidates. Try recruiting those who already participated in the concept surveys, interviews, and focus groups. In addition, look for new people who are in your target market.

Request a certain number of hours per week participation over the length of the beta program. As an incentive to participate in beta testing, you can give the commercially available product away for free or at a discount.

Beta Test Plan Sample

Goals and Objectives
- Gather feedback on product features and functions
- Test the product in diverse user situations
- Gather testimonials

Program Information
- Start date: 5/1/2010
- Duration: 6 weeks
- Quantity: 25 beta sites

Beta Customer Qualification
- Type of user: Middle income, professional
- Experience level: Uses this type of product daily
- Location of beta site: Continental U.S.

Beta Recruitment
- Contact people who completed a concept survey
- Contact people who attended the focus group
- Contact other people in the target market

Product Package
- Shipping box
- Product
- Cover letter
- Installation instructions and quick start document
- Problem report form

Beta Feedback

Regular feedback from your beta customers is crucial. Be prepared to ask specific questions regarding installation, usage, documentation clarity, and how well the product solves a problem or satisfies a need. You can direct beta testers to fill out a feedback form on your website, or call them to discuss the details.

Questions to ask may include:

- Was the product easy to install?
- Was the product easy to use?
- How well did the product solve your problem or meet your needs?
- What features are the most important?
- How is the quality of the user documentation?
- What is your overall assessment of the product?
- Would you recommend this product to someone else?
- What are your comments and suggestions?

From Beta to Final Development

When your beta test is complete, send a thank-you letter to the participants, and ask them to fill out a survey to summarize their feedback. With the beta test results, decide which features and functions, if any, need to be modified before you launch your commercial product. A change might mean modifying designs, test plans, and documentation. Changes might also mean a slip in your production and shipment schedule.

While you want to ship the product as early as possible, it's best to fix any important features and issues which affect quality. Go through the entire cycle of design, production, and testing if need be. The product is ready for release when it performs as specified. To reduce development time, you may exclude certain features from the current version. New features can be added to later versions.

How many of your products should you manufacture? The answer depends in part on your budget and in part on your risk tolerance. Beta test results often reveal customer enthusiasm. Talk to distributors and retailers to find out how many products of your type are selling. Remember retailers often start out stocking a small trial amount. As an estimate of the number of products to manufacture, think about the number of buyers you can reach with your marketing programs.

Chapter 18:
Marketing Development

In the factory we make cosmetics; in the drugstore we sell hope.

Charles Revson

Topics in this Chapter:

- Branding Your Product
- Product Naming
- Add Value and Protection with a Trademark
- Marketing Theme
- Packaging Your Product
- Packaging Steps
- Packaging Tips

During product development, you need to develop marketing strategies. Otherwise, the completed product just sits in a warehouse while you work on marketing.

Marketing and product development are interrelated. If you are developing with a team or outside consultants, work on product development and marketing in tandem. If it's just you, you need to divide your time.

For example, if I'm working on a project by myself, I designate certain days for marketing and other days for development. Thursday and Friday may be for marketing, such as creating advertising and promotions, while the other days I'm in full development mode. This method allows you to stay focused and develop the entire product in a balanced and integrated manner.

Branding Your Product

Branding is a messaging technique to instill a positive emotional reaction when people think about your product. Branding distinguishes your product from the competition. Branding also builds familiarity, leading to a purchasing preference.

For example, the Coca-Cola logo prompts people to think about having fun as well as having a refreshing beverage. This impression is reinforced by advertising showing people partying while drinking Coca-Cola.

We identify a brand by a variety of elements such as its product name, logo, images, colors, fonts, sounds (e.g., song, chimes, distinctive motorcycle engine), symbols, shapes, slogans, word choice (e.g., sophisticated, slang, folksy, earthy), and/or user experience.

There are bottles of water and then there's Perrier. Yes, Perrier is just sparkling water but its brand confers sophistication and class.

In the 1990's the Chevy truck was just another truck until General Motors started using the song "Like a Rock" by Bob Seger in TV and radio advertising. They also repeated the tagline "Like a Rock" in print advertising. Chevy trucks soon soared to number one in sales. When the campaign ended in 2004, sales then dropped like a rock.

The key to effective branding is using consistent and repetitive marketing messages in advertising, brochures, business cards, packaging, promotional items, trade show signage, website, and customer service. The messaging must convey something customers can relate to so they think your product is a reflection of themselves. In essence, branding communicates a promise your product leads to fame, fortune, recognition, romance, safety, and other motivators.

Do all products need branding? Not necessarily. Many people are motivated primarily by low price. Therefore, if your strategy is to cater to this market segment, and you want to keep your costs to a minimum, branding is not a major issue. Nor would branding be an issue if you were selling private-label products with a retail store brand name.

Product Naming

You should select a product name by the time you start beta testing. Selecting a product name does not have to be difficult. Look at your list of product benefits and positioning as a guide.

Names like DieHard for a battery and Close-Up for toothpaste are good examples of the product benefit within the name. Other examples of combining words into names include the Hewlett-Packard LaserJet and Adobe PageMaker. Another way to create a name is to combine and fuse words together such as Eveready and Velcro (velvet and crochet). Start with your product's benefits and brainstorm from there.

Use a name that is easy to pronounce and spell. Use a search engine such as Google with your product name as the keyword to see if the product name is taken. Go to the USPTO website and search the trademark database for names. Check the web domain name to see if it's available by typing in your web browser www.productname.com to see if someone else's page comes up.

Add Value and Protection with a Trademark

Trademarks play a valuable role in marketing your product. Think of trademarks as the legal aspect of branding. A trademarked product helps build trust, reputation, and loyalty. Whenever you see a trademarked product from Sony, Hershey Foods, or General Electric, you intuitively know what you're getting before ever opening the package.

A trademark benefits you by:

- Adding value to your product brand and company
- Keeping competitors from copying your brand name
- Protecting your product's reputation

Having a registered trademark makes it easier to sue for damages in the event of infringement. In addition, a registered trademark gives you the right to obtain a website domain address with the same name. Internet law is still in flux and this may change.

A trademarked brand name allows a company to distinguish itself and prevent others from using a similar name that may tarnish its good reputation. As a result, trademarks are valuable company assets.

There should be no confusion between a trademarked name and another product. For example, the product "Krazy Glue" is trademarked. If you advertised your product as "Krazi Glue" or "Crazy Goo" you'd probably receive a "cease and desist" letter from the trademark's owner, because your product name is likely to confuse consumers. For an easy test, say the words out loud. If the name you've chosen sounds like an existing trademark, you're most likely facing an infringement. Ultimately, the decision of infringement and damages lies in the courtroom.

Another test in determining if your trademark application is acceptable, is to not dilute an existing trademarked brand's reputation. For example, Sony has a trademark on its Walkman portable electronics products. If a new pet product is called the Dog-Walkman, not only would there be a cause for concern about confusion, but Sony might not want to be associated with a pet product.

Search for Trademark Availability

A trademark must be distinctive and not a common word or phrase. A trademark may consist of a word, letter, number, symbol (logo), color, shape, or combination of these. In some instances, distinctive sounds and smells can be trademarked.

To perform a trademark search, go to the U.S. Patent and Trademark Office website (www.uspto.gov) and select "trademarks." Enter the product name you have in mind and see if it exists. In addition, use search engines such as Google or Yahoo, enter your product name and review the results for anything that looks or is pronounced similar to your product name.

The key is to make sure your product name would not be confused with any existing trademarks. If your product name sounds or looks similar to the name of an existing trademark, you could be challenged.

Filing a Trademark

In the United States, trademark ownership is usually granted to the first to use the mark, rather than first to file. I suggest that once you come up with an available product name, add the "TM" symbol and display it on your website or printed materials. Adding a "TM" symbol to your product name (e.g., Productname™) puts the world on notice to your claim. Use the trademark in your advertising, brochures, business cards, flyers, labels, t-shirts, and on your website.

After you determine your product is marketable, file for a federal registered trademark. Before filing, the trademark must be "in use" meaning you must first display the product name with the trademark symbol on a flyer, website, or product label to the public.

To obtain a federal registered trademark, file with the U.S. Patent and Trademark Office. The registration process can be performed online (www.uspto.gov) using the Trademark Electronic Application System (TEAS).

The federal trademark filing fee is currently $375 ($325 if filed electronically). Once a federal trademark is granted, you may use the symbol "R" inside a circle (e.g., Productname®). The trademark lasts for ten years. You may renew for additional ten-year periods as long as the trademark is in use.

Your other option involves filing for an "Intent to Use" trademark for $100. This is helpful to reserve a trademark in the future while having nothing in-use at this time. As part of the process, you must sign a sworn statement that you have a real intention to use the trademark. When your product is ready, you'll still need to place the trademark in-use and then file an application.

To obtain a trademark for your business name (known as a "Service Mark"), file with your state's Secretary of State. If your company name is unique and you're doing business in more than one state, you are advised to register for a federal trademark using the steps described above. A service mark can also protect an event, such as the Olympic Games, which has the five rings trademarked.

When you own a trademark, it's up to you to monitor for infringement. I suggest searching the Internet for any products using your product name. In addition, you can use Google Alerts (www.google.com/alerts) to automatically track your trademarked name. If a potential trademark infringement exists, talk to an attorney who specializes in intellectual property.

Marketing Theme

To evoke branding you need to start with a theme. Connect your theme to the product positioning and have it centered on whatever your customers are seeking.

Perhaps you have seen positioning of a product as expensive and/or high quality, often with a theme of richness. For example, the mustard Grey Poupon is positioned as a premium product. The theme involved a Rolls Royce limousine as a luxury icon. The message is that by tasting Grey Poupon, you feel as if you are experiencing luxury.

The San Jose Sharks of the National Hockey League have the theme of a snarling shark with black and teal colors. Their market research revealed women prefer teal and men prefer black. The Sharks made their logo, team jersey, and website follow this theme. Interestingly, even when the team had played poorly, their merchandise sales were among the best in sports.

Base your marketing communications on a theme such as:

• Animals	• Mountains
• Architecture	• Oceans
• Family life	• Sports
• Farming	• Sun and stars
• Flowers	• Technology and innovation
• Fun, friends, and parties	• Travel and world geography
• Luxury	• Historic events, people, periods

Marketing Theme

Brainstorm the theme, look, and feel of your marketing communications.

Overall Theme
Think of a few different themes which would appeal to your audience (e.g., the look, setting, the story you want to tell):

Images
Brainstorm the type of images to compliment the theme (e.g., photos, drawings, graphics, color combinations):

Headlines
Make a list of possible headlines. Effective headlines often include a statement of benefits or the asking of a question. Look at other products and see what grabs your attention as a starting point:

Taglines / Slogans
Brainstorm possible catchy and memorable taglines or slogans (e.g., The milk chocolate melts in your mouth, not in your hand; Got Milk?; Where's the Beef?). Creating a slogan is not easy, but think of your positioning and then Just Do It:

Body – Main benefit points
For each of your product's main benefits and advantages, make a list of phrases to use in your messaging (e.g., *Product* saves time and is fun to use):

Body – Main copy points
List the main messages you want to communicate (e.g., unique product features, a special reputation, or a limited opportunity):

Packaging Your Product

Packaging can be as important as the product itself. This is especially true for retail products. Shoppers often make assumptions and purchase decisions based on the packaging. It's just human nature and there's no way around it. Packaging serves four key objectives:

- Containing and protecting the product
- Preventing theft
- Getting attention, persuading, and informing
- Positioning the product to reflect price, quality, and convenience

Your first packaging consideration should be product distribution. If you're selling retail, the package must have an outstanding shelf presence. The package must command attention to lure a shopper browsing products. Before designing your packaging, talk to retailers about their requirements such as format, size, and weight. On the other hand, if you're selling business-to-business or shipping direct to the customer, packaging flair is less important. Still, packaging quality must match the quality and price level of the product. For example, you would not wrap an expensive Rolex watch in a paper bag.

Product packaging consists of:

- **Outer packaging** – contains the product and provides information. Information printed on the package or label may include product name, company name, logo, sales copy, instructions, warnings, list of product components or ingredients, testimonials, awards, location made, price, and barcode.

- **Inside packaging** – protects and holds the product in place (e.g., cardboard, foam, plastic).

- **Master carton (case)** – holds and protects a quantity of the product. Information printed on the master carton includes company name, product quantity, weight, handling instructions, and barcode.

UPC Barcode

Retail packages use the industry standard Universal Product Code (UPC) barcode. The UPC consists of twelve characters representing the product manufacturer, product, and a check digit. GS1, a worldwide standards organization, manages UPC (www.gs1.org). The United States group is called GS1 US (www.gs1us.org).

To obtain a UPC bar code, there are two main methods. One is to become a member of GS1 US. To become a member you need to fill out an application online. Expect to pay an initial fee of $750 and up for a block of 100 UPCs, and then a $150 per year renewal fee. After you sign up, you're assigned an identification number licensed for your company's use. Use this number to create your own UPC.

The other method, if you're just starting out, is to obtain a single barcode from a third-party vendor for $50 to $90. For example, the company Simply Barcodes (www.upccode.net) offers UPC barcodes for $89. They assign you the number and for another $25 generate the barcode artwork. I have not worked with them, so do your research.

Once you're assigned a UPC number, add a barcode to your packaging artwork. Some graphic design software applications can create barcodes. If not, you can visit a barcode-generating website. For a small fee ($10 to $30) you enter the code on the website and a barcode graphic file is displayed or emailed to you. Send the barcode graphic file to the graphic designer.

Many websites are available to generate barcodes. Use a search engine to find them. I've successfully used Bar Code Graphics, Inc. (www.barcode-graphics.com).

If your product is a book, you do not need a UPC, but you need to acquire an International Standard Book Number (ISBN) from RR Bowker (www.bowker.com). ISBNs are issued as a minimum of ten numbers in a block. For more information, go to the ISBN website (www.isbn.org).

I suggest testing the barcode before you finalize the packaging. Take a printout of the barcode to a retail store. Ask if they can do a quick scan for you. If it works, the cash register shows the barcode's numbers. If it's not readable, the print quality of the barcode may not be suitable or the code is incorrect.

Packaging Elements

The following are components in packaging. Check off the elements used for your product type (✓).

Product Container
- ❑ Cardboard or Chipboard box
- ❑ Glass bottle
- ❑ Metal can
- ❑ Plastic bottle, box, or case

Outer Package Material
- ❑ Cardboard
- ❑ Chipboard
- ❑ Glass
- ❑ Metal
- ❑ Plastic

Outer Package Design
- ❑ Company information
- ❑ Product information
- ❑ Expiration date
- ❑ Graphics
- ❑ Industry certifications
- ❑ Instructions
- ❑ Legal disclaimers
- ❑ Logo
- ❑ Part and/or Serial number
- ❑ Patent number
- ❑ Product awards
- ❑ Sales promotion
- ❑ Testimonials
- ❑ UPC barcode
- ❑ Warnings
- ❑ Warranty

Outer Package Type
- ❑ Plastic Bag with header
- ❑ Blister pack (plastic housing over cardboard)
- ❑ Box or Carton
- ❑ Clamshell (two plastic halves folded together)
- ❑ Shrink-wrap over product

Interior Material
- ❑ Cardboard
- ❑ Foam
- ❑ Plastic

Interior Contents
- ❑ Accessories
- ❑ Coupon / Rebates
- ❑ Instruction guide
- ❑ Promotional materials
- ❑ Registration card
- ❑ User manual
- ❑ Warranty card

Package Placement
- ❑ Hang from a rack
- ❑ Inside a vending machine
- ❑ Point of sale display
- ❑ Ship direct to customer
- ❑ Sit on a shelf or counter

Master Carton

Retailers order in quantities by the case. A case may include 4, 8, 12, 32, or other amount of products. The case is a cardboard box known as a master carton. Perhaps you've seen boxes opened at the supermarket with a dozen ketchup bottles or eight boxes of cereal. Talk to a retailer to see how many units per master carton are typical for your type of product.

The master carton protects the product and packaging. If you have a retailer in mind, check their website if they have shipping guidelines in terms of master carton dimensions, sturdiness, taping, and printing.

To save money, use a standard corrugated box from an office supply or packing materials company. The type of box depends on retailer guidelines, how fragile the product may be, and weight. If your product does not fit a standard box, ask your packaging manufacturer to provide a quote for a custom master carton.

The box must be sturdy enough to handle shipping abuses. Both UPS and FedEx have packaging guidelines. Even if you do not use them, their websites provide useful guidelines on shipping materials and proper packaging suggestions.

As a simple test, place your products in their packages and put them in the master carton. Drop the box on a hard surface from a height of four feet. Do it repeatedly and then open the container to see how the products and packages survived.

Place your company name and barcode on the master carton. When just starting out I suggest creating a label to apply to the box instead of printing directly on the box. You can also use a packing slip inside a clear cover with its destination address facing out.

If the product is perceived as very valuable, it might attract theft. In this case, do not list the product name on the master container itself. If you're shipping your product outside the country, check with Customs officials for specific guidelines.

When sales volume is high enough, then ship products by the pallet. A standard pallet is 40 by 48 inches. Therefore, your master carton must be able to stack evenly on a pallet and sturdy enough to withstand stacking.

Packaging Steps

Package design should be consistent with your other marketing materials and follow the same branding guidelines. Everything your customer sees should have the same look and feel in terms of images, fonts, style, color, and message.

You can save a lot of money on package design if you use standard items such as a box, bottle, can, bag, tag, or other materials. Otherwise, there are setup charges and other costs for custom packaging. Keep in mind, the timeline to create new packaging can easily take four weeks or longer.

To create packaging, use the following steps as a guide:

- Review packaging of similar products and list the elements of the package. Note which elements appear attractive and which do not.
- Make a list of packaging requirements and sketch possible designs.
- Discuss packaging requirements with your target retailers and distributors Ask retailers how and where your product type is typically displayed and master carton requirements.
- Contact packaging vendors and discuss your project. Look in the Yellow Pages for Packaging or "Package Design and Development" headings. Look for contract packagers at the Packaging Digest website (www.packagingdigest.com) and the Contract Manufacturing and Packaging Association website (www.contractpackaging.org). In general, it's best to find a local company or one with a local sales representative so you can meet in person. In addition, a packaging company located near your product manufacturer reduces your shipping costs.
- Ask packaging vendors to provide packaging samples to review the materials and quality.
- For a quote, provide the packaging manufacturer with a prototype, any accessories, and any inserts such as documentation.
- Request a price quote based on your forecasted quantity and budget.
- Contact a graphic designer experienced with product packaging to create the look and layout. Discuss your packaging needs and product positioning. Ask for a dieline (template) from the packaging vendor to help with the design layout.
- Develop packaging content such as sales messages, product information, and testimonials for the graphic designer.
- For retail products, take mock-ups to a retail store to see if your packaging stands out.
- Approve the final design, and have the graphic designer send artwork to the packaging manufacturer.

Product Launch Flowchart

Whom should you first target? Focus on Innovators and Early Adopters within your target market because they're less price sensitive and tend to be more forgiving of product deficiencies. They're eager to buy new products and you need to generate sales as quickly as possible.

Tailor communications to position your product as new and innovative. Exact messaging depends on your target market. For example, attract them with messaging such as cool, innovative, newest technology, and stylish design. Even if your product does not involve new technology, there are people in every social group who are Early Adopters. They're interested in buying new products to make them stand out from the crowd.

How do you actually find the Innovators and Early Adopters? It's not easy. As discussed earlier, marketing is part art and part science. Your initial marketing might be scattered. As you generate sales, gather as much customer information as you can (e.g., job title, hobbies, geographic location, and business type). Then, focus your marketing and sales to the types of buyers who have purchased your product. Keep narrowing your focus until you find your true target market.

If you want to sell through retailers and distributors, which do you target initially? Before accepting your product, many large retailers and distributors want to see a successful sales track record and evidence you can deliver on big orders. Start with small retail stores and distributors, then work your way up.

In addition, your launch strategy must mirror the way customers buy. Communicate with customers at each stage of their buying process.

Use the following marketing tactics to take a customer from awareness to purchase:

- **Awareness** – Facilitate awareness with advertising, direct mail, press releases, product reviews, retail packaging, special events, and sales prospecting.

- **Interest** – Generate excitement and interest with special deals, promotions, and strong benefit messages.

- **Purchase** – Make your product available where your target market shops or at popular websites; offer a reasonable price; and a money-back guarantee.

- **Satisfaction** – Approval occurs when a product performs as promised (meets or exceeds perceptions and expectations).

- **Word of Mouth** – Provide a slogan, positioning statement, or concise phrase of benefits the customer can easily repeat to others.

- **Re-order** – Gain repeat orders by shipping your product with order forms, placing your telephone number and website address on your product, sending coupons, and mailing reminders.

Finalize Your Product

Monitor final development with the launch checklist you created earlier. If you're working with a number of people, the launch checklist serves as a sign-off from those responsible for development, marketing, quality assurance, and manufacturing. Review the following items on a daily basis as you near launch:

- Parts ordering
- User documentation
- Product production
- Test results
- Packaging production

Finalize your marketing and sales programs so they are ready to roll when the product is ready. Give yourself plenty of lead-time to design, develop, edit, and submit each communications element. Organize these marketing and sales items before launch:

- Print advertising (might have long lead times)
- Online advertising
- Brochures
- Business cards
- Direct mail
- Press releases
- Sales letters
- Website

Countdown to Launch

Bring all the following activities and elements together in the days leading up to the launch:

- Assemble product, packaging, and shipping materials.
- Submit a press release to an online press release service, as well as direct to your target audience magazines, newspapers, distributors, retailers, your list (prospects and customers), and upload to your website.
- Send a press kit or product launch kit to your distributors and retailers.
- Ship products to pre-arranged customers (e.g., samples and demos to end-users, distributors, and retailers).

- Make sales calls to prospects.
- Execute marketing programs such as postcard mailings, email blast to your personal list, or attend trade shows.

Announce the Launch with a Press Release

By the time the product is released from manufacturing, all marketing and sales activities should be planned and ready to execute. A press release is an announcement to the media to generate awareness.

Gain more press coverage by linking your product launch to a current or historical event. For example, if you've invented a new type of communications device, you could launch the same day Alexander Graham Bell invented the telephone. There are many historical events with anniversaries every day. Search the Internet using the keywords ["your product type" and "historical events"]. For example, in Google use the keywords ["light bulb" and "historical events"]. Then, look for events near your launch date.

The timing of your product launch may coincide with an event such as a trade show. In this case, your press release would announce your new product to be unveiled at a particular trade show or conference. If you launch at a trade show, have signs at your booth highlighting your new product. In addition, ask the trade show managers to place signs around the trade center, inserting flyers into show directories, or sponsoring a show event.

If your product has a long sales cycle, marketing and sales activities should begin months before the product is ready for commercial release. In this case, announce well in advance the launch date with a press release and notice on your website. For example, your message might be, "The General Availability of Product X is planned for October 1, 2010." If the exact launch date is uncertain, you can say for example, "Fall, 2010." When the product is available, change your website to read, "Product X began shipping on October 1, 2010."

Press Release Submission

Today, a majority of press releases are submitted electronically. There are online distribution services that distribute press releases to the major news services, publications, and news websites instantly.

Distribution services forward your press release to their member media organizations. Media organizations then review each press release and decide whether to publish it or not. Some distribution services are free and others charge up to $500. The paid services usually have a broader member base. Review a distribution service's member list to make sure they include your target market before signing on. If the free services include your target market, start with them.

Free and fee-based press release distribution services include:

- Business Wire (www.businesswire.com)
- Emailwire (www.emailwire.com)
- !PR Services (www.exclamationpr.com)
- Press Release Network (www.pressreleasenetwork.com)
- PR Newswire (www.prnewswire.com)
- PR Web (www.prweb.com)
- Xpress Press (www.xpresspress.com)

In addition, send your press release to individual publications that serve your target market and cover your product type. Submitting directly increases your acceptance rate. Make a list of possible publications then search their website for "submit news" or "press release" or "submission process." They'll usually provide a form for your press release and contact information. To make it easy, cut and paste information from your word processor into the appropriate fields in their form.

Include photographs of your product, preferably taken by a professional photographer who provides the photographs as digital files. For press releases submitted by email, include product photos in high-resolution for print publications (300 dpi JPEG format), and low-resolution images for web display (72 dpi JPEG format). Some online forms allow you to attach a photo to your press release.

Media publishers have lead times related to the frequency and size of the publication. For instance, quarterly publications generally have a three-month lead-time. In this case, submit the press release three or four months before the launch date. On the other hand, daily newspapers or online publications may have a lead-time of hours or days. In this case, write "For Immediate Release" at the top of the press release.

Press Release Format

FOR IMMEDIATE RELEASE:

CONTACT:
Contact person
Company name
Phone number
Fax number
Email address
Website address

Headline

City, State – Date – Opening Paragraph (inform THAT your new product is available)

Paragraph (key product advantages and benefits, where the product is available)

Paragraph (quotes from yourself or testimonials from known people)

Paragraph (summary of your company)

Closing (include your website address, contact name, phone, and email)

(indicates end of press release)

Press Release Format

A professional public relations person can write and submit a press release for you, but if you feel comfortable writing, make sure you:

- Write concisely (one or two pages)
- Make use of keywords in the headline and body your target market uses when searching on the web for your product type
- Place key facts up front in the early paragraphs
- Avoid words that sound like advertising lingo or hype
- Avoid jargon
- Include contact information (name, telephone, email, website)

To help format your press release, look at others for your product type. Find these with an Internet search engine with keywords ["your product type" and "press release"].

If you print your press release, and there's more than one page, indicate "more" at the bottom of the first page, and "Page 2" at the top of the second page.

Supply Product Information

A press release provides basic information, but additional data is often needed by the media. You want to make it easy for the media to write a story about your company and products. Depending on your industry, you might need to create either a press kit or product launch kit.

Press Kit

A press kit, sometimes referred to as a media kit, brings together all your product and company information. Create a press kit containing:

- **Fact sheet** – A summary of important company and product information.
- **Photographs** – You and your products, and possibly the output or results of your product.
- **Press releases** – Press releases you have already submitted.
- **Product reviews** – Reviews of your product in newspapers, magazines, or blogs.
- **Press quotes** – Published remarks made in newspapers and magazines (print and online) about your product or company.

Product Launch Kit

Your distributors, retailers, and customers need detailed information about your product before they're persuaded to place an order. A product launch kit brings together important information about your product.

There's no standard format, but the product launch kit is usually a document (printed or an electronic file) with product, marketing, and sales information. In addition, the product launch kit may include product brochures, product reviews, product samples if appropriate, and competitive information.

Product Launch Kit

Use this template as a guide to creating your product launch kit.

Product Description
Describe your product in terms of benefits, features, and specifications:

Positioning
Indicate the product position in the market and advantages your product offers as compared to the competition:

Technology
Describe any technology making your product new and exciting:

Pricing
Either provide a price list or indicate customers should contact you or a sales representative directly:

Packaging
List part numbers, the contents of the package, and any available accessories and their part numbers. Indicate the weight of the package individually and the weight of the master carton:

Ordering Instructions
Provide ordering instructions such as going to a website, placing a fax order, or by telephone:

Contact Information
List whom to contact for more information. Include telephone numbers, email address, mailing address, and website:

Create a Press Room on Your Website

Turn a press kit or product launch kit into electronic files available from your website. Use Adobe PDF files for documents and JPEG for images. Have a link on your home page to a page called "Press Room." On the "Press Room" page, allow downloads of your product launch kit, press releases, product reviews, fact sheets, and photos. This saves you the cost of printing, postage, and shipping materials. Those interested can acquire the information instantly.

If your product has an expensive price tag, have a press kit printed to provide a perceived value of quality.

Boost Sales with Product Reviews

A great way to obtain publicity is with product reviews. A product review is perceived as credible and trustworthy.

Product reviews do not happen by accident. Perhaps you've seen a "New Product" section in magazines and websites. The reviews were most likely the result of a company or ad agency submitting information to the publication.

Product reviews are free, with the only cost being an investment of your time. You want to make it as easy as possible for someone to review your product. Therefore, to improve the chance of getting a positive review, create a Reviewer's Kit.

A Reviewer's Kit includes:

- **Cover Letter** – A request for a product review along with product highlights.

- **Instructions** – The suggested steps to use and review your product.

- **Product Fact Sheet** – A summary of important product information (product name, category, benefits, features, advantages, specifications, and pricing).

- **Company Fact Sheet** – A summary of important company information (company name, contact information, website, mission, and brief history).

- **Photographs** – Images of your products, and possibly the output or results of your product.

- **Press Quotes** – Published remarks made in newspapers and magazines (print and online) about your product or company.

To receive a review of your product, follow these steps:

- Search for magazines, newspapers, and websites that cover your product type (e.g. Better Homes and Gardens, Popular Mechanics), business publications (e.g. Entrepreneur, Fast Company) and your local newspaper (Business or Local section).

- Find the name of the publication's editor or columnist of the "New Products" section.

- Contact the publication and ask for the process to have a product reviewed. Some of their websites have a section called, "How to Request a Review."

- Submit the Reviewer's Kit (or follow their guidelines to request a review).

- Be available to answer questions.

After a review is performed, add the reviewer's comments to your website, packaging, brochure, and direct mail. To add the reviewer's company logo, check with the company for permissions and guidelines.

Launch Summary

Congratulations! You have finally realized your vision and have launched your product! Launching a new product is like giving birth to a child. When a child is born, you don't say, "Okay, it's born, my job is finished." Now is the time to nourish it, promote it, and earn the rewards from your hard work. Your customer wins with a great product. You win by knowing you're helping others and by making money for yourself. Turn to the next chapter to learn more about distribution and product marketing.

PART FIVE –
SELL THROUGH RETAIL, DISTRIBUTORS, TV, WEBSTORES, AND MORE

Formulate and stamp indelibly on your mind a mental picture of yourself as succeeding. Hold this picture tenaciously. Never permit it to fade. Your mind will seek to develop the picture...Do not build up obstacles in your imagination.

Norman Vincent Peale

Chapter 20:
Getting into Retailers and Distributors

I probably have traveled and walked into more variety stores than anybody in America. I am just trying to get ideas, any kind of ideas that will help our company. Most of us don't invent ideas. We take the best ideas from someone else.

Sam Walton, Founder of Walmart

Topics in this Chapter:

- What Retailers Want
- How to Approach Retailers
- Fulfillment and Inventory
- Selling to Retail through Showrooms
- Hiring a Sales Rep
- Build a Retail Track Record with Wizard Distribution
- Selling Your Product on QVC and HSN
- Selling Your Product on an Infomercial
- Selling Your Product through Catalogs and Webstores
- Selling Your Product as a Private Label
- Selling Your Product as a Promotional Item
- More Distribution Channels
- Market and Sell at Trade Shows
- Personal Selling
- Selling Your Product as an OEM

What Retailers Want

While you might want your product sold at Walmart, this is not always the best place to start. Before approaching the large chain stores, start with small independent stores and small distributors to gain a track record of sales. Distributors and retailers generally order a small amount for a test. When the product sells, they order more.

In general, distributors and retailers look for products with:

- Perceived value to the end-user (e.g., solves a problem or meets a need or want).
- A large sales potential and high margin to generate a profit (e.g., margins can range from 35% to 70% for durable goods, and 10% to 25% for consumables).
- Nice packaging similar to products they currently carry.
- A company able to produce the product in the volume they need.

As an example, Costco buyers are looking for products that:

- Are made of high quality.
- Provide great value at a reasonable price.
- Have a large potential sales volume.
- Meet the needs and wants of their members.
- Have a certain degree of uniqueness.

Support, in the form of in-store demos, point of sales displays, advertising, and promotion is also a key selection factor. Retailers want support and welcome just about anything you can do to help generate sales. Ask retailers for their specific desires.

How to Approach Retailers

Before you approach a retail buyer, be prepared to provide the following:

- ❑ Color brochure of the product (professionally designed and printed on quality paper) – product description with benefits, features, any awards, testimonials, and contact information.

- ❑ One page cover letter (printed on your business letterhead) – highlights of your product: description, benefits, who the product is for, its need in the market, how the need is not being met, and pricing.

❑ Product Fact Sheet (printed on your business letterhead).
  - Product name
  - Product category
  - Short product description (focus on benefits to the end-user and retailer)
  - Suggested retail price, wholesale costs, minimum order size, warranty
  - Type of retail packaging including size, weight, and how the product will be displayed (merchandising)
  - Master carton information including size, weight, and number of units
  - Lead time to ship to the retailer
  - Any certifications (e.g. UL, CSA, CE)
  - Any intellectual property you hold (e.g. patents, trademarks, copyrights)
  - Names of competing products and your competitive advantages
  - List of any retailers currently selling your products
  - Marketing plans (methods to drive traffic to the stores)

❑ Company Fact Sheet (printed on your business letterhead).
  - Company name
  - Contact information
  - Website address
  - Mission
  - Brief history
  - Dun & Bradstreet D-U-N-S number (www.dnb.com)

❑ Product samples with packaging (often requested later).

You should have the above information ready by the time you make contact. When you have these materials ready, take the following steps to approach a distributor or retailer:

- Determine which retailers carry your product type. Search local retailers and the Internet. Use a search engine with keywords such as ["your product type" and "retailer"]. Take note of how competing products (and products in the same aisle) are priced and displayed.
- Call companies and ask to talk with the Buyer or Category Manager who handles your product type. For small independent stores, talk to the owner. Ask for policies and procedures for carrying new products.

- Often, retailers direct people to a company webpage with information about new vendor applications.

- Submit the information and material requested.

- Follow-up with a telephone call to make sure they received your information. Then, ask about the next steps.

Keep in mind most buyers do not have time for presentations. They want to review your application first, and then decide if they want to talk further. When you talk to a buyer, be prepared to answer their questions:

- What sales do you expect from your product? (This will be compared to the products they currently stock.)
- How quickly can you supply products?
- What quantity can you supply on a monthly basis?
- Do you have UPC barcodes?
- What's the best way to merchandise (display) your products?
- How will you communicate or advertise to customers?
- Do you have funding to support in-store promotional programs (e.g. demos, point-of-purchase displays)?

Note: Retailers will not finance your inventory. As a matter of fact, it can take 90 days to get paid after shipment.

Walmart Local Purchase Program

Walmart has a Local Purchase Program to provide small businesses the opportunity to sell their products at local or regional stores and clubs. This is generally for those who do not have the capacity to distribute products on a national level. If the test is successful, they will order more products and continue to expand on a region by region basis.

The first step is to go to your local Walmart and ask to talk to the store manager. The store manager will want to see product samples and pricing information. If they are interested, you'll receive a Local Supplier Questionnaire.

To be considered for Walmart, be prepared with:

- A Dun & Bradstreet Supplier Evaluation Report (a financial risk assessment report, www.dnb.com)
- Product liability insurance
- A UPC barcode for your packaging

As with any major retailer, you'll increase your chance of being accepted if you have some track record of sales and the financial ability to manufacture products for inventory. For further information, visit Walmart's supplier website (www.walmartstores.com/Suppliers/).

Open Vendor Days

Some retailers have "Open Vendor Days" to allow small businesses to present new products. You'll likely have just 15 minutes to make your pitch. Search the internet with keywords ["open vendors days" and *"retailer name"*]. As an example, CVS and Walgreens have annual events:

- CVS – Open Buy Days event (www.cvsopenbuydays.com)
- Walgreens – New Vendor Days event (www.successfulcpgselling.org)

Assistance for Women and Minorities

Many retailers have special programs for minorities and women who want to be suppliers. For example, Costco has a Diversity Vendor Program. Search for retailers with keywords "Minority Vendor Program" or "Vendor Diversity."

For additional information, visit the National Minority Supplier Development Council website (www.nmsdcus.org). To assist women, there's the Women's Business Enterprise National Council (www.wbenc.org).

Fulfillment and Inventory

You have a few options for shipping your product – do it yourself, use a fulfillment company, or have the manufacturer ship directly to the customer. Compare costs and efficiency to determine the best method for you. If your retailer requires order transactions via electronic data interchange (EDI), make sure you select a fulfillment company with this capability.

A fulfillment company (sometimes called a fulfillment house) stores your product in inventory, takes customer orders, and ships to your customer. Since they are always available to take orders and ship your product, they're good to use. Typical costs may include per order charges, quantity of items shipped, data entry, shipping materials (boxes), plus postage. In addition, charges may include receiving merchandise, inventory storage, reporting, and insurance.

When you start using a fulfillment company, and if you're selling products direct to the customer, test the process. Act as a customer and order your product or have a friend do it. See if the process is smooth, the shipment arrives as promised, the packing slip is correct, and the product and packaging are undamaged.

Find fulfillment companies by searching the Internet with keywords ["your product type" and "fulfillment"]. Amazon offers a fulfillment service for orders from Amazon and non-Amazon sources. For more details see Amazon Services (www.amazonservices.com) and click on Fulfillment.

Retail and Distribution Planning

Use this template to help organize your retail and distribution planning.

- Name the regions your product plans to be sold initially (e.g., just in your area, the coastal regions, mountain areas, state, entire country, world):

- Name the distributors and retailers to carry your product type (e.g., local stores, regional distributors):

- Uncover the typical margins for your product type (ask distributors and retailers for the normal range):

- Name where inventory will initially be stored (e.g., your home, fulfillment center, the manufacturer):

- Determine the methods for shipping your product (e.g., regular post, FedEx, UPS, fulfillment center, direct from the manufacturer):

Selling to Retail through Showrooms

Showrooms offer you a great opportunity to reach retail buyers with your finished product. A showroom is a product representative company who leases space at a marketplace. The showroom owners exhibit and sell product lines to retail buyers.

For example, at the Dallas Market Center, there are hundreds of showrooms with a variety of products. Retail buyers go from showroom to showroom looking for new products. The buyer can view products, obtain information, and place orders.

Marketplaces are typically located in large buildings or convention centers. The largest United States marketplaces are in the following cities:

- Atlanta AmericasMart (www.americasmart.com)
- Chicago Merchandise Mart (www.mmart.com)
- Dallas Market Center (www.dallasmarketcenter.com)
- Las Vegas Market (www.lasvegasmarket.com)
- Los Angeles Mart (www.lamart.com)
- New York Market Center (www.230fifthave.com)

Another type of showroom is a standalone store in a business district displaying products to professionals. For example, a furniture showroom is open to interior designers who are looking for design ideas. When a designer sees products of interest, a showroom representative places an order with manufacturers or distributors.

Products carried by showrooms include apparel, accessories, baby items, books, collectibles, cosmetics, crafts, furniture, garden, gifts, housewares, jewelry, lighting, personal care, and pet products.

Selling your product at a showroom provides an avenue to get into the retail market. Your first step is to find which showrooms carry your product type. With the marketplaces listed above, go to each website and click on Showrooms (sometimes called Exhibitors). Then search by product category. For each product category there is a list of showrooms with company contact information.

Next, contact the showroom representative and describe the benefits of your product. Ask for their process to have your product accepted and their business terms. When discussing your product, focus on the market need, the benefits provided, competitive advantages, and pricing.

If a showroom carries your product, a sales commission ranges from 5% to 25% of the wholesale price. In addition, there is a showroom fee from $50 to $750 per month.

It's a good idea to attend marketplace events to see how showrooms operate. During an event, showrooms are busy catering to retail buyers. Therefore, it's best to contact showroom representatives when the event is completed.

Hiring a Sales Rep

Would you like to have a nationwide sales force selling your product? Hiring Independent Sales Representatives (Rep) makes this possible.

A Rep, also called an Independent Manufacturers Representative, is an individual or a company with several staff members. Reps manage multiple product lines based on a customer type, market, and in a certain geographic territory.

The Rep does not buy and sell your product. Rather, the Rep prospects, negotiates, and closes deals with your customers. Reps meet with buyers at trade shows, showrooms, by telephone, video conference, or face to face. The customer may be a retailer, distributor, dealer, corporation, or end-user of your product. When a purchase is made, you ship the product and send an invoice to the customer.

Reps offer the advantage of being able to sell your product into places you can't since they have established contacts within a particular industry. You also benefit because Reps are only paid when they sell. The commission ranges from 5% to 25% depending on the norms for an industry.

Will a Rep take on your product?

It depends. If you have little or no track record of sales, most Reps do not want to be "pioneers" or "missionaries" opening new markets. Then again, if your target customer fits perfectly with their existing contacts, they might be open to representing your product.

For example, if your new product is intended for Bed Bath & Beyond, Michaels, and the Container Store, and the Rep regularly calls on these retail buyers, then they might take the risk. For a new product without a track record, the commission you offer might need to be higher than average as an enticement.

Keep in mind, the Rep's primary responsibility is selling, not marketing. You need to develop the marketing strategies to create awareness and sales leads.

Finding Reps

To hire a Rep, there are ways to find them including:

- Use an internet search engine with the terms "Independent Sales Rep," "Independent Manufacturers Rep," or "Directory of Manufacturers Reps."
- Ask the retailer (buyer or the buyer's assistant), "I'm trying to sell my product to your company, can you give me the name of a Rep you work with."
- Go to trade shows related to your industry. Reps usually exhibit for companies at small and regional shows. Usually the Rep's business card is stapled to the back of brochures and catalogs.
- Place an ad in trade magazines. For example, "Manufacturer of household products seeks a commission-based Independent Sales Rep to sell to the major retailers."

There are organizations where you can find Reps including:

- Manufacturers' Agents National Association (www.ManaOnline.org)
- Manufacturers Representatives of America (www.mra-reps.com)
- Association of Independent Manufacturers' Representatives (www.aimr.net)
- Electronic Representatives Association (www.era.org)

Your Ideal Rep

Before you begin the interviewing process, you need to put in writing the characteristics of an ideal Rep. You should define some or all of the following depending on your situation:

- **Contacts** – What contacts must the Rep currently have? For example, the Rep must know the buyers for dental products at Walgreens, CVS, Rite Aid, Target, and Walmart.
- **Territory** – What geographic territory must the Rep cover?
- **Competition** – List the competitors the Rep should not represent. (You don't want a Rep working with competitor's products.)
- **Price** – The Rep should currently sell products in the same price range as your product. If your product sells for $50 and the Rep sells only $1,000 products, it's not a good fit.

- **Benefits** – It's best if the Rep sells similar benefit-oriented products. If the Rep is primarily selling safety type products and yours is a time-saving product, it might not be a good fit.
- **Technical Skills** – If your product is technical, list the qualifications needed to effectively communicate the product's features and functions.

When you interview a Rep, in addition to the above requirements, ask questions to uncover the following:

- Information about the Rep Company such as years in business and number of sales people.
- Names of manufacturers and product lines they currently represent.
- Primary markets and customer types (% of sales in those areas).
- Gross sales generated over the last year.
- For a person who would be your prime Rep, inquire about their education, years of experience, and job history.

When evaluating Reps consider the following:

- **Priority** – Is the Rep focused on selling, or are they into all kinds of other activities such as manufacturing their own products, running their own business, into other ventures, or taking extensive vacations?
- **Character** – Does the Rep appear to be trustworthy with integrity?
- **Stage of Career** – Are they ready to retire within a year (you waste your training time)? Are they new to the Rep Company (ask when they joined the company)? Are they in a career transition (ask how long they plan to stay with the company)?
- **Rep Size** – Do you need a large Rep company with sales people in all parts of the country, or only in certain markets?
- **Referrals** – Call referrals to uncover how well the Rep has performed and the ease at working together.

Working with a Rep

Keep in mind, Reps are motivated by commissions, the image of the company they represent, product quality, new products, and support.

In order to evaluate the business opportunity, the Rep often inquires about the following:

- Overview of your company
- Product information
- Target market
- Sales history
- Commission rate
- Description of desired Rep and skills needed
- Support provided to the Rep

When you and the Rep decide to work together, the next step is to negotiate and sign a Sales Representation Agreement. The terms cover the commission, territory, markets, when the Rep is paid, contract duration, as well as a number of legal clauses. Make sure the agreement specifies the Rep cannot carry any competing products. To clarify, make a list of the current competitors.

Once you hire a Rep, you need to support them. Support includes product training, sales tools, brochures, product samples, and marketing. You and the Rep need to be clear on marketing responsibilities. As an example, you provide advertising in national magazines while the Rep takes care of trade shows.

To keep the relationship strong, there should be regular communications. You want to know from the Rep sales activities as well as trends in the market. You should inform the Rep about any product issues, new products, and marketing activities.

Reps can be a great way to generate product sales. The period of time to find, hire, train, and generate sales can take a minimum of two to three months. Therefore, start the process early in order to have a Rep on-board when the product is ready to launch.

Build a Retail Track Record with Wizard Distribution

Typically, retailers want to know you are making sales before they take you on as a vendor. If you have a new product without a history, isn't this a Catch-22?

A solution is Wizard Industries, a unique distribution company focusing on new products from emerging small brands. They help new inventors and existing companies by providing access to retailers. Wizard has no exclusive agreements or binding contracts.

The owner, Billy Carmen, developed a patented distribution and product exposure system making it easy to get new products to market. You register at the

Wizard website for free (www.WizardDistribution.com), enter product information, and ship them a small inventory of product samples. Upon a sale, you are paid in 30 days.

A powerful component of the system is called Sample Rewards. With Sample Rewards, a consumer who wants your product can receive it for free if they recommend it to a retailer who ends up carrying the product. You and Wizard win by expanding distribution, and the customer wins with a free product. This is a clever grassroots method to move your product into retailers.

To broaden the awareness of new products, Wizard produces the Product News Channel (www.ProductNewsChannel.com) and Product News Journal (www.ProductNewsJournal.com). Both the online news channel and print publication aid in the communication of new product news. There is no cost to you for a news story such as a new product launch.

For additional exposure, they offer several paid services including press release writing and distribution, and custom press and demonstration video production.

To learn more about selling your product through Wizard Industries, go to their website www.WizardDistribution.com. To get started, click on the 'New Vendor Setup' tab.

Selling Your Product on QVC and HSN

Wouldn't it be great to sell thousands of your products in just 3 minutes on QVC? If you have the right type of product, this can happen.

Since products are sold on TV, they should look good and be easy to demonstrate. Here's what sells on QVC:

- Beauty
- Bed and Bath
- Christmas toys
- Collectables
- Consumer electronics
- Fashion
- Fitness
- Food and cookbooks
- Home improvement, décor, textiles, and cleaners
- Jewelry
- Kitchen gadgets and appliances
- Music
- Patio and Garden

If your product fits into one of these categories, you're on the right track. If your product is for kids and teens, baby items, fur, alcohol, guns, knives, books (other than cookbooks), software, videos, or a service, then QVC is not interested.

To be considered, you must have a finished packaged product. QVC does not help with development or manufacturing. You need to have manufacturing in place and inventory ready to ship. For a first showing, they request inventory valued between $50,000 and $75,000 retail. For example, if your product retails for $20, you provide 2,500-3,750 units.

QVC buys your product at wholesale and marks it up. So if your product retails for $20, your wholesale price might be somewhere around $10. The markup depends on the type of product.

Manufacturing capability is a decisive factor for selection. QVC wants to know you have high volume production capacity in the hopeful event the product takes off. Ask your manufacturer the quantities they can produce on a monthly basis and on a two week notice.

To learn more about getting your product into QVC, go to their vendor website (www.qvcproductsearch.com). When you're ready, submit a vendor application online. It takes from four to six weeks until you hear back.

While it's possible for an inventor to approach QVC directly, I suggest using an agent if this is your first product. An agent saves you time and energy, presents your product in the best possible light, and positions your product in front of the right buyer without waiting in line.

Kim Babjak is a QVC agent and eight-year veteran selling products on QVC. Contact her at www.KimBabjak.com.

HSN

Home Shopping Network (HSN) works similarly to QVC. You need a finished product and inventory. The product should be something that solves a problem, is unique, and easily demonstratable.

They do accept pre-production prototypes for review. Make sure the prototype is of the highest quality to improve your chance for acceptance.

For a vendor application and answers to frequently asked questions, see their website (www.hsn.com/corp/vendor). After you submit an application, it takes about 30 days to receive a response.

Selling Your Product on an Infomercial

You might be wondering if infomercials are the way to go for your invention. In the broadcast industry, infomercials are known as direct response television advertising (DRTV).

The objective of an infomercial is to sell products directly to the consumer. But the big money begins when infomercial companies sell their products to retailers.

There are two main paths for an inventor to get involved with an infomercial. One is to create you own infomercial, buy airtime, and fulfill orders. However, this can cost you $100,000 and up.

The second path is to turn your invention over to an infomercial company. For a royalty of 2% – 5% the company does everything, including product development, manufacturing, infomercial production, airtime, order taking, and shipping. A higher royalty is possible if your product is already fully developed and manufactured.

Here's the catch: You don't get paid until all their expenses are recovered. This means your royalties don't begin until they reach a break-even point (which could be 100,000 to 1 million units).

In general, the royalty formula is:

Royalties = (Sales – Expenses) x Royalty Rate

Because of the huge infomercial expenses, you're probably better off looking for a licensing deal with a manufacturer. With licensing, the only deductions are for returns and allowances (incentives to retailers). The other benefit of licensing is that you receive royalties with the very first sale, and perhaps receive an advance. To evaluate which is best for you, talk to infomercial companies and manufactures to compare potential sales revenue, expenses, and royalty rates.

If you are interested in pursuing infomercial companies, the product characteristics they are looking for include:

- Visual and easily demonstratable
- Offers benefits to the end-user
- Is in the development stage and not currently in retail stores
- Best if the product has a consumable element for repeat purchases

In addition, they prefer if your invention fits into one of the following best-selling categories:

- Beauty
- Personal Care
- Fitness
- Health
- Automotive
- Housewares
- Kitchen
- Sporting Goods
- Hobbies

Be prepared before you contact an infomercial company. They want to see some type of prototype (not just an idea on a piece of paper). You can show your invention by emailing them good product photos or a link to a website. In addition, you should be ready with the following information:

- The market need for the product (consumer problems, pains, desires)
- Product description
- Benefits
- Features
- The target customer
- Likely price points
- How it's different and better than other products

There are many infomercial companies with a wide range of service offerings. Companies that take on a product and do everything without an upfront fee include:

- Media Enterprises (www.mediaenterprisesinc.com)
- Sylmark (www.sylmark.com)
- Thane International (www.thaneinc.com)
- Tristar Products (www.tristarproductsinc.com)

Most of these companies have a submission form on their website. Instead, I recommend you call and ask for a contact person. Tell them you have a prepared document that completely explains the invention along with photos. If you have a patent, the patent should protect your invention. Without a patent, ask if they will sign a non-disclosure agreement before you submit your information. If they will not sign an NDA, provide only general information such as the need in the market and benefits to the consumer, but without a detailed list of features and functions.

Selling Your Product through Catalogs and Webstores

Catalogs are another terrific way to get your finished product into the market. The great news today is catalog companies market and sell via printed mailings and online webstores. Approach catalog companies using the same approach as any retailer (see the above section on how to prepare and approach retailers).

To search for catalogs, go to Catalogs.com (www.catalogs.com). Then click on a category related to your product and review the catalogs for a fit.

In addition, search the Internet using keywords ["your product type" and "catalog"]. For example, in Google use the keywords ["car parts" catalog]. Then, examine the catalog listings to see which have similar products.

Another method to find catalogs is at the National Mail Order Association website (www.nmoa.org). They provide information on catalogs as well as direct mail.

When you find a suitable catalog, go to their company website and look for a "New Vendor" or "Product Submission" page. If you can't find submission information, use their contact form and ask about the process to become a new vendor. If you prefer to call, ask for a Buyer or Merchandising Manager for help.

Catalogs to review include:

- Frontgate (www.frontgate.com)
- Hammacher Schlemmer (www.hammacher.com)
- Herrington (www.herringtoncatalog.com)
- Oriental Trading Company (www.orientaltrading.com)
- Pacific Spirit (www.pacificspiritcatalogs.com)

Webstores

There are several companies selling products without a printed catalog, but rather using online webstores. These online-only catalogs are known simply as "webstores."

Webstores usually operate by means of two business models. One method is to list your product for sale, take orders, and pass the customer information to you (known as drop shipping). You then ship the product to the customer.

The other type of webstore carries inventory. You ship a quantity of products to the webstore, and then they sell it and ship to the customer. Either type of webstore can work. It depends if you want to be involved with shipping products to customers or not.

To find a webstore to carry your product, search the Internet using keywords ["your product type" and "webstore"].

When selling through a catalog or webstore, you can also sell from your own website. You normally sell at the retail price, while the catalog or webstore sets their own price.

Selling Your Product as a Private Label

In 2009, the Private Label Manufacturers Association (www.plma.com) reported, "Store brands now account for one of every five items sold in U.S. supermarkets, drug chains and mass merchandisers. They represent more than $65 billion of current business at retail and are achieving new levels of growth every year."

Private labels are alternatives to branded products sold by a retailer. Examples include Kirkland Signature brand sold at Costco, Sam's at Walmart, as well many other generic products.

Private labels are typically comparable in terms of materials, ingredients, or appearance. Retailers sell a private label if the brand has a large established customer base and is already heavily advertised. Retailers are motivated to sell private labels because of the higher margins. If the retail margin for a brand is 40 to 50%, the margin of a private label is often 60 to 70%.

When a retailer decides to sell a private labeled product, they either contact a specific supplier or announce a bid. The bid is usually submitted via an online auction.

Private labels are typically not for a unique new invention. If your invention does the same thing as a national brand with a significant cost savings, then a retailer might be interested. Approach retailers using the same methods as explained earlier. The difference is to describe the product as a low cost alternative to brands they are currently selling.

Selling Your Product as a Promotional Item

The advertising specialty industry is a great market to sell your products. Maybe you've seen the mugs, pens, golf items, journals, tee shirts, and other novelty items given away by companies to promote awareness and generate sales.

Companies spend big money on promotional products to have their logos, website, and telephone number in the hands of their prospects and customers. Promotional product sales generated over $19 billion in 2008.

How the Industry Works

A company such as IBM, contacts a logo business for ideas on a marketing campaign. The logo business is the distributor and center of the promotional products industry. The distributor provides the company with suggestions and product ideas to help meet their objectives.

When the customer decides on the type of product for a logo, the distributor places an order from a supplier. The supplier is you, the product owner. The supplier prints the logo, or other artwork, on the products and ships to the distributor. The distributor makes sure product quality is up to standard and delivers to the company.

Getting Your Product in the Door

To sell your product as a promotional item, there are two main organizations you should become familiar with: Advertising Specialty Institute (www.asicentral.com) and Promotional Products Association International (www.ppai.org). Both have plenty of information and resources. Look into ASI and PPAI to see which organization best caters to your product type. You need to become a member of at least one of these organizations.

Advertising Specialty Institute (ASI) has about 90% of the industry's suppliers and distributors as members. As a product supplier, you must have an ASI identification number to sell in this market. Having an ASI number makes you legitimate in the eyes of distributors. Membership cost for a supplier is $799 with a $250 application fee.

According to Laura Fisher of ASI, "With a membership, your company and product information are available online to the distribution network. ASI also provides a number of educational and marketing opportunities to entice distributors including trade shows, magazine advertising, and lists for direct mail."

Promotional Products Association International (PPAI), a non-profit organization, works with suppliers and distributors around the world. PPAI connects suppliers and distributors by means of tradeshows, magazines, and educational programs. By becoming a PPAI member, you receive the Universal Promotional Identification Code (UPIC). With a UPIC, you are accepted as a qualified supplier. In addition, membership enables access to distributor contact information.

Gwen Gann of PPAI says, "As a supplier member, you place your profile online which includes your product line details and company information." Membership starts at $600 based on your sales volume.

Courting the Distributors

Once you have an ASI or PPAI number (or both), your objective is to make distributors aware of and interested in your products. There are a number of paths to reach the over 20,000 distributors including:

- Call distributors and meet directly. Many are open to see the latest products in the market.
- Exhibit at advertising specialty trade shows to attract the distributors in attendance.
- Rent a list of distributors and mail a letter of introduction, product literature, and follow-up with a phone call.
- Hire a sales rep company who already has established relationships with distributors. The sales rep introduces your product and receives a commission on orders.

Playing the Game

Distributors choose to work with suppliers who have an ASI or PPAI number, are credible, and can turn an order around in two weeks or less. It's important to create relationships with distributors so they know you and your products. If a distributor calls to place an order, make sure payment terms are clear. For first time orders, ask for payment up front. For follow-on orders, you can provide credit terms after you check their credit and references.

It's an unwritten rule, but suppliers should never go around distributors and talk to end-user companies directly. "Distributors will find out and you can forget about getting business from them again," said Ryan Kaback of Custom Logos in San Diego. Therefore, don't sell direct or you'll likely be left out in the cold.

To determine if selling your product as a promotional item is for you, answer these questions:

- Can your product be sold as a promotional item?
  Talk to logo companies in your area for opinions. To find a logo company, look in the phonebook under "Advertising Promotional Products."
- Can a logo or other artwork be printed on your product?
- Can you ship an order in two weeks or less?
- Can you provide great products and customer service?

If you've answered "yes" to all the above questions and you're willing to make an investment to create awareness with distributors, then you could be on the winning path to carve out a piece of this $19 billion industry.

More Distribution Channels

In addition to the above mentioned channels of distribution (methods to sell your product), there are several other retail and distribution avenues available to you.

Stores that used to carry just one type of product now carry several. Years ago, drugstores only sold drugs. Now drugstores sell appliances, stationary, school supplies, teddy bears, food, and more. The point is that your product might sell well in several types of retailers.

Retailers carrying more than one type of product include:

- Auto – Advance, AutoZone, Kragen, O'Reilly
- Beauty – Sally Beauty Supply, Ulta
- Books – Barnes and Noble, Books-a-Million, Borders, Hastings
- Cards and Stationery – Hallmark (Gold Crown)
- Convenience – Circle K, QuikTrip, 7-11, Town & Country, Wawa
- Department stores – Dillard's, JC Penney, Macy's, Sears
- Drugstores – CVS, Walgreens
- Electronics – Best Buy, Radio Shack
- Grocery – Krogers, Meijer, Publix, Red Lion
- Hobby and Craft – Hobby Lobby, Michaels

- Home and Hardware – Home Depot, Lowes
- Jewelry – Sterling (Kay), Tiffany, Zales
- Office products – Office Depot, Office Max, Staples
- Pet supplies – Petco, Petsmart, Pet Supplies Plus
- Sporting goods – Academy, Bass Pro Shops, Dick's, Sports Authority, Sport Chalet
- Video and music – Blockbuster, Hollywood Video, Movie Gallery

As if this wasn't enough, the carts and kiosks seen in the shopping malls, events, and airports are another type of retailer.

Most carts and kiosks are businesses buying and selling products, while some are inventors selling their products. Studies indicate products for carts and kiosks are best priced under $20. Optimal price points seem to be at $12 and $3. The best selling products are accessories, dolls, toys, foods, sweaters, and scarves.

Market and Sell at Trade Shows

Did you know the famous Pet Rock got its start at a trade show? In 1975, Gary Dahl took his rock in a gift box to a housewares trade show. A buyer from Neiman Marcus was impressed and ordered 5,000 units and the rest is history.

To decide which trade shows are for you, see what established companies with similar products are doing. Go to their websites and review the events they attend. Additionally, check trade show listings (noted below) to determine which events focus on your product type.

There are two main types of trade shows: marketing direct to the customer, and marketing to a retail buyer.

Exhibiting to the end-user customer is typically done at trade shows, fairgrounds, swap meets, or related to an event. You rent a booth and bring products for the purpose of selling.

Exhibiting to a retail buyer is usually at an industry conference or trade show. In this venue you do not normally bring products to sell, but rather generate interest and hopefully take sales orders from buyers. Then you'll obtain a purchase order from the retailer's purchasing department, ship the product to the retailer's warehouse, send an invoice, and collect a check in 30 to 90 days.

Exhibiting at trade shows is often expensive. Expenses include creating the booth display, shipping the display to the trade show, marketing activities, and travel. Therefore, to justify a trade show, calculate the potential sales, minus expenses, to see if a profit is possible.

Keep in mind, in the early stages, expenses such as trade shows are an investment to generate awareness for future product sales.

Gather Sales Leads

The main objectives to exhibiting are to make sales and collect leads. Since not everyone is ready to make a purchase at the show, collect contact information so you can follow-up and make a sale later. To collect leads you may offer a free report, brochure, technical whitepaper, provide a free trial, or have a contest. I suggest, before you exhibit, attend trade shows related to your product and see what methods exhibitors are using to generate sales and collect leads.

Before exhibiting at a show, ask the organizers if they offer a card swipe machine to collect contact information from attendee's badges. This allows attendees who are interested in your product to easily provide their contact information. At the end of the show you'll receive an electronic file containing data of people who swiped their cards. In addition, be sure to bring paper forms to collect detailed information including name, address, email address, needs and wants, when they are ready to buy, quantities, and names of the decision makers if they are a business.

To attract people to your booth, the trade show organizers usually offer a number of marketing tactics to generate awareness and interest for your product. A popular method is to obtain a mailing list, which enables you to send a postcard to attendees before the show. As a tactic, the postcard has an offer they can claim when they stop by your booth. The offer should be of value to attendees and tied-in to your product. The offer could be a free sample, free trial, special discount, or promotional item giveaway (e.g. calculator, coffee mug).

Another tactic to generate awareness is to issue a press release coupled with an announcement during the trade show. The announcement could be a new product, special pricing, giveaway, appearance by a celebrity, etc. Check with the show organizers to see what services are available.

Trade Show Communications

When exhibiting, make sure your signage and brochures highlight the product's benefits rather than just its features. So, if your product is an energy saving device, your sign might say, "New Product Saves 45% in Electricity at Half the Cost." You should also have signage to collect leads. For example, have a headline: "Win a

Free iPod" with instructions, "Place your business card in the bowl for a chance to win an iPod Nano."

When people walk by, you want them to stop and visit your booth. Don't just stand there and say nothing or only say, "Hello." You've spent a lot of time and money to set up a booth. Ask a question which they have to answer "Yes."

For the energy product example, you might say to a passerby, "Are you interested in saving energy costs?" They are most likely to say "Yes." Then say, "Good, let me show you in two minutes how you can save money." When talking with people, be friendly, complimentary, and ask questions to uncover their needs and wants.

Finding Tradeshows

To find a tradeshow, use online directories to search by type, location, and date. General trade show directories include:

- Tradeshow Week (www.tradeshowweek.com)
- Trade Show News Network (www.tsnn.com)
- Global Sources – click on Trade Shows (www.globalsources.com)

Tradeshows geared toward inventors include:

- Minnesota Inventors Congress (www.minnesotainventorscongress.org)
- InventBay Expo (www.inventbay.com)
- Yankee Invention Exposition (www.yankeeinventionexpo.org)

For current information on trade shows and other resources, please visit www.ProductCoach.com and click on Resource Links.

Personal Selling

Selling is the process of facilitating a customer transaction – your product in exchange for their money. Uncovering market needs from a sales viewpoint is commonly known as prospecting. Prospecting may include making outbound calls, meeting people face-to-face, and answering inbound calls.

Part of the selling process involves creating the proper mindset. We can become anxious when promoting our product because it may feel like there's a lot on the line. When you converse with someone in person, email, or on the telephone, your objective is to reduce pressure. People shift into defensive mode if they think you're only trying to sell them something. They do not want to be sold, they want to buy. You must adopt the role of problem solver. Instead of approaching someone with the intent to sell, which also puts pressure on you, just go into the situation to determine if there's a need for your product. You have no agenda other than to ask questions. Tell the person you're there to provide education about your product. If they have a need for your product, great, if not, that's okay too.

One of the keys to selling is building a contact list. Start with your beta testers, focus group attendees, and survey recipients. Then add those who respond to your press release, advertising, direct mail, trade shows, free newsletter on your website, and other marketing programs.

To manage this information (e.g., names, addresses, telephone numbers, and email addresses) set up a contact database. There are many contact databases available and some of the better known are *Act!* and *SalesLogix* from Sage Software, *Goldmine* from Front Range Solutions, and *Maximizer* from Maximizer Software. They offer the benefit of tracking customer information, setting reminders, monitoring performance, and much more. As an alternative, Microsoft Office, Outlook and Excel provide a basic method of tracking customers.

Elevator Statement

You might encounter potential prospects while traveling, on the telephone, or at business events. At all times you should be ready to deliver a quick statement pitching your product. People call this an elevator statement, elevator speech, or elevator pitch.

The use of the term "elevator" is from the scenario or a chance encounter in an elevator with an important person (e.g. company president, retail buyer, potential customer, magazine editor, or investor) and you only have up to 20 seconds to get them interested in your product.

The elevator statement is short and sweet but is not a tagline or positioning statement. Think of the elevator statement as a brief conversation to entice the other person.

Elements of the elevator statement include:

- Benefits provided to the end-user (save time, save money, make money, improve their health, improve safety, improve self-esteem).
- Who the product is for (target market).
- The name of your product.

Here's a sample guide to create your statement:

- "I created a new product that helps [target market] [benefits]."
- "The product is called [product name]."
- "People tell me it's great because now for the first time they are able to [benefits]."

As an example:

- "I created a new product that helps senior citizens hang picture frames themselves."
- "The product is called EZHang123."
- "People tell me it's great because now for the first time they are able to brighten their rooms and enjoy the memories of their family and friends."

After your statement, ask a question:

- "Can I send you a sample?"
- "Can I send you a brochure?"
- "Can I send you a link to my website?"
- "Do you have a friend or family member who might be interested?"

If they answer "Yes," then ask for a business card, email address, or telephone number. If they ask for more information, be prepared to talk about your product's benefits, features, how it works, pricing, special discounts, how it's better than the competition, testimonials, quality, and warranty.

In addition to a verbal communication tool, the elevator statement can be used (or modified) in written form on your website, for social networking websites, and in advertisements.

Selling Your Product as an OEM

As an original equipment manufacturer (OEM) you make and sell your invention directly to a company who then sells the product under their brand name. This is especially common in the computer industry. For example, a Hewlett-Packard computer might contain a microprocessor from Intel, video card from NVIDIA, and hard drive from Seagate.

As an OEM, the item you sell could be a finished product, module, or part. The brand name company integrates items, from one to many companies, to form a complete product. These companies seek outside suppliers to get to market quicker and for savings in research and development.

In addition, companies license components from other companies when they can't design around a patent. Did you know a typical DVD player consists of technology from several companies consisting of about 400 patents?

The advantages to operating as an original equipment manufacturer are low marketing expenses, no need to produce fancy retail packaging, and being able to sell large quantities at a time. The disadvantage is being at the mercy of companies who can easily switch suppliers if a better deal arises. If one company does not re-order, you can lose a large chunk of revenue.

Keep in mind, while you operate as an OEM, you can still sell your product through retailers. This is common today. The computer products mentioned above sell as both OEM and retail.

To sell your item as an OEM, look for companies with complimentary products. They might be working on a product in which your invention saves them time and development expense. Approach companies with a proposal showing how your product expands their product line and generates more profit.

Some companies are actively seeking OEM suppliers (joint venture) and make public announcements. You can find the announcements with internet search terms ["seeking OEM suppliers"] or ["seeking OEM makers"].

Note: The definition of OEM varies according to industry. In some cases, the company who makes the branded product is called an original equipment manufacturer. The reasoning is that they purchase components and modules from OEM suppliers. Therefore, the branded company is the "original" or top-level producer of the finished product.

Chapter 21:
Marketing and Sales Checkup

If everything seems under control, you're just not going fast enough.
Mario Andretti

Topics in this Chapter:

- Marketing and Sales Tracking
- Sales Losses
- Customer Satisfaction
- Competition Review
- Patent Infringement Review
- Product Review

After launching your product, you need to continue with marketing and sales activities to generate revenue. But is what you're doing working? To determine the effectiveness of your actions, you need to monitor and track your activities. If revenue is lower than expected, you need to change one or more things such as the product, pricing, sales tactics, or marketing programs.

Marketing and Sales Tracking

Marketing and sales tracking helps you determine if the unit volume or revenue is meeting your objectives. Think of the buying process.

If you're not getting leads, there's a problem creating awareness. If you're getting leads, but only a small number are converting to sales, your sales methods might need improvement. If your product is a consumable that is supposed to be re-ordered, and they're not, there could be a problem with the product or the re-ordering process.

To identify trends, keep track of your marketing and sales activities by placing them into a log using a program such as Microsoft Excel.

Items to track include:

- Date marketing program publicly appears
- Marketing program (e.g., email to your newsletter subscribers, direct mail to *Popular Mechanics* subscribers, or Google AdWords)
- Number of leads generated (e.g., email requests for more information, website unique visitors, calls in response to an advertisement, direct mail response cards received, or contacts made at a trade show)
- Number of units sold
- Revenue generated
- Cost of marketing program

Marketing and Sales Log						
Date	Marketing Program	Num Leads	Num Units Sold	$ Revenue	$ Cost	$ Profit

Sales Losses

Another way to fine-tune your product and business practices is to ask questions of those who decided not to buy. These are people who contacted you (sales leads) but for whatever reason did not place an order.

When it seems apparent a prospective customer does not want to buy your product, call and ask why. Let them know you realize you can't help them with your product, and that's okay. You just want to know the honest reason why they did not buy.

Whatever they tell you, do not defend yourself, just listen. Use this feedback to enhance your product, your marketing, and sales methods. Questions to ask include:

- Did you buy another product?
- What was your biggest complaint about our product?
- Was our company easy to work with?
- What improvements would you suggest?

To conclude, thank them for their time and give them your name and telephone number in case they have not purchased another product or become dissatisfied with the competitor's product.

Customer Satisfaction

You might assume people love your product for one reason, but they really like something else instead. For example, I figured customers purchased my wireless modem because of the features, pricing, and ease of use. Yes, those were strong factors, but 24-hour support was actually the deciding purchase factor because it gave customers peace of mind. As a result, I emphasized 24-hour support in future marketing messages.

Customer feedback in the form of surveys (mail or email) or telephone calls reveal how they're using your product and provide valuable suggestions for improvements. I suggest surveying all customers and then calling a few.

There are web-based survey tools in which you set up the questions and email a link to your customers. The customer clicks the link and answers the questions. At the conclusion, the survey tools provide a summary of the answers. Popular survey tools include Survey Monkey (www.surveymonkey.com) and Zoomerang (www.zoomerang.com).

Call customers and ask why they purchased your product. They may be surprised you're calling, but some will be eager to talk. First, thank them for purchasing your product. Inform them you're seeking feedback to improve the product. Let them know you only have a few questions, but ask if this is a good time to talk.

Questions to ask include:

- What was your reason for buying the product?
- Why did you choose the product over others?
- What do you primarily use the product for (if it's not obvious)?
- What type of business are you in (if selling to businesses)?
- What, if any, improvements would you suggest?
- Has the company been easy to work with?

To conclude, thank them for their time and provide your name and phone number in case they have questions or come up with suggestions later.

Competition Review

How has the competition reacted to your product? Different competitors react differently. They might:

- Change their product price
- Talk about your product in a disparaging way
- Change their marketing and sales strategies and tactics
- Add or change product features
- Do nothing

Monitor competitors on a regular basis. Pick a day once a month to visit competitor websites to read their press releases, product information, and financial information. If they offer a newsletter or automatic email service, sign up for it.

On the Internet, there are alerting services to tell you when a webpage has changed. For example, if a competitor changes their price or adds a new product, their website reflects a change.

A company such as WatchThatPage (www.watchthatpage.com) sends you an email showing you the changes. In addition, Google has an alerting service to allow you to monitor keywords (www.google.com/alerts). When a new webpage is created or changed, with the keywords you specify (such as a competitor's name), you'll receive an email notification.

Patent Infringement Review

Once a month you should scan the market for products that might be infringing on your patent. Look for products at retailers, in catalogs, retailer websites, and directory websites such as:

- Buy.com (www.buy.com)
- Catalogs.com (www.catalogs.com)
- Google Products (www.google.com/products)
- Nextag (www.nextag.com)
- Walmart (www.walmart.com)

For any product resembling your patent, you should buy the product and examine its features. In addition, read their website, advertisements, packaging, and user manual.

Patent Infringement Log			
Company	Product Name	Description	Where Found

Contact your patent attorney with information about any product infringing on your patent. Your attorney will compare the product to your patent's claims. Usually a first step is to send a letter to the infringing company to put them on notice and to stop producing their products. Companies typically either ignore the letter or provide a counter-argument.

Most infringement cases are settled out of court. As a remedy to an infringing product you can offer the company a license agreement in which they continue to sell products and pay you a royalty.

If you can't afford to sue a company for infringement, there are organizations that take cases on a contingency basis (they are only paid by a percentage of the winnings). General Patent Corporation (GPC) is an example of a company helping inventors fight against infringers. Founded by Alexander Poltorak, GPC has successfully won infringement cases. For more information, visit their website (www.generalpatent.com).

Product Review

Do you need to improve your product? The information you collect from customer feedback, marketing and sales tracking, and competitive analysis helps you figure out what to improve for your next product release. If there are product defects causing poor reviews, lost sales, or product returns, then resolve the issue and re-launch the product as a new version.

Make product improvements to stay competitive and only if they'll have an impact on future sales. When customers and prospects make suggestions, ask if they'd still buy the product without this feature. If the answer is yes, then it may be unnecessary to include certain feature sin the next product version.

To create an updated product version, go through the **Market-Step** process again. Don't worry, it will be much easier the next time around.

This is the end of the main section of the book. There are more advanced topics in the Appendix.

I hope the material has helped you. To continue the learning process, please visit my website www.ProductCoach.com.

Thank You and Best Success,

Matthew Yubas

APPENDICES

I never perfected an invention that I did not think about in terms of the service it might give others. I find out what the world needs. Then I go ahead and try to invent it.

Thomas A. Edison

Appendix A:
Investigate Your Competition

Topics in this Appendix:

- List Competitors
- Collect Detailed Data
- Organize Data
- Evaluate the Competitive Environment
- Combat Competitors

A competitor is any company or individual selling a similar product or solution to your target market. You'll want to perform competitive research to know how to outsell them. In addition, if you seek funding or licensing, you need to explain your product's advantages over the competition and how to sustain those advantages.

Collecting information provides important insight about how to minimize competitive threats. In the next five sections, I'll walk you through the process of researching and analyzing competition.

List Competitors

Start by making a list of your potential competitors. Research sources include magazines, journals, newspapers, retailers, product review websites, and the competitor's website. Yahoo (www.yahoo.com) is a great place to see companies listed by category. In addition, use the free patent search engine to find competitors with similar products (www.uspto.gov). Another free online service is Webster's Online (www.webdir.net).

You can also effectively search for competitors using the North American Industry Classification System (NAICS). NAICS, operated by the United States Census, provides categories and statistics of business activities in North America. This system is replacing the Standard Industrial Code (SIC). Use NAICS to find lists of companies with products comparable to yours. The NAICS Association has a free search engine (www.naics.com).

Competitive Products and Prices		
Company	Product	Price

To use the NAICS, first find the classification for your product type. For example, if your product is a screwdriver, go to their website (www.naics.com), click on Code Search, enter "screwdriver" and note the returned code, 333991.

Using this code, go to Webster's Online (www.webdir.net) and search by NAICS code. When you enter 333991, screwdriver manufacturers are listed.

You might see many competitors. You are mainly concerned with companies that give you the most competition. Key competitors are those that offer quality products with a known brand name, provide good value, have a large share of customers, or have growing revenue. Narrow your list to your key competitors.

Collect Detailed Data

With your list of key competitors, collect company and product details. Read product reviews in magazines or online, visit your competitors' websites, read their press releases, talk to marketing consultants, talk to sales people where the product is sold, and last but not least, use their product.

For computer products and accessories, check the CNET website (www.cnet.com) for its large database of reviews. You might also pay attention to blogs and Internet discussions on *Yahoo Groups* or *Google Groups.* You might read what people like and do not like about particular products. If a competitor is a public company, obtain their annual report and 10-K reports. Study these reports for product information, discussions of competition, and financial statements. As you gather information, think of the following:

- Why do customers buy the competitor's product (e.g., brand name, quality, price, service, innovation, style)?
- What are the unique features of my product versus the competition?
- What are the deficiencies of my product versus the competition?

Reasons People Buy from the Competition	
Product	Reasons People Buy This Product

Organize Data

After you've gathered competitive information, organize and summarize it. This information will be used when we determine how to combat your competition.

For your major competitors (known brand, most customers, highest revenue, highest quality products) use the following format to organize data.

Summary of Each Key Competitor
Company name:
Product name(s):
Website address:
Stock symbol (if public):
Year founded:
Target market:
Perception in the market:
Product positioning:
Product pricing:
Marketing programs in use:
Distribution method:
Product strengths:
Product weaknesses:

Evaluate the Competitive Environment

The **Market-Step** Competitive Environment Evaluation (see next page) is a look at competition as a whole. For each question on the following worksheet, check the box that best describes your competitive situation. Answering these questions helps reveal your competitive environment.

For example, in "Number of Competitors" if there is only one competitor, put a checkmark in the box under "Few."

When completed, look at your checkmarks. If most are positioned on the right side, then your product is in a desirable competitive environment. If most checkmarks are positioned on the left side, then your product is in an undesirable environment and likely need to find ways to combat your competition.

Competitive Environment Evaluation				
[Undesirable]				[Desirable]
Number of Competitors (e.g., 30 is many, 3 is a few)				
Many				Few
❏	❏	❏	❏	❏
Dominant Competitors (large market share and known brand names)				
Many				None
❏	❏	❏	❏	❏
Competitive Fighting (frequent marketing promotions, price wars)				
Intense				Mild
❏	❏	❏	❏	❏
Market Segment Growth (average is 5%, high growth is 25% per year)				
Shrinking				Growing
❏	❏	❏	❏	❏
Market Segment Size (100 customers can be small, 100,000 is big)				
Small				Big
❏	❏	❏	❏	❏

Combat Competitors

When competition is intense, your product needs competitive advantages to entice prospective customers. Keep in mind, your product is more than just the physical device. The total product includes documentation, support, and perhaps accessories. There are a number of areas to combat competitors.

Your competitive advantage might include one or more of the following:

- Lower price (along with your lower costs)
- Higher price based on quality, exclusivity, or luxury
- Greater product benefits
- Demonstrated higher quality
- Innovative features or style

- Greater overall value using a mix of features, quality, and price
- Better availability or convenience
- Excellent customer service
- Better marketing communications (e.g., advertising, promotions)
- Greater sales activity (e.g., more people, more territories)

What advantages does your product idea offer compared to the competition (e.g., faster, less expensive, longer lasting, higher quality, makes more money, saves more time, more fun, greater safety)? Inform your prospective customers about these advantages on your website, sales letter, brochure, and other communications.

Competitive Advantages	
Product	Your Advantage

You can also combat competitors by uncovering the weaknesses in their strengths. Companies often rely heavily on their strengths to win sales. So, if you can find fault with their strengths you have an advantage.

For example, if your competitor is claiming their product has more features, you could communicate all those extra features are a disadvantage because they're harder to learn, increase costs, and slow users down.

If a competitor claims their product is more technically advanced, you could point out some advanced products are more complicated, harder to use, and are more prone to failure. List what your competition boasts as their best product assets, and think how it could be communicated to your prospective customers as a weakness.

Strengths Into Weaknesses	
Comp. Product	Their Strengths into Weaknesses

In summary, use your competitive investigation to create advantages in your product as well as marketing and sales strategies. Think like a competitor. What would they do if your product hit the market? Would they lower prices, add new features, or increase marketing? Create countermeasures ahead of time so you can initiate actions rapidly to offset competitor moves.

Appendix B:
Select Your Target Market

Topics in this Appendix:

- Why Select a Target Market
- Target Market Factors
- Methods to Select a Target Market
- Your Target Market
- Other Targeting Methods

A target market is the market segment you can best serve and earn the highest possible profit. A target market can be a group of people or businesses sharing common characteristics, such as hobbies, occupations, or industry.

For example, a target market could be coin collectors, female golfers, or computer manufacturers. These broad segments can be further narrowed down to coin collectors who live in San Francisco, female golfers over age 55 who live in Texas, or computer manufacturers with 1,000 or more employees.

Why Select a Target Market

Initially, you might have many market segments of people or businesses potentially interested in your invention. That's good, but you'll want to narrow it down to one primary market segment you can effectively reach based on your marketing budget. Choose a target market according to its potential for success. If you measure success in terms of profit, then your target market is the one that delivers the greatest profits.

You need to select a target market because you do not have the time or money to sell to everyone. For example, if your product is golf clubs, you could not afford to advertise in every magazine and newspaper in print and online. While you could advertise golf clubs in a hockey magazine because some hockey players play golf, you can be sure advertising in a golf magazine reaches your target audience.

The following Markets and Segments diagram illustrates the process to select a target market. From the entire market, you'll brainstorm a few segments thought to be the best source of sales. Next, analyze each segment and identify the most attractive segment as the target market.

Markets and Segments

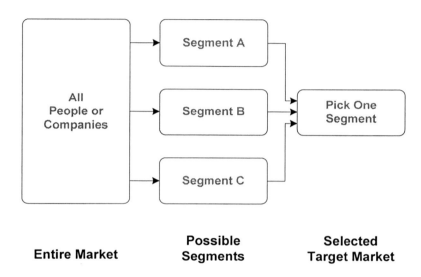

Entire Market   **Possible Segments**   **Selected Target Market**

Selecting a target market allows you to design a product with benefits and features to specifically appeal to a certain group. Don't try to be everything to everybody.

Target Market Factors

When you have different market segments to consider, a few factors need examining because each target market factor can influence your choice. Let's look at the following factors, and then use them to select your target market.

- **Segment Size** – A measurement of the total number of people or companies in a market segment.

- **Buyer Interest** – The result of your interviews and surveys of a particular market segment. It's the percentage of those who have responded favorably.

- **Segment Potential** – The total number of potential interested buyers in each market segment. Segment Potential equals the Segment Size multiplied by the percentage of Buyer Interest.

- **Buyer Price Sensitivity** – The selling price a market segment is willing to pay. Some segments only buy something if it's on sale or there's a deep discount. For others, if you show your product satisfies a need or saves money, they'll pay any reasonable price.

- **M/S Expense** – The marketing and sales expenses needed to reach a market segment. The less the expense the more favorable.

- **Market Growth** – An indicator of how fast the market is growing in terms of people or companies. For example, Las Vegas is a fast-growing city. So if your idea meets a need for people or companies in Las Vegas, then market growth is in your favor.

- **Buyer Readiness** – The time it takes for a customer to make a purchase. For example, if you're selling to a market segment consisting mainly of bureaucracies, purchase decisions could take a long time. Market segments making quick purchase decisions are more desirable.

- **Competitiveness** – The number of competitors and the fierceness of the competition. Does your segment require you to compete with Sony, Panasonic, and Sanyo? Or, can you tailor your idea to a segment where there are no major players?

- **Familiarity** – The degree to which you understand the workings of a market segment. Market segments where you're familiar with the technology, trends, distribution, and customer behavior are more desirable.

Methods to Select a Target Market

There are two methods I've developed to select a target market. The first is the **Market-Step** Profit Potential Method, which is a calculation of profit in each market segment. The market segment with the highest profit potential becomes your target market. We'll go through an example and then have you perform this calculation later.

Profit Potential Method

Use the following steps to determine the profit potential of a market segment:

- **Segmentation** – Make a list of possible market segments.
- **Determine Segment Size** – The total number of people or companies in each market segment.
- **Determine Buyer Interest** – The percent interest from concept surveys and interviews in each market segment.
- **Calculate Segment Potential** – Multiply Segment Size by percentage of Buyer Interest.
- **Determine a Selling Price** – Use survey information and comparative competitor pricing as a starting point to determine a selling price.
- **Calculate Potential Revenue** – Multiply Segment Potential by Selling Price.
- **Calculate Segment Profit** – Revenue Potential minus Unit Costs and M/S Expenses.

If one market segment has the highest profit potential, then this is your target market. If more than one market segment has comparable profit potential, then use the following Positive Factors Method to determine a target market.

Positive Factors Method

The second way to determine a target market is the **Market-Step** Positive Factors Method, which is the total number of favorable target market factors. This method is used to support your profit potential calculations.

Use the target market factors and rank each segment based on how it favors you. For each factor use a "+" if factor favors you, a "o" if the factor is neutral, or " – " if the factor does not favor you. Therefore, a segment with the most plusses and least minuses is the most attractive market segment and is your target market.

The Positive Factors Method uses the following target market factors:

- **Segment Size** – The larger the better.
- **Buyer Interest** – The higher percentage the better.

- **Buyer Price Sensitivity** – The higher the selling price the better.
- **M/S Expense** – The lower the marketing and sales expense the better.
- **Market Growth** – The greater the market growth the better.
- **Buyer Readiness** – The faster a customer takes to make a purchase the better.
- **Competitiveness** – The less intense and least amount of name brand competitors the better.
- **Your Familiarity** – The more familiar with a market segment the better.

Example of Market Segments for Screwdrivers

Let's use a new type of screwdriver for our example. You believe the market segments are Carpenters, Auto Mechanics, and Homeowners over the age of 65.

The next step is to determine the size for each of these market segments. Using the Internet, library, and other research tools, look for the total number of people in each group. Use keywords such as "market size" or "market growth" in a search engine. For Carpenters, a search might be ["market size" and "carpenters"].

In this example, use the following market research assumptions to select a target market.

- **Segment Size** – Assume your research reveals there are five hundred thousand Auto Mechanics, one million Carpenters, and ten million Homeowners over the age of 65 in this country. These numbers represent the segment size.

- **Buyer Interest (Percent)** – From conversations, interviews, and surveys, you conclude 80% of Auto Mechanics would like the new screwdriver, as well as 30% of Carpenters, and 10% of Homeowners over the age of 65.

- **Number of Interested Buyers** – To determine the number of potential interested buyers, multiply the segment size times the percentage of interested buyers. This is an estimate of how many people are interested in your idea in each market segment.

		Segment Size	Buyer Interest	Interested Buyers
Auto Mechanics	=	500,000	80%	400,000
Carpenters	=	1,000,000	30%	300,000
Homeowners 65+	=	10,000,000	10%	1,000,000

Given these numbers, you might automatically assume the Homeowners market is your target market. Other factors such as marketing and sales expenses, and price sensitivity, influence the selection.

Target Market Selection by Profit Potential Method

Segment Choices	1 Auto Mechanics	2 Carpenters	3 Homeowners 65+
Segment Size:	500,000	1,000,000	10,000,000
x % Interest:	80%	30%	10%
= Potential:	400,000	300,000	1,000,000
x Selling Price:	$25	$20	$10
= Revenue:	$10,000,000	$6,000,000	$10,000,000
− Unit Costs:	$1,600,000	$1,200,000	$4,000,000
− M/S Expenses:	$1,400,000	$1,800,000	$5,000,000
= Profit:	$7,000,000	$3,000,000	$1,000,000
Your Selection	✓		

To calculate the profit potential for the Auto Mechanic segment:

- Assuming the appropriate Selling Price for this segment is $25, then Revenue is the number of Interested Buyers times the Selling Price which is 400,000 x $25 = $10,000,000.

- You estimate your Unit Costs are $4 each, therefore the Total Unit Costs is the number of Interested Buyers times the Unit Cost which is 400,000 x $4 = $1,600,000.
- You estimate your M/S Expense to reach this market segment is $1,400,000.
- Therefore, Segment Profit is Revenue minus Total Unit Costs minus M/S Expenses which is $10,000,000 – ($1,600,000 and $1,400,000) = $7,000,000.

Performing the same calculations for each segment reveals the Auto Mechanics would likely be the most profitable.

Let's look at the second method to determine a target market. Positive Factors Method uses target market factors to select a target market. Each factor is equally weighted in importance.

Target Market Selection by Positive Market Factors			
Segment Choices	1 Auto Mechanics	2 Carpenters	3 Homeowners 65+
Segment Size:	o	o	+
Buyer Interest:	+	o	-
Price Sensitivity:	+	+	-
M/S Expenses:	+	o	+
Market Growth:	o	+	+
Buyer Readiness:	+	o	-
Competitiveness:	o	+	o
Your Familiarity:	+	o	o
Total +	5	3	3
Total –	0	0	3
Score	5	3	0
Your Selection	✓		

Recall that Auto Mechanics were very interested in the new screwdrivers. Therefore, you entered a "+" next to Buyer Interest. In terms of marketing and sales expenses, you telephoned the most popular trade journals in each of the three market segments. Advertising in the auto mechanic trade magazines is the least expensive out of the three segments. As a result, you entered a "+" next to M/S Expenses. The same research is performed for each factor.

Looking at the following table, you see that the Auto Mechanic segment has the most positive factors and least amount of negative factors. Therefore it is the target market.

To summarize this example, you started with the thought there are three market segments: Carpenters, Auto Mechanics, and Homeowners over the age of 65. Then, you evaluated each segment by determining a profit potential. You evaluated each by rating the positive target market factors. The most profitable and most favorable led you to conclude Auto Mechanics are the best target market.

Your Target Market

Now it's your turn to select a target market. Use the information from your market research, surveys, and interviews to determine a target market. Use the Profit Potential Method and Positive Factors Method as a guide.

Target Market Selection by Profit Potential Method		
	1	2	3
Segment Choices			
Segment Size:			
x % Interest:			
= Potential:			
x Selling Price:			
= Revenue:			
– Unit Costs:			
– M/S Expenses:			
= Profit:			
Your Selection			

Target Market Selection by Positive Market Factors			
	1	2	3
Segment Choices			
Segment Size:			
Buyer Interest:			
Price Sensitivity:			
M/S Expenses:			
Market Growth:			
Buyer Readiness:			
Competitiveness:			
Your Familiarity:			
Total +			
Total –			
Score			
Your Selection			

Other Targeting Methods

Selecting a target market is not an exact science. Selection is part planning, part experience, and part experimentation. In addition to the methods already described, here are a few others to try:

- **Method A –** Target several markets at once and narrow the choice down to the one producing the best results. For example, select the three most likely market segments. Then, divide your marketing budget and apply one-third to each segment. Use marketing communication tools to create awareness, lead generation, and sales in each segment. Set a time limit such as six months. The type of customers who have generated the majority of revenue becomes your target market.

- **Method B** – Offer your product only on your website. Register your website with various search engines and review the demographics of visitors. Have a form allowing people to request product information. One of the questions on the form asks demographic information such as job title, industry, age range, or other information to help narrow your market selection. The characteristics of those who generated the majority of revenue defines your target market.

- **Method C** – Select the same target market as the leading competitors. Their target can be inferred from their advertising, packaging, and marketing messages. Most likely your competitors have tried other markets and have found the current market they serve is the best. When selecting the same target market, you need to offer some advantages to offset the awareness and reputation of the competition. As you acquire customers, survey them to better understand their characteristics and preferences. In addition, use the feedback to improve your product and to enhance marketing communications.

Appendix C:
The Market-Step Product Plan

Topics in this Appendix:

- Market-Step Product Plan Contents
- Market-Step Product Plan Sections

A business plan is used to raise money or guide business operations. However, to self-manufacture and market your product, it's essential to have a detailed product plan.

A product plan describes how your product meets the needs of customers, how you'll market your product, and how you'll produce sales. Overall, a product plan guides your product development, manufacturing, launch, marketing, and sales. To help you create a product plan, use my Market-Step Product Plan format. (This plan format is not for licensing or assigning your invention.)

The flow of the **Market-Step Product Plan** includes:

- **Uncovering the Facts** – Market need, market environment, and customer characteristics

- **Creating a Vision** – Goals, objectives, and strategies

- **Actions** – Marketing and sales tactics by sales cycle

- **Assessment** – Monitoring and evaluating progress

There are nine sections to the **Market-Step Product Plan**. Read the descriptions and examples in each section, and then write your plan.

This **Market-Step Product Plan** is available as a Microsoft Word template included with the Invention Templates package, and is available from my website (www.ProductCoach.com).

Market-Step Product Plan Contents

1. Purpose
2. Market Need
    - 2.1. Need
    - 2.2. Gap
    - 2.3. Solution
3. Customer
    - 3.1. Customer Characteristics
    - 3.2. Customer Decision-Makers and Influencers
    - 3.3. Customer Buying Criteria
    - 3.4. Customer Buying Process
4. Market Environment
    - 4.1. Market Segments
    - 4.2. Market Segment Size
    - 4.3. Market Segment Revenue Potential
    - 4.4. Opportunities
    - 4.5. Threats
    - 4.6. Market Success Factors
    - 4.7. Industry Influencers
5. Goals and Objectives
6. Strategies
    - 6.1. Target Market
    - 6.2. Product Strategy
    - 6.3. Positioning
    - 6.4. Value Proposition
    - 6.5. Pricing Strategy
    - 6.6. Communications Strategy
    - 6.7. Sales Strategy
    - 6.8. Distribution Strategy
    - 6.9. Product Support Strategy
    - 6.10. Partnership Strategy
7. Tactics by Sales Cycle
    - 7.1. Awareness and Lead Generation
    - 7.2. Customer Interest
    - 7.3. Sales
    - 7.4. Customer Support

Market-Step Product Plan Sections

1. PURPOSE

Purpose is a statement to communicate the product plan's intent to investors, advisors, management, partners, or co-workers.

- **Action**: Describe the purpose of your product plan.
- **Example**: "This document is a product marketing plan to launch our new TurboX toy."

2. MARKET NEED

Market need describes the need for your type of product, the gap that exists in the market, and how your product fills this gap to solve the problems or satisfy a need or want.

2.1. Need

What is the problem, need, or want currently not being addressed in the market? People are aware of their needs or sometimes must be shown how your product uncovers something missing in their lives.

- **Action**: Describe the need for your type of product.
- **Example**: "In the toy market, children easily get bored with their toys. They want a product that can morph into a new look and function with interchangeable parts. They want a toy that does not fall apart."

2.2.   Gap
Gap is a weak solution offered by competition or a lack of any solution.

- **Action**: Compare what customers need and want, to what's currently available.
- **Example**: "Toys for male children break easily and are considered boring after just one hour. Parents become frustrated about purchasing a toy the child no longer uses."

2.3.   Solution
A solution provides a customer with something that is better, faster, reduces pain, raises esteem, provides increased safety, generates more revenue, cuts costs, or provides higher value to their customers.

- **Action**: Describe how your product solves the customer's problems, fills the gap, and is better than other available products. Name support services or other products to be included to provide a complete solution.
- **Example**: "The TurboX uses the latest high-strength plastics for long-term durability. Extra durability makes small interchangeable parts possible. These interchangeable parts allow for new features and functions in an almost unlimited set of configurations."

3.   CUSTOMER
Understanding your prospective customer's world allows you to develop products to fit their needs. This allows you to create marketing and sales campaigns to grab attention and motivate buying decisions.

3.1.   Customer Characteristics
Customers can be individual consumers, organizations, or both. Their characteristics are expressed in terms of demographics and psychographics. Demographics include age, sex, income, education, and occupation. Psychographics include lifestyle, personality, religion, and social class.

- **Action**: Name the demographics and psychographics of a typical customer in each potential market segment. In addition, name the characteristics of a secondary customer type.

- **Example:** "The end-user of our TurboX are male children, ages five to ten who live in the suburbs of cities with populations over 50,000."

3.2.   Customer Decision-Makers and Influencers

Decision-makers and influencers are people who directly influence the purchase decision of a potential customer. These people should be addressed in your marketing and sales strategies and tactics. They include the head of household, purchasing manager, chief financial officer, sales manager, and retail salesperson.

- **Action:** Name the decision-makers and influencers in each potential market segment.
- **Example:** "The decision-makers for the TurboX are parents, while influencers are retail store salespeople, friends, and the child."

3.3.   Customer Buying Criteria

People select a product for its ability to solve a problem, satisfy needs and wants, price, value, availability, brand name and style.

- **Action:** Describe what customers would expect from your product based on surveys and analysis of future trends.
- **Example:** "The customer for the TurboX wants bright colors, rugged design, interchangeable parts, ease of use, low price, and at least a one-year warranty."

3.4.   Customer Buying Process

We all go through a process to select a product. We determine some important buying criteria, gather information, select possible product candidates, and make a purchase. Customers in each market segment have a certain buying process. This might be a determining factor in deciding your target market.

- **Action:** List the steps customers would go through to buy your type of product. Determine how they'd gather information, how they'd become aware of your product, where they'd look for it, who they'd talk to, how they'd make the final buying decision, and what form of payment they'd prefer.
- **Example:** "When a five to ten year old child sees an advertisement for a TurboX, he tells his parents he wants one. If the parents agree, the child

and parent(s) go to a toy store to look at the toy. The parent checks for safety information, compares prices to similar products, and asks the salesperson questions."

4.   MARKET ENVIRONMENT

The market environment is the arena where your product type competes for customer attention. It includes your customer market segments, market trends, market drivers, competitors, and industry influencers.

4.1.   Market Segments

A market segment is a group of customers with common characteristics, needs, and wants. Market segments include industry type, location, buyer preferences, and age. A target market is a market segment you can best serve and earn the highest possible profit.

- **Action**: Evaluate a few market segments as potential target markets. Then evaluate each segment based on market size, revenue potential, opportunities, and threats.
- **Example**: "The potential market segments for the TurboX are single mothers, single fathers, or married couples. In all segments, there's at least one male child between the ages of five and ten."

4.2.   Market Segment Size

Market segment size is the total number of people or organizations within a market segment.

- **Action**: Determine the size of each of your market segments.
- **Example** "There are 15 million single mothers, 10 million single fathers, and 50 million married families."

4.3.   Market Segment Revenue Potential

Revenue potential is the total possible revenue from a market segment. Revenue potential is derived by the total number of potential buyers multiplied by the rate of purchase and multiplied by the product selling price.

- **Action**: Calculate the maximum revenue potential (forecast) on a yearly basis, in each market segment, over the next three years. If you do not know a selling price, use an average amount of competitors or similar products.
- **Example**: "Revenue Potential = 10 million (potential buyers) x 2 (purchases per year) x $1 (selling price) = $20 million."

4.4.   Opportunities

Opportunities are new trends from government regulations, economic changes, new technology, and social changes.

- **Action**: Name the opportunities in the marketplace for your type of product.
- **Example**: "The current trend is for parents to buy entertaining multi-functional toys for their children in order to free up more time for themselves."

4.5.   Threats

Threats include competitors, new technology that eliminates the need for your product, or government regulations that outlaw your type of product. Threats can exist now or be realized in months or years to come.

- **Action**: Name threats in each market segment and note how credible the threat is to your product or business. In addition, name possible substitution products that may replace the need for your product.
- **Example**: "A major competitor is negotiating to purchase a key distribution company. This will make it difficult to sell our product through distribution."

4.6.   Market Success Factors

Market success factors are industry norms (generally accepted or officially stated) and customer expectations when buying your product type. [Also known as Market Drivers.]

- **Action**: Name the key issues important in each of your market segments.

- **Example**: "Packaging must be bright and colorful. Advertising must be aimed at both the children and parents. Distribution through Company X is required."

4.7.   Industry Influencers

Industry influencers are people, companies, and agencies influencing purchase decisions. They include industry analysts, magazine product reviews, regulatory agencies, news agencies, or famous individuals.

- **Action**: Name the industry influencers in each of your market segments.
- **Example**: "Before buying toys, people read *Consumer Reports* and *Yahoo Groups* on the Internet."

5.   GOALS AND OBJECTIVES

With your understanding of the market and the behavior of customers in those markets, you need to set clear, winnable goals. Goals are specific, measurable, and have a due date. Typical goals include revenue, profit, and market share.

- **Action**: Name the goals and objectives for your product.
- **Example**: "Product revenue must be $3 million after the first year of introduction, and $5 million in the second year." Or, "After the first year, TurboX will have a 25% market share of the male children toy market."

6.   STRATEGIES

Once market research is performed and potential customers are understood, it's time to develop strategies to meet the goals and objectives of your product. A strategy is a description of what you want and how to obtain it. Create strategies for each of the following:

6.1.   Target Market

A target market offers the most opportunities and least amount of threats. Initially, your target market may not be clear. In this case, you may try to go after a few market segments and see how many customers you'll attract. Keep in mind, it becomes costly and inefficient to go after customers in too many market segments. So, after launching your product, review revenue and expenses from each segment of customers, and then focus just on the most profitable segment. For more details, see Appendix B, Select Your Target Market.

- **Action:** Select a target market that's the most profitable, offers the most opportunities, and has the least amount of threats.
- **Example:** "Our target market consists of married adults between the ages of 25 to 45, owns a small business, and uses the Internet to purchase toys for their children."

6.2.   Product Strategy

A product strategy is the key benefits, features, and functions your product must have to generate sustainable sales. It includes a timeline of when the product is available, as well as any upgrades, accessories, and future spin-off products. It includes a statement about using continuous improvement or leapfrog technology to improve the product's value and keep ahead of the competition.

- **Action:** Name your product strategy.
- **Example:** "TurboX will launch September 2010. The product is made with the best materials to withstand temperature extremes, vibration, and moisture. It has an advantage over the competition by offering interchangeable parts to allow the user to customize the features. Accessories to enhance the colors will be available two months after product launch."

6.3.   Positioning

Positioning is how you want your product perceived in the marketplace as compared to the competition. Perceptions include the most expensive, the least expensive, the best value, the market leader, the most dependable, the most convenient, the easiest to use, the most comfortable, and so on.

- **Action:** Describe how you want your product perceived.
- **Example:** "TurboX is positioned as the most enjoyable, toughest, and safest children's product in the U.S. market."

6.4.   Value Proposition

A value proposition is a statement of the value your product adds to your customer's business (for business products) or improves a personal lifestyle (for consumer products).

- **Action:** Describe the value your product adds. Think from your customer's point of view because they'll ask, "What's in it for me?" when considering your product.

- **Example:** "TurboX provides hours of entertainment value at one-third the price of going to the movies."

6.5.   Pricing Strategy

A pricing strategy is determining what customers are willing to pay and at the same time sufficient to meet your revenue or profit goals. Pricing is based on factors such as what the market will bear, profit margin, positioning strategy, and competitive comparison. Pricing strategy also depends on market conditions, channel discounts, sales commissions, and your goals and objectives.

- **Action:** Describe the retail price, channel price, and any discounts.

- **Example:** "A price point to provides us a 30% margin and a 40% margin to distributors and retailers." Or, "A price 5% below comparable competition."

6.6.   Communications Strategy

A communications strategy for your product is the method for raising awareness, producing sales leads, generating interest, and motivating a purchase. Communications include advertising, banner ads, billboards, coupons, direct mail, press releases, press kits, public relations, presentations, special discounts and incentives, partner programs, and trade shows.

- **Action:** Determine the communications needed to create product awareness, generate leads, and motivate a purchase.

- **Example:** "Two months before product launch, half-page ads are placed in trade magazines. On the product launch date a press release is sent out using Businesswire. Press releases are issued monthly based on product announcements and new business relationships.

Additional leads are generated from email lists purchased from trade magazines. All leads are followed-up with an email and a phone call."

6.7.   Sales Strategy

A sales strategy is the methods used to sell your product. Methods include field sales, inbound direct response telesales, outbound cold-calling, web-selling, and word-of-mouth referrals. Usually, a combination of these methods is generally most effective.

- **Action**: Describe the sales method for your product.

- **Example**: "Trade magazine ads are used to create awareness and direct response leads. The leads are followed up with a telesales person for qualification. Qualified leads are handled by an account representative who takes a consultative approach to look for sales opportunities. A purchase order is received and the product is shipped from a warehouse with 30-day terms."

6.8.   Distribution Strategy

A distribution strategy is the method for getting your product to the customer and for getting paid. Distribution includes shipping your product to a retailer, distribution center, direct to a customer, or downloading a file from a website. Methods of getting paid include credit card, check, cash, or purchase order with credit terms.

- **Action**: Describe the distribution method and names of distributors needed for your product.

- **Example**: "The product is available for download from our website. The user makes a selection, adds the product to a shopping cart, and then checks out. A credit card is entered, verified, and the amount is deposited to the business checking account. The user is presented with download instructions and receives a thank-you message upon completion."

6.9.   Product Support Strategy

A product support strategy is the method to address customer service needs before and after the sale. It includes the required levels of support such as tier one, two, and three. It includes how customers make contact, such as an

800 number, email, or a combination of these. The strategy outlines information systems and response times needed to satisfy customers.

- **Action**: Describe the support required for your product.
- **Example**: "Initial support contact is handled by email. An automated response is emailed to the sender to inform them their query was received. A support person attempts to ratify the issue within twenty-four hours. If the issue cannot be resolved, the issue is routed to a manager for examination."

6.10.   Partnership Strategy

Partnerships may or may not be appropriate for you. Partnering is used to offer a complete customer solution, provide access to certain distribution channels, and strengthen perception in the market. Partners include suppliers, industry analysts, agencies, key customer accounts, and companies offering complementary products or services.

- **Action**: Determine which organizations are suitable for a partnership.
- **Example**: "Partnering with ToyMax provides a key distribution channel for TurboX."

7.   TACTICS BY SALES CYCLE

Tactics are the action programs to bring the above strategies to life. Each tactical program costs something. Determine the total amount you're willing to spend on marketing and sales. Then, create action programs, and allocate a dollar amount to each item as shown in the following examples. The **Market-Step** Product Marketing Plan arranges the tactics by stages of the customer buying process:

- Awareness and Lead Generation
- Customer Interest
- Sales
- Customer Support

7.1.   Awareness and Lead Generation

To generate a sale, customers must first become aware of your product. Tactics include advertising, promotions, direct mail, press releases, product reviews, trade shows, and your website. The following is a sample action plan to generate awareness and sales leads.

Awareness and Lead Generation Programs		
Programs	Actions	Cost
Advertising	• Place ads in magazines A, B, C on a monthly basis	$20,000
Direct Mail	• Mail to target organizations within the region	$10,000
Press Releases	• Product launch • Partner relationships • New technology	$8,000
Product Reviews	• Get product reviews in magazines that cover the target market	$ 500
Promotion	• Contests • Premiums • Discounts	$1,500
Trade Shows	• Participate in spring and fall trade shows • Look into partner programs (shared booths, shared pre-show mailings, etc)	$25,000
Web	• Post product information and enable download of brochure when the prospect provides contact information • Exchange links with vendors and distributors • Get placement in search engines • Buy Google AdWords	$10,000
TOTAL		$75,000

7.2. Customer Interest

The second step in the sales cycle involves generating real interest in your product. Tactics include free samples, free trial periods, information seminars, partner programs, incentives to distributors, and incentives to retailers. The following is a sample action plan to generate interest.

Customer Interest Programs		
Programs	**Actions**	**Cost**
Prospect Evaluation	• Provide free trial period and free shipping	$5,000
Distributors	• Send product samples • Join their partner program	$5,000
Reference accounts	• Contact major customers to build reference accounts • Solicit testimonials	$5,000
Partnering	• Set up annual user conferences and annual sales meetings	$10,000
TOTAL		$25,000

7.3. Sales

Now that you've generated awareness and interest, the third step involves prospecting your potential customers. Tactics include inside telesales, Internet sales, and face-to-face field sales. The following is a sample action plan to produce sales.

7.4. Customer Support

Customer support is often needed after the sale to help with installation, general use, and customer satisfaction. In addition, customer support is useful before the sale to help with a customer's technical issues.

Programs include training for Customer Support staff, setting up a call-tracking database, and periodically assessing customer satisfaction. The following is a sample action plan to facilitate customer support.

Sales Programs		
Programs	**Actions**	**Cost**
Outside Sales	• Follow-up qualified leads • Build relationships • Close sales	$50,000
Inside Sales	• Take incoming calls • Make outbound follow-up calls to direct mail responses and leads from advertisements, web, and trade shows	$20,000
Distributors	• Produce a distributor kit: ordering info, price list, brochures, competitive info	$10,000
TOTAL		**$80,000**

Customer Support Programs		
Programs	**Actions**	**Cost**
Training	• Provide training for sales and support staff	$20,000
Systems	• Call-tracking database • Customer satisfaction surveys	$50,000
TOTAL		**$ 70,000**

TOTAL MARKETING AND SALES EXPENSE $ 250,000

8.   PROFIT SUMMARY

Provide a forecast of future sales, cost of goods sold, gross profit, marketing and sales expenses, and net profit. Use a spreadsheet to perform profit forecast calculations and place the results in this section. The following is a sample Profit and Loss statement.

Profit and Loss Statement	
Sales Revenue	3,250,000
Cost of Goods Sold	(2,000,000)
Gross Profit	1,250,000
Operating Expenses:	
Marketing and Sales	250,000
Salaries	200,000
Administrative	50,000
Total Operating Expense	(500,000)
Net Profit Before Taxes	750,000

9.   MONITOR AND EVALUATION

Your product plan should outline how to monitor your progress. You'll need a procedure of regularly examining your product's progress and making course corrections as required. Initially, you may do this on a weekly basis, and then as the product matures, on a monthly basis.

9.1.   Marketing and Sales Effectiveness

Monitoring marketing effectiveness is measuring the success of your marketing programs. Describe how you'll track sales leads from each marketing program and then analyze success.

- **Action:** Describe the marketing and sales statistics needed to monitor on a weekly and monthly basis. Use a spreadsheet and look for trends.

- **Example**: "The number of leads from advertisements, direct mail, and website visitors, are tracked on a weekly basis. Inbound and outbound sales called are tracked on a weekly basis."

9.2.   Sales Win / Loss Analyses

Sales win / loss analyses are interviews with customers and prospects to determine why you won and lost sales. You can ask customers why they purchased your product. And, ask lost customers why they did not buy your product. Use the feedback to enhance your product, marketing and sales strategies, and tactics.

- **Action**: Describe how you'll monitor your sales progress.
- **Example**: "New customers are called one month after a purchase to determine the underlying reasons why they made a purchase. Prospects, who decided not to buy, are called on a monthly basis to find out why. Results are feedback to the marketing department."

9.3.   Customer Satisfaction

You'll need to monitor customer satisfaction. It's often the case people complain among themselves but only a small percentage present problems to the company they bought the product from.

- **Action**: Describe how to be proactive in uncovering the working and non-working product features. Use the feedback to enhance your product, marketing, and sales strategies and tactics.
- **Example**: "New customers are called two weeks after a purchase to discuss ease of installing and getting up to speed. In addition, they'll be called two months after purchase to discuss product satisfaction. Customers are asked about product quality and their likes and dislikes about the product. In addition, they are asked for suggestions and comments."

9.4.   Competition Review

Competitors might make changes as a result of your new product. They might change their price, increase marketing, or do nothing at all.

- **Action:** Describe how to monitor activities of current and potential competitors.

- **Example:** "Competition is reviewed on a monthly basis. The competitor's press releases, advertising, promotions, sales methods, and changes to pricing are examined."

Product Plan Notes

The technically superior product does not always win. Winners are good products supported by the great marketing and sales systems. In your product plan, describe the way your customer thinks, buys, and makes decisions. Clearly identify how your product meets a need and how to overcome competition. Then, discuss the strategies and tactics to acquire new customers and maintain satisfaction.

Appendix D:
Product Math

Topics in this Appendix:

- Profit and Loss
- Return on Investment
- Break Even
- Margins and Discounts

This section covers some mathematical formulas related to creating and marketing your invention.

Profit and Loss

Profit and Loss is an accounting income statement showing how well your product performed or a forecast of how it might perform over a month, a quarter, or a year.

The general format of a profit and loss statement for a given time period is the following:

Profit and Loss Statement	
Sales Revenue	50,000
Cost of Goods Sold	(10,000)
Gross Profit	40,000
Operating Expenses:	
Marketing and Sales	10,000
Salaries	10,000
Administrative	3,000
Total Operating Expense	(23,000)
Net Profit Before Taxes	17,000

Gross Profit = Sales Revenue – Cost of Goods Sold
Net Profit = Gross Profit – Operating Expenses

Essentially, profit is revenue minus expenses for a time period. To further expand the term profit, financial people use the term EBITA which means Earnings Before deduction of Interest, Tax, and Amortization expenses.

The items to consider as you determine your business profit or loss include:

Revenue
- Product Sales
- Subscriptions (recurring revenue)
- Maintenance and Support
- Licensing

Expenses
- Equipment
- Sales and Marketing
- Administrative and Support
- Salary and Benefits
- Legal and Professional
- Office and Supplies
- Miscellaneous Expenses

Return on Investment

Return on Investment (ROI) is a quick measure of the financial gain versus an amount invested over a time period. This measure is used for projecting future results or determining actual results.

For new products, the investment includes development, marketing, sales, production, administrative, salary, and office expenses. You may also want to consider opportunity costs such as the income you're foregoing while working on your invention. By calculating an ROI, you can determine if proceeding with development makes sense.

ROI should be higher than a risk-free investment such as a Treasury Bill, certificate of deposit, or money market fund. If the ROI for your product is less than the return from investing in a standard certificate of deposit, for example, then it's probably not worth developing the product. If you intend to obtain funding from investors, they will expect a certain ROI for their risk. The following is a simple ROI formula:

$$ROI = \frac{Gain - Investment}{Investment}$$

For example, your expected profit for the first year is $200,000 and your investment is $180,000. Therefore,

ROI = ($200,000 – $180,000) / $180,000 = $20,000 / $180,000 = 11%

As a result, 11% is your product's return on investment. Compare this to a financial risk-free indicator such as a certificate of deposit for the same time period.

Break Even

Break Even is the number of product units sold to make revenue equal to costs. This is a handy number for determining a minimum sales volume needed to begin making a profit.

The formula uses Fixed Costs that do not vary with sales volume (e.g., rent, utilities, salaries). The formula also uses Variable Costs such as those needed to produce each product (e.g., materials, packaging, sales commissions). Units sold above the Break Even number represent your profit.

$$Break\ Even = \frac{Fixed\ Costs}{Selling\ Price - Variable\ Costs}$$

For example, total fixed costs per month are $10,000, your product has a selling price of $50, and the variable costs to produce each product is $10.

Break Even = $10,000 / ($50 - $10) = 250 units

Margins and Discounts

In terms of selling products, margin is the percentage of profit between cost and selling price. The following are a few scenarios when working with distributors and retailers.

Determine a Wholesale Price

In this scenario you're selling directly to a retailer. The retailer will want to know the wholesale price (retailer's cost). To obtain a wholesale price, you need to set a retail price and understand the likely retailer margin. To uncover the retailer margin, look for industry data and ask the retailer the range of margin they need. Use the formula:

$$\text{Wholesale Price} = \frac{\text{Retail Price}}{1 + \text{Retailer Margin}}$$

For example, you determine a retail price of $19.95, and the retailer wants a margin of 40%. Therefore,

Wholesale Price = $19.95 / (1 + .40) = $19.95 / (1.4) = $14.25

Your Maximum Costs

In this scenario you're selling to a distributor who then sells to a retailer. You need to determine the maximum cost of manufacturing your product so that everyone (retailer, distributor, and you) can make a profit.

If your costs are too high, it won't make sense financially to develop your product. At the same time, if your costs are too high to go through a distribution channel, consider selling direct to end-users.

Let's look an example where we have a retail price in mind, and we want to determine the distributor cost, retail cost, and your maximum product cost. To do this, we'll work backwards from the retail price.

$$\text{Wholesale Price} = \frac{\text{Retail Price}}{1 + \text{Retailer Margin}}$$

For example, the Retail Price is $19.95 and the Retailer Margin is 40%. Therefore,

Wholesale Price = $19.95 / (1 + .40) = $14.25

This means the retailer needs to buy the product at no higher than $14.25.

If you sell through a distributor, who then sells to a retailer, there's an additional layer of pricing. Let's assume a distributor also wants a 40% margin. Use the formula:

$$\text{Distributor's Cost} = \frac{\text{Distributor Selling Price}}{1 + \text{Distributor Margin}}$$

Note: The Distributor Selling Price is the same as the retailer's Wholesale Price.

Distributor's Cost = $14.25 / (1+ .40) = $10.18

Therefore, $10.18 is the Distributor's Cost and also your selling price.

To determine if you can make a profit, set a profit margin to cover your expenses and room for a net profit. Expenses include administrative, marketing, selling, and taxes. Check with an accountant to find out the typical profit margin for your type of business. You can also search the Internet for standard business ratios which include statistics on typical profit margins.

For example, with a Selling Price of $10.18 (to the distributor), and by setting a profit margin of 30%, your maximum product cost is $7.83.

$$\text{Your Cost} = \frac{\text{Your Selling Price}}{1 + \text{Your Margin}}$$

Your Cost = $10.18 / (1+ .30) = $7.83

To summarize the example:

Retail Price	$ 19.95
Wholesale Price	$ 14.25
Distributor Cost	$ 10.18
Your Cost	$ 7.83

For everyone to make a profit, your unit product costs can be no higher than $7.83. This number represents your manufacturing cost, packaging, inventory, and other costs related to producing your finished product.

Determine a Profit Margin

From an accounting point of view, you should determine a profit margin. Each industry has a certain profit margin that's typical of a healthy business. Check with an accountant to find out what's typical for your product type. Given your product costs and selling price, therefore:

$$\text{Profit Margin} = \frac{\text{Selling Price} - \text{Product Costs}}{\text{Selling Price}}$$

For example, your cost to produce and package your product is $10, and the selling price is $12.50.

Profit Margin = ($12.50 - $10.00) / $12.50 = 20%

Therefore, each unit sold produces a 20% margin.

Discounted Pricing

Let's suppose you want to offer a discount pricing structure based on volume purchases. To determine a retail price for a percent discount use the formula:

Retail Price = Retail Price x (1 – Discount)

The key is to determine at what quantities you'll offer a discount. I like to have discounts based on the ratio of 1:2:5. This means there's a discount at quantity levels such as 10, 20, 50 or 100, 200, 500 units. This ratio repeats itself and may start at any point. Be sure to check there's still room for a profit at the lowest levels of discount.

For example, your Retail Price is $10 for one product. Discounts are offered in the following structure:

- 30% discount for quantities of 10 to 19:

      Selling Price   = Retail Price x (1 – Discount)
                      = $10 x (1-30%)
                      = $10 x (.70)
                      = $7

- 40% discount for quantities of 20 to 49:

    Selling Price   = Retail Price x (1 – Discount)
                    = $10 x (1-40%)
                    = $10 x (.60)
                    = $6

- 50% discount for quantities of 50 or more:

    Selling Price   = Retail Price x (1 – Discount)
                    = $10 x (1-50%)
                    = $10 x (.50)
                    = $5

In this example, at a selling price of $5, the margin needs to be checked to make sure there is room to generate a profit.

Appendix E:
Funding Your Idea

Topics in this Appendix:

- The Need for Money
- Types of Funding
- The Investors
- Stages of Funding
- What Type of Funding Do You Go After?
- To Receive You Must First Give It Up
- Prepare for Funding
- Steps to Obtain Funding
- When Do You Seek Funding?
- The Investor's Process
- How Investors Evaluate You and Your Idea
- Funding Rejection
- SBA-Backed Loans
- Other Funding Possibilities
- Additional Funding Tips
- Funding Resources

OK, you have a great idea but it'll cost thousands of dollars to finance. Now what? Raising money is a normal part of doing business, especially if you intend to develop, grow, and expand.

The Need for Money

Money allows you to develop, market, and sell your idea. Initially, startup money is needed for market research, equipment, prototype development, and filing intellectual property. As you move further along in development, you'll need money for employees, consultants, more equipment, supplies, prototypes, and marketing programs.

Overall, money is needed for the following:

- Market research
- Prototype development
- Product development
- Patent filing and legal fees
- Product launch
- Management team
- Employees and consultants
- Advertising and promotion
- Computer equipment and software
- Rent
- Utilities
- Supplies
- Taxes

Investors understand the need for money since many businesses fail due to undercapitalization (lack of money). Investors want to know what you're going to do with the money once they give it to you. They'll want to make sure you're clear about how to allocate it properly to develop the business and you won't be using it to take a vacation. You'll need to show how much you require, what you're going to use it for, how long the money will last, and how much revenue your products will generate.

How much money do you need? Realistically estimate the amount required to develop and market your invention. Make a list of everything needed and then allocate a dollar amount for each item. Remember, some expenses are one-time events (e.g., marketing reports, equipment to build a prototype, filing for a patent) and others are recurring (e.g., office rent, utilities, salary). Calculate the total expenses needed for the first and second years.

Types of Funding

Funding basically comes in two flavors: debt and equity. Debt is money you borrow and pay back; equity involves giving up partial ownership in exchange for money.

Debt

Debt funding is a loan you must repay. Typically, lines of credit are used for working capital and term loans are used to buy fixed assets. The typical term of a loan can be from one to ten years. The start of repayment can begin the following month or the following year. When you meet with a lender, the loan officer will create a reasonable repayment plan.

Equity

Equity funding involves selling a part of the business in exchange for money. For example, this is accomplished by forming a corporation, then issuing shares of stock to yourself, and then a percentage to your equity investors. Another method of equity financing involves bringing in partners for partial ownership in exchange for money and expertise.

The Investors

In general, you should seek investors according to what stage your business is at and how much money you need. Money can be acquired from a variety of sources. Your initial source of funding often comes from friends and family. Other sources include Angel Investors, Venture Capitalists, Investment Bankers, and Investment Brokers. When asking for funding, demonstrate you have a viable product idea with a well thought-out business plan.

Friends and Family (debt and equity)

It might be risky to infringe upon personal relationships, but friends and family are sources of funding. You have to consider what could happen to the relationship if you lose the money they invested.

Some of your friends and family can probably afford to gamble a few thousand dollars here and there. You'll need to determine whether they want to invest with a loan or with equity and become partial owners.

For equity investors, provide a written agreement stating the amount invested and number of shares of stock they've been issued. Debt investors need a written agreement with loan amount and repayment terms.

Angel Investors (equity)

Angels are typically wealthy individuals acting alone or pooling their money in an investment group. Instead of going to Las Vegas to gamble, they risk funding new businesses with the expectation of a high return. Angels are usually business people who have made enough to retire but are still interested in the excitement of business.

Angels are usually only comfortable investing in a certain type of technology or market. Therefore, it's best to find Angels who specialize in your type of product industry. Before Angels provide funding, they'll perform due diligence on you and your idea.

Angels who operate individually may invest from $50,000 to $250,000. On the other hand, a pooled group of Angels may invest up to $3 million. The amount they fund is usually enough to carry your business for one to two years.

In exchange for their investment, Angels receive a percent equity ownership in your business. In five to seven years after handing over the funds, Angels hope to recoup from five to ten times the amount they invested.

Venture Capitalists (equity)

Venture Capitalists are managers of a fund. Wealthy individuals and organizations put money into the fund hoping for a large return for their risk. In fact, they seek a greater return on investment than what they could normally receive in the market over the same time period.

The Venture Capitalist (VC) manages the fund by investing in new businesses that are willing to give up equity in exchange for money. The goal for the VC is to grow the fund by getting the new business to go public or be acquired. When a new business goes public through an initial public offering (IPO) or is acquired, the proceeds are sold and placed back into the fund. The VC anticipates an IPO or acquisition will occur in three to seven years. Acquisitions occur more commonly than an IPO.

VCs provide more than just money. In some cases, they provide expertise in management, marketing, and have key contacts who may become large customers. The VCs have a vested interest in growing your business.

Depending on your expertise, your role may become minor as new management comes in to run the business. You still have equity in the business and when the business goes public or is acquired, you receive cash or publicly traded stock you can sell.

Bankers (debt)

Bankers help businesses grow by lending money. Bankers perform careful analyses to make sure you can pay off the loan based on your business generating a positive cash flow. Therefore, most Bankers do not fund startups, preferring instead to see a positive track record of revenue and paying bills in a timely manner.

In almost all cases, Bankers seek a personal financial guarantee so you don't take the money and retire to the Cayman Islands. Personal financial guarantees include assets such as real estate, stocks, bonds, and mutual funds. In addition, Bankers loan money when it's backed by the value of your inventory or accounts receivable, but it depends on the Banker. Keep in mind, Bankers can provide general advice, but they do not get involved in managing your business.

Note: Plan ahead. It can take from six to twelve months from the day you first look for money to the time you receive it. This means you'll need cash flow or other liquid assets to keep you afloat.

Stages of Funding

The need for money varies according to which stage your business is at. Funding stages include:

- **Seed capital** – Money for initial research and business planning. Seed capital is likely to come from you, friends, family, and Angels.

- **Start-up capital** – Money for rent, market studies, prototype equipment, supplies, etc., for the first year or so of operation. Start-up capital is likely to come from you, friends, family, and Angels.

- **Mezzanine capital** – Money to help your business grow, move to a better office, launch a marketing campaign, or purchase new equipment. Mezzanine capital is likely to come from Bankers and Venture Capitalists.

- **Bridge capital** – Money to bridge the gap between your current funding and the next level of funding. Bridge capital is likely to come from Bankers and Venture Capitalists.

What Type of Funding Do You Go After?

Whether you go after debt or equity funding depends on your comfort level. Ask yourself a few questions:

Pursue Debt?

- Do I have personal collateral to guarantee the loan?
- Am I willing to lose my collateral, such as a house, in the event the business fails?
- Can I make the monthly payments to pay off the debt?

Pursue Equity?

- Am I willing to give up some control in exchange for funding?
- Am I willing to take advice from equity investors?
- Am I willing to share the profits?
- Am I willing and able to make a series of presentations to investors to excite them about my idea?

If you're comfortable with loans and have collateral, seek a loan from a bank or from friends and family. If you're lucky enough to know someone who is not adverse to risks and losses, see if they'd lend some money without requiring collateral. Otherwise, equity is your funding route.

To Receive You Must First Give It Up

Who likes the thought of giving up a piece of their business? Not many, but if you want equity funding, that's how the game is played. On the positive side, the investors know how to grow money, can lend advice, and have key business contacts. I like the phrase: "A rising tide floats all boats." In the context of funding, you make money and your investors make money. Everyone wins.

How much ownership you give up depends on the value of your business and how much an investor contributes. The value of your business today is based on the potential future revenue or profit. The valuation process is performed by an experienced finance professional.

For example, let's assume your business is valued at $750,000 based on future revenue. Suppose you need $250,000 from an equity investor.

A $250,000 investment plus the original value of $750,000 creates a new business value of $1,000,000. Ownership is a percentage of investment to the total value. Your ownership is $750,000 divided by $1,000,000 or 75%. The investor's ownership becomes $250,000 divided by $1,000,000 or 25%.

Business Value After Funding		
	Before Funding	**After Funding**
1. Business value: 2. Investor adds: 3. New value:	$ 750,000	 $ 250,000 $1,000,000
Your ownership %: Your ownership $:	100% $ 750,000	75% $ 750,000
Investor's ownership %: Investor's ownership $:		25% $ 250,000

As you can see by this example, receiving equity funding decreases the percentage of your ownership. However, your dollar ownership remains the same after the investment and grows as the value of the business grows.

This example is a simplification, but it's the general approach for determining percent ownership. In addition, each time you seek more funding, your percent ownership decreases. As market conditions change, the value of the business changes – up and down.

The good news is that as more money comes into your business from investors and customers, the value of your business increases. So, even though your percent ownership decreases, your dollar value should increase. Don't be afraid to give up equity, it could lead to more money for you.

Prepare for Funding

You'll need to do some homework before seeking equity or debt funding. Two key activities involve creating a business plan and forming a management team.

Initially, while you're exploring your invention's marketability, the business entity can be just a sole proprietorship. Then, once you believe the market is viable, form a corporation. In general, if you're seeking equity investors, consider forming a C-corporation so you can issue shares of ownership. You may not think you want equity investors now, but things may change later. Check with a business attorney about what makes sense in the long term.

At some point you'll need a management team, but you may start with advisors. An advisory team offers guidance and shows investors you have people to provide leadership in every aspect of your business.

Ideally, the advisory team includes a technical person, a financial person, a legal person, and a marketing strategy person. In addition to being competent in their fields, advisors should be able to introduce you to key customers, distributors, or suppliers. The team is comprised of people you know personally or are referred to you. Together, they form the core of your business and help you brainstorm strategies and tactics.

Your advisory team might want to be paid up front or might ask for a small percentage of the business in the form of stock options. Later, when you obtain funding, you can hire the advisors as full-time management, or hire new managers and keep the advisors as consultants or board members. The advisors may want a less active role in managing and assume a general oversight role, or participate on your board of directors.

Steps to Obtain Funding

Billions of dollars are invested in businesses every year. Obtaining funding takes persistence and determination. Follow these steps and you're on your way:

- Determine the marketability and feasibility of your idea
- Form an advisory team
- Make a list of your funding needs (research, development, etc) and a dollar amount
- Form a business entity
- Determine what type of funding you want (debt, equity)
- Understand the needs of your investors (return on investment)
- Write a business plan to entice investors
- Contact investors and form a business relationship
- Submit a proposal
- Negotiate terms of funding

When Do You Seek Funding?

When you want funding, investors like to see you are prepared. Here are a few tips about approaching investors:

- Invest some of your own money in prototype development or marketing research. Since investors are taking a risk, they like to see you are taking a risk as well.

- Investors like to see validation of your idea by others. If possible, show you already have interested customers from pre-sales, letters of intent, or positive responses from surveys or beta tests.

- File any patent, trademark, or copyright applications. Investors like to see intellectual property, which forms a competitive advantage and adds business value.

- Approach investors when a business plan is complete.

- Have a business entity in place such as a C-corporation. Investors fund businesses rather than an individual.

The Investor's Process

Investors proceed with caution, even if they like you and your idea. You'll need to prove your case before they open up their checkbook. As a first step, investors typically want to review a proposal consisting of an introductory letter and business plan executive summary. If they like the proposal, investors will:

- Evaluate your business plan
- Perform due diligence on you and the viability of the product idea and business concept
- Have you make a presentation
- Make an investment decision
- Structure a funding plan
- Provide your business with the money

How Investors Evaluate You and Your Idea

Being a credible person is as important as having a great idea. Investors judge you and everyone involved on character. You must have a reputation as honest and respectable in your personal and business life. You must honor your commitments and deliver more than you promise. Investors look at your credit history, including your ability to pay on time, any bankruptcies, liens, as well as lawsuits.

Investors review business plans in terms of how your product will make a profit, how you'll grow the business, how you're able to manage the business, and how you'll pay off investors.

Business plan formats vary, but the following format will satisfy most investors:

1. Cover Letter
2. Executive Summary
    a. The Market
    b. The Business Model
    c. The Management
    d. The Money
3. The Company
4. Mission Statement
5. Management
6. The Opportunity
7. Products and Markets
8. Sales and Profit Summary
9. Funding Requirements
10. Investment Proposal

Investors evaluate your business plan based on Market, Business Model, Management, and Money. Investors want to know:

The Market

- Is there a need or want for your product?
- Who is the target market and what are the demographics of the customers?
- For a business buyer, what's the benefit of your product (e.g., lower costs, higher revenue, higher margins, increased customer retention)?
- For a consumer buyer, what's the benefit of your product (e.g., better health, lower costs, prestige, fun to use, saves time)?

- Is there an exciting and significant market for your product (e.g., new trends, high growth, capitalize on new technologies)?

- What are the advantages of your product over the competition? How can you sustain the advantages and create new advantages?

- Do you have access to distribution channels?

The Business Model

- What is the business model and how do you plan to grow the business (e.g., licensing your idea to a manufacturer, selling your product to a retail chain, collecting monthly subscription fees)?

- Is there a compelling, well-articulated strategy for capturing and defending a significant market share?

- Is there proprietary technology or other strong barriers to entry?

The Management

- Does the management team have experience and can they execute their plan (e.g., experience in the industry, grown a similar business before, have a proven record)?

- Are you open to advice and coaching?

The Money

- What are the product costs and selling price?

- How many units can you sell the first year?

- When will the business be profitable?

- How much money do you need?

- Once you receive funding, how will you use the money (e.g., R&D, marketing, administration)?

- Equity investors want to know: What's the exit strategy for the company (e.g., acquired by a competitor, acquired by a company offering complementary products, or taking your business public)?

Funding Rejection

Equity investors reject funding proposals that are not thoroughly and properly prepared. Here are some common reasons for rejection:

- The business plan is poorly written. It was not written with an investor as the intended audience.

- The business has only a small growth potential. Many equity investors want to see at least a 20% to 50% return above the current rate of a safe investment such as a Treasury bond or certificate of deposit. The percent return varies depending on market conditions.

- Investors do not understand your product idea or your industry.

- You do not have enough experience. Investors want you to have industry experience. They also want to see experience owning a business, or being involved in managing a business.

- Lack of commitment. Investors want to see you're fully committed to developing your idea and generating revenue. They prefer you've invested some of your own money.

- Difficult to protect your idea. Investors want to know your idea cannot be easily copied by existing or new competition. They prefer something that is hard to duplicate, or legally protected with patents, trademarks, or copyrights.

Debt lenders are primarily concerned about repayment. The lending officer considers the following:

- Have you invested in your business that's at least 25% to 50% of the loan you're requesting? A lender will not finance 100% of your business.

- Do you have a good credit record, work history, and letters of recommendation?

- Do you have sufficient experience and training to operate a successful business?

- Does the business have sufficient cash flow to make the monthly payments?

SBA-Backed Loans

The Small Business Administration (SBA) does not provide loans, but guarantees a percentage of a loan made by a bank or investment company. Lenders like this because the SBA covers a percentage of the loss in the form of unpaid interest if you can't pay back a loan. Just because the SBA covers a loss, it doesn't mean a lender will be less stringent evaluating you and your business.

SBA loan programs are generally intended to encourage longer term small business financing, but the actual loan maturity is based on the ability to repay and the purpose of the loan. In addition, short-term loans are also available through the SBA to help small businesses meet their working capital needs.

For an SBA-backed loan, seek an SBA lender in your area. Contact them to find out what's involved with getting a loan. Be sure to ask what types of SBA loans are available. There are three types of approved SBA lenders:

- **Preferred lenders** – They can make a final decision without SBA approval, which means approval time is quicker than for other types of SBA lenders.

- **Certified lenders** – They need the SBA to make the final decision, which means the approval process is longer.

- **Participant lenders** – They rarely make SBA loans.

For more about SBA loan programs, go to their website (www.sba.gov) and select: Services > Financial Assistance > SBA Loans

Other Funding Possibilities

I've included some other interesting forms of funding. They might be appropriate if your business is already generating revenue but needs additional funding.

- **Factoring** – Factoring involves an exchange of your accounts receivables for funding. Think of this as a stepping stone before qualifying for a traditional bank loan. With factoring, you're essentially selling your receivables at a discount so you can obtain cash now rather than waiting for customers to pay you. Private companies that offer this service are responsible for all collections and may charge a fee from 2% to 10% based on the amount they collect.

- **Purchase Order Advances** – Purchase Order Advances are similar to factoring except you're trading your customer purchase order asset to gain some funding. This type of funding usually has high rates, so use it judiciously.

- **Convertible Debt** – Convertible Debt is a loan converted to equity instead of paying back the loan. You can usually find a better interest rate with convertible debt than a traditional loan, but you'll need to make sure giving up equity is right for you.

- **Limited Partnerships** – Limited Partnerships allow you to take on partners who'll invest money without being liable for losses other than their original investment. You bear all of the financial risk, but you maintain full control. Check with state laws and an attorney before pursuing this method.

- **Private Placement** – Private Placement involves offering stock in your business privately without going through an intermediary or registering your company under Federal securities laws. Private Placement takes the form of equity, secured promissory notes, or limited partnerships. Check with state laws, an attorney, or CPA before pursuing this method.

Additional Funding Tips

Here are some more tips to help you obtain funding for your invention:

- If you're a woman or a minority, look into the various business grants and loans available.

- If your partner is a woman or minority, consider transferring the primary business ownership to qualify for special grants and loans.

- Look for grants and loans funded by your county and city government. There are often programs available to stimulate the local economy.

- Build credibility by seeking a small loan and then paying it off in a timely manner.

- Have your business plan reviewed before submitting it to an investor. Ask a local businessperson, a college professor, or a business consultant to provide comments and suggestions.

- If you need someone to write a business plan and you're short on funds, try trading your skills for theirs.

Funding Resources

Angel Capital Electronic Network (ACE-Net)
An investor network sponsored by the SBA
www.activecapital.org

Small Business Investment Company Program (SBIC)
Investment firms licensed by the SBA
www.sba.gov/aboutsba/sbaprograms/inv/esf/inv_sbic_financing.html

Tech Coast Angels
California angel group
www.techcoastangels.com

Global Financial Network
A financial search engine
www.cfol.com

BusinessFinance.com
A source for funding options
www.businessfinance.com

StartUpBiz.com
Business information
www.startupbiz.com

Housing and Urban Development
Assistance to small and disadvantaged businesses to sell products and services to the government
www.hud.gov/offices/osdbu/index.cfm

Appendix F:
Business Startup

Topics in this Appendix:

- Business Entity Advantages and Disadvantages
- Business Entity Considerations
- Business Startup Checklist
- Further Startup Guidance

Launching a product requires setting up and maintaining a business. Your business involves developing and marketing your product, raising money, generating a cash flow, following rules and regulations, and paying taxes. Legally, your business must be a certain type of business entity.

Business Entity Advantages and Disadvantages

Select the type of business entity that limits your liability, reduces taxes, is structured toward raising money, and is easy to set up. You may choose from a number of legal business entities.

In the early stages, as you research your idea's marketability, I suggest keeping your costs low by operating as a sole proprietorship. Then, when you seek funding or are about to produce your product, form a corporation or LLC. When in doubt, discuss business setup with an attorney who specializes in business formation.

The following are the advantages and disadvantages of different types of business entities. Note that business formation rules vary by state. Search for your state's Secretary of State for specific details, requirements, and filing fees.

Sole Proprietorship

A sole proprietorship is the easiest form of business to set up and maintain. Legally, your business and personal assets are one and the same. Profit or loss generated by the business is reported on Schedule C or F of your personal tax return. You can run the business either as an individual or as a married couple. Either way, you should have a separate bank account for business and personal use.

As a sole proprietorship, you're allowed to hire employees, but I suggest having work performed by independent consultants or a contracting agency in the beginning. If you hire employees you'll need to obtain a tax ID number, set up a payroll system, and pay additional taxes.

Advantages:

- Very little paperwork
- Business losses can be deducted from your personal income to reduce your overall tax obligation
- You have full control over the business

Disadvantages:

- No liability protection, which means if your business is sued, losses can be deducted from the business and your personal assets (but you can buy liability insurance, which is explained in the next section)
- Any debts are repaid from business and personal holdings
- Raising money may be more difficult

General Partnership

A general partnership is an agreement between two or more people who share ownership of a business. They share profits and losses according to their percentage of participation. From a tax perspective, each partner's share of profit or loss is reported on Schedule E of your personal tax return. If you start a partnership, I suggest creating a partnership agreement where you clearly spell out duties, responsibilities, and an exit clause.

Advantages:

- Easy method of forming a business for two or more people
- Business losses can be deducted from your personal income to reduce your overall tax obligation

Disadvantages:

- Each partner is held personally liable for all claims, debts, and taxes against the partnership
- Insurance is needed in the event a partner dies (to buy out partner's estate)
- Duties and responsibilities of each partner are not always maintained

Limited Liability Partnership

A Limited Liability Partnership operates similarly to a General Partnership except there are both general partners and limited partners. A limited partner is an investor but cannot participate in managing the business. In the event of a financial loss sustained by a business, the limited partner is limited to the amount invested. If a limited partner participates in business management decisions, the limited partner is then treated as a general partner and responsible for all losses.

Corporation

There are C-corporations, S-corporations, and Professional Corporations. A corporation is comprised of shareholders, directors, and officers. The shareholders are the owners who elect a board of directors to oversee the business. Then, the board of directors hires officers such as the president and vice presidents to manage the business. This may sound like a lot of people, but the shareholders, directors, and officers could consist of just a husband and wife.

Keep in mind, there are public and private corporations. A corporation becomes public when it files with the Securities and Exchange Commission to trade its stock in the market. Your private corporation is held in control without being influenced by the public market.

Articles of Incorporation are filed with the state to form a corporation. Each state has slightly different rules to govern corporations. Talk to a business attorney to discuss the advantages and disadvantages of filing in your home state or another state such as Delaware or Nevada that has certain tax benefits.

C–Corporation

In general, the commonly used term "corporation" is usually a C-corporation. With a C-corporation, any profits the business earns are taxed at the corporate rate. In addition, any money you take out of the business in the form of salary, bonus, or dividends, is also taxed. This is known as double taxation. Note: You're not required to take a salary, bonus, or declare dividends. Your strategy might only be to grow and sell the business.

Advantages:

- Liability is generally limited to the assets of the corporation (personal assets are protected)
- It's easier to raise money compared to other business entities in which equity is exchanged for shares of stock
- There can be many classes of stock issued such as common and preferred classes
- There can be an unlimited number of shareholders
- Medical insurance premiums are tax deductible

Disadvantages:

- More paperwork is required than other business entities
- Can be ten times more costly to set up and maintain than a sole proprietorship or partnership
- More regulations to observe
- Double taxation – the business is taxed at the corporate rate and you pay taxes on your salary, bonus, or any dividends

S–Corporation

A corporation can be set up as a Subchapter S-corporation. An S-corporation generally has the same liability protection as a C-corporation. The main difference is that profits and losses are reported on your personal income tax return similar to a sole proprietorship or partnership. As a result, there is no corporate tax, dividends to pay out, and no double taxation.

Another difference is the limits on the type of stock an S-corporation can issue. This may be a disadvantage when seeking investors.

Advantages:

- No double taxation compared to a C-corporation
- Business losses can be deducted from your personal income to reduce your overall tax obligation

Disadvantages:

- Stock is limited to one class
- There's a limit of 75 shareholders
- Shareholders cannot be a corporation, partnership, or foreign entity
- The limitations on stock may be a problem for investors who want to take the company public later

Professional Corporation

If the business consists primarily of professional services, regulations require the corporation be formed as a Professional Corporation. Professional services include accounting, architecture, finance, legal, and medical. Talk to an attorney who has experience setting up a professional corporation in your state. If you're in business primarily to sell products, a Professional Corporation is not applicable to you.

Limited Liability Company (LLC)

An LLC has characteristics of both a corporation and a partnership. Your liability is limited to the assets of the business, which provides you with personal protection. Compared to a corporation, an LLC has "members" instead of stockholders and "membership interests" instead of stock. Members must all be U.S. citizens or resident aliens. The profits and losses of an LLC are shared and reported on your personal income tax return similar to a sole proprietorship, partnership, or S-corporation.

Advantages:

- No double taxation
- Limits on liability are similar to a corporation

- Business losses can be deducted from your personal income to reduce your overall tax obligation
- No limit to the number of members

Disadvantages:

- Requires at least two members (some states allow one member)
- Membership interests are limited to one class
- More costly to set up and maintain than a sole proprietorship or partnership

Business Entity Considerations

If you intend to raise money in exchange for stock, many investors prefer a C-corporation as opposed to an LLC or S-corporation. If you want the protection of a corporation and are not seeking investors, then an S-corporation is suitable. Remember, you may convert an S-corporation to a C-corporation later.

When you discuss business formation with an attorney, take the following issues into account:

- Setup costs
- Taxes
- Limiting your liability
- Protecting your assets
- Continuity of the business in the event of death
- Raising money
- Insurance coverage
- Number of owners
- Amount of paperwork
- Benefits such as medical coverage

Liabilities

The term "liability" covers a range of business matters. Liability means you're responsible for issues such as financial debts, product failure, or a personal injury on the job. As mentioned above, business entity structures, such as the C-corporation, help shield your personal holdings from business liabilities.

The term "limited liability" means your personal losses do not exceed your investment in the business. For example, if your business is a corporation and is sued, and the losses exceed the available business assets, your personal assets are not at risk. You do risk losing whatever money you invested into the business.

In general, there are four ways to reduce the risk of liability:

- **Business entity** – Setting up a corporation or a Limited Liability Company provides more liability protection than a sole proprietorship or partnership.

- **Insurance protection** – Your business can be sued for issues such as product liability, personal injury, errors, or omissions. Any fines imposed could be high enough to put you out of business. For protection, there are business insurance plans to cover a business from losses. Discuss liability in detail with an insurance agent who specializes in business insurance. Note, some trade shows require liability insurance before being permitted to set up a booth and exhibit.

- **Customer waivers and releases** – If you've used a software or web-based product, you probably have come across the need to agree to certain terms before you may use the product. These agreements help reduce company liability. They do not release the company from recklessness or negligence. These waivers and releases indicate that in the normal course of using the product there are certain limits of recourse by the customer if there's a problem. Talk with an attorney to see if waivers and releases apply to your product.

- **Product certifications** – Passing regulations or receiving certifications might be required for your product. Whether certifications are required or not, I recommend having an independent test lab check for product issues that could be hazardous to your customer. Identifying and fixing issues before product launch can limit the risk of liability.

Business Startup Checklist

Here's a checklist of activities for starting up your business:

- ❏ Evaluate the marketability of your idea.
- ❏ Determine your funding requirements (see Appendix E, Funding Your Idea).
- ❏ Select a name for your business.
- ❏ Write a business plan.
- ❏ Determine the business legal structure (sole proprietorship, partnership, or corporation).
- ❏ Call your City Clerk, County Clerk, or Secretary of State office to determine the requirements for a business license, certification, or permit.
- ❏ If your business is a sole proprietorship or partnership, and operating under a name other than the owner(s) name, then you need to file a "Fictitious Name" also known as a DBA (Doing Business As). Contact your City Clerk or County Clerk for specific instructions.
- ❏ Call the Internal Revenue Service at (800) 829-4933 or visit their website (www.irs.gov) to obtain a federal employer identification number (EIN). An EIN is not needed if you are a sole proprietor without employees.
- ❏ Call your state Board of Equalization or state Department of Treasury to determine the requirements for collecting sales tax.
- ❏ Open a checking account for your business.
- ❏ If you plan to hire employees, check with the U.S. Department of Labor website (www.dol.gov) to review employee rights. For additional help, contact the Employment Development Department in your state.
- ❏ To protect the name of your business, contact your Secretary of State to register a service mark.
- ❏ Establish a website and email account.
- ❏ Order business cards and stationary.
- ❏ Establish a method to track revenue, expenses, and inventory with a system such as Quicken or QuickBooks, made by Intuit.
- ❏ Establish a method to track your customers' contact information with a system such as Microsoft Outlook.

Further Startup Guidance

Additional resources for business startup include:

- Federal Trade Commission Business Guidance
  (www.ftc.gov/ftc/business.htm)

- National Association of Women Business Owners
  (www.nawbo.org)

- Small Business Administration / Small Business Development Center
  (www.sba.gov) / (www.sba.gov/sbdc)

- U.S. Chamber of Commerce
  (www.uschamber.com)

Appendix G:
Non-Disclosure Agreement

Inventor(s) _____ and

Participant(s) _____ agree:

1. The parties have been or expect to engage in discussions about their respective businesses that may involve the disclosure of Confidential Information generally regarding:

_____.

2. "Affiliate" means any other entity that controls, is controlled by, or is under common control of a party hereto.

"Confidential Information" means information obtained by the Receiving Party from the Disclosing Party (including, without limitation, information discovered by the Receiving Party while on the premises of the Disclosing Party) that (a) derives economic value, actual or potential, from not being generally known to or readily ascertainable by other persons who could obtain economic value from its disclosure or use, and (b) is the subject of efforts that are reasonable under the circumstances to maintain its secrecy.

Notwithstanding the foregoing, Confidential Information shall not include any information that the Receiving Party can conclusively show (i) is or becomes available in the public domain through no fault of the Receiving Party; (ii) was in the possession of the Receiving Party before receipt from the Disclosing Party; (iii) is received from a third party that legitimately acquired such information without restrictions as to its use or dissemination; (iv) was independently developed by the Receiving Party; or (v) as may be required by law.

"Disclosing Party" or "Receiving Party" shall mean either party to this Agreement, as the case may be, and shall include any Affiliates of each party.

3. The Receiving Party shall not disclose any Confidential Information to any other person or entity without the prior written consent of the Disclosing Party.

4. The Receiving Party shall exercise at least a reasonable degree of care in safeguarding and protecting the Confidential Information from disclosure or unauthorized use.

5. The Receiving Party shall not copy, reproduce, divulge, publish, or circulate Confidential Information to any of its employees or professional advisors other than those who have a need to know.

6. The term of this Agreement shall be one year and thereafter this Agreement shall automatically be extended for successive one-year terms unless terminated by either party upon written notice.

7. All obligations hereunder shall survive for a period of five years after termination.

8. The Receiving Party shall return to the Disclosing Party all copies of all Confidential Information immediately upon receipt of a request from the Disclosing Party for the return of the Confidential Information.

9. Nothing in this Agreement shall be construed or interpreted as granting any license, copyright, or other interest in or to any Confidential Information. The Disclosing Party shall retain title to all intellectual property and proprietary rights in the Confidential Information.

10. Each party acknowledges that the other party may now market or have under development, products that are competitive with products or services now offered or that may be offered by the other party. Any disclosures pursuant to this Agreement shall not serve to impair the right of either party to independently develop, make, use, procure, or market products or services now or in the future that may be competitive with those offered by the other.

11. This Agreement shall be governed by the laws of the State of
_____.

12. This Agreement may be executed in one or more counterparts, all of which together shall constitute one and the same instrument.

13. Neither party may assign any of its rights or obligations under this Agreement without the prior written consent of the other party, except in connection with a merger or acquisition of all or substantially all of the assets of the assignor. Subject to the foregoing, this Agreement shall endure to the benefit of and bind the successors and assigns of the parties.

IN WITNESS WHEREOF the parties have caused this Agreement to be executed as of the _____ day of the month of _____, in the year _____.

SIGNATURES

Inventor's Name: _____

Address: _____

City, State ZIP: _____

Signed: _____ Date: _____

PARTICIPANT(S)

Participant's Name: _____

Address: _____

City, State ZIP: _____

Signed: _____ Date: _____

Participant's Name: _____

Address: _____

City, State ZIP: _____

Signed: _____ Date: _____

Appendix H:
License Agreement Explained

Topics in this Appendix:

- Introduction
- Recitals
- Definitions
- Grant of License
- Termination
- Compensation
- Right to Audit
- Improvements
- Representations and Warranties by Licensor
- Representations and Warranties by Licensee
- Indemnification
- Product Liability Insurance
- Patent Infringement Lawsuits
- Schedules
- Quality Control
- Confidentiality
- General Provisions

There is no one standard license agreement. License agreements vary by company and attorney, but contain much of the same language. The following are explanations of typical license agreement provisions to help you translate the legalese.

Introduction

The Introduction section or opening statement, lists the names and addresses of the licensee (company) and licensor (inventor).

Recitals

Recitals describe the business of the licensee and the desires of the licensor.

- For example, "The licensee is in the business of developing, producing, and marketing kitchen appliances. The licensor desires to license to the licensee a new Widget."

Definitions

Definitions provide the foundation to the agreement. Definitions often include:

- **Invention** – Description of your invention being licensed.
- **Territory** – Geographical territory the licensee plans to market and sell the product (list of countries, regions, or worldwide).
- **Net Sales** – Net Sales (or net revenue) is commonly defined as product sales revenue less any returns, rebates, refunds, and discounts.
  Tip: Make sure company expenses for development, advertising, marketing, and sales commissions are not deducted to calculate net sales.

Grant of License

The grant section covers what you, the inventor licensor, are providing to the company licensee.

- **Rights Granted** – Describes the rights you are giving to the licensee to produce, market, and sell your product.
- **Territory** – Describes the exclusive right to market the product in certain geographical areas.
  Tip: Make sure you only allow exclusive rights to a region the company already has marketing and sales operations. For example, if the company wants worldwide rights but only markets and sells in North America, do not provide worldwide rights. If the company claims to be expanding to other regions, wait until they expand and then you can add an addendum to the original agreement. In the meantime, you can seek a license agreement with other companies in other territories.

- **Field of Use** – Describes the markets or industry the licensee is allowed to produce, market, and sell the product. If your product has multiple uses, you can restrict the licensee to certain markets.
  Tip: If a company targets consumers and your product can be sold to both consumers and businesses, then make sure Field of Use indicates exclusivity only in consumer markets. Then, for example, you are then open to obtain a licensing deal with another company that markets to businesses.

- **Term** – Describes the duration of the agreement. For example: "The term of this Agreement is for a period of five years and shall automatically renew for one year periods provided the Guaranteed Minimum Annual Royalty is paid before the anniversary date or either parties give written notice to terminate the Agreement."

- **Sublicense** – Describes consent (or withholding of consent) to allow the licensee to sublicense to another company. The sublicense company might have more expertise than the licensee in a certain field or territory. It's best if the grant states written consent is required by you before allowing a sublicense to occur. For some reason you might not like the sublicense company.

Termination

Describes actions or inactions by either party triggering the license agreement to be terminated. Make sure the license agreement covers your right to terminate if:

- The company breaches any part of the license agreement.
- The company files for bankruptcy.
- The company fails to pay you the guaranteed minimum annual royalties.
- The company is sold or acquired. (You might not want to be associated with the new owners.)
- The company is convicted of a felony.

Compensation

Compensation can include royalties, advances, and a license fee.

- **Advance** – Describes a one-time non-refundable amount against future earned royalties paid to you at the time the license agreement is signed. You keep the amount regardless of what happens in the future with the license agreement. You begin to receive royalties when the royalty amount due is greater than the advance amount.

- **License Fee** – Describes a one-time non-refundable amount paid to you at the time the license agreement is signed. You keep the amount regardless of what happens in the future with the license agreement. The License Fee is not against future royalties.

- **Royalty** – Describes the percentage earned for net sales of your product. For example: "In consideration of the right and License granted herein, Licensee shall pay a royalty on Net Sales at the rate of five percent (5%) of Net Sales."

- **Royalty Payment Schedule** – Describes when you are paid. You should be paid royalties at least on a quarterly basis. In this case, sales are calculated over a span of three months and you are paid royalties 30 days after this period.

- **Guaranteed Minimums** – Describes the minimum royalties you receive on an annual basis. If at the end of a year, royalties from sales do not reach the minimum amount, then you receive a lump sum payment to make up the difference. If the company does not pay the guaranteed minimum there should be a statement indicating you have the right to terminate the license agreement.

Right to Audit

If you believe the royalty payments are incorrect, then a Right to Audit provision allows you to hire an independent auditor to investigate product sales and royalty payments.

- **Results of Audit** – Describes the penalty or interest rate if the company has under-reported royalties.

- **Payment of Audit** – Describes who pays for the auditor's services. Some agreements state that if the error is within a small amount, such as 2%, then you pay the auditor. If the error exceeds the amount then the company pays the auditor.

Improvements

The agreement should state the company has the right to make changes to the product, but has to notify you in writing. For any change you or the company makes, you retain all intellectual property rights. If new intellectual property is created, it becomes part of the license agreement.

Representations and Warranties by Licensor

This states you are in fact the owner of the invention and intellectual property. If this turns out to be false, the company can terminate the license agreement and sue you for financial damages.

If the company wants a warranty that your invention does not cause a patent infringement lawsuit, this can be tricky. To protect yourself, this section should state, "To the best of my knowledge the invention does not infringe on a patent." You should review warranties with a patent attorney who can provide an opinion about the likelihood of an infringement.

Representations and Warranties by Licensee

You should request a statement that the company will develop the invention into a product in a timely manner. In addition, the company will make a strong effort to aggressively market the product in the assigned territories and obey all regulations and laws.

Indemnification

Indemnification means, in general, one party pays for damages caused by the other party. Usually it works both ways. If you are sued as a result of product defects caused by the company, the company covers the cost of a lawsuit. If you cause a problem, and the company is sued, you pay for all damages. In addition, there should be a statement indicating the company must purchase Product Liability insurance to cover the cost of product defect lawsuits.

Product Liability Insurance

The company should pay for product liability insurance and maintain the policy throughout the term of the license agreement. Product liability insurance is used to protect against lawsuits or other claims as a result of defects or failure of product to perform as stated. The amount of coverage is often between one and ten million dollars, but depends on the type of product and target market.

Patent Infringement Lawsuits

Keep in mind, patents do not infringe on patents. Products in the market infringe on patents. It's possible your finished product might infringe on someone else's active patent. If your product infringes on a patent, the agreement should state the company pays for defending an infringement lawsuit.

It's also possible another product will infringe on your patent. The agreement should state if your patent is being infringed, you are not required to sue the infringer. Infringement lawsuits can easily cost $100,000 in legal fees. The agreement should specify if you choose not to sue the infringer, the company has the right to sue on your behalf. If you sue an infringer and win, you collect the award. If the company sues the infringer and wins, the company collects the award and you receive a percentage (such as 20%).

Schedules

There needs to be a schedule in the license agreement indicating an approximate date the product will launch into the market. You obviously want to collect royalties as soon as possible. If the due date is not met, you have the option to terminate the agreement and receive specified monetary damages.

Quality Control

A quality control provision gives you the right to inspect the product before it is shipped to the customer. The company should agree to send you samples to inspect. In addition, the agreement should state you receive samples to inspect once a year. (The number of reasonable samples often depends on the cost to produce and ship.)

Some agreements say you have final authority on quality, while others state you are allowed to make suggestions but the company has the final authority to determine quality. I suggest you and the company define an acceptable product ahead of time to reduce the chance of an argument. Obviously, you don't want a sloppy product, but you also don't want to be a perfectionist holding up production.

Confidentiality

A provision stating you and the licensee need to keep information about the license agreement confidential.

General Provisions

At the end of the license agreement are general legal provisions. These are usually standard but are very important to understand and negotiate as needed. Some of the common provisions are:

- **Arbitration** – Describes a dispute will be resolved with arbitration and not a court. This is to reduce time and costs.

- **Assignment** – Describes either party cannot assign or transfer rights to a third party without written consent from the other party.

- **Attorney's Fees** – Describes if a dispute arises and legal actions occur, the losing party must pay the winning party's legal fees.

- **Entire Agreement** – Describes the license agreement is the only agreement between licensee and licensor. The license agreement supersedes any other prior written or oral agreements.

- **Force Majeure** – Describes in the event of some unforeseen disaster, the agreement can be put on hold.

- **Governing Law** – Describes laws be interpreted and enforced if a dispute arises according to the laws of a named state.

- **Headings** – Describes the headings used in the agreement have no special meaning. (Headings are titles and subtitles within the agreement document.)

- **Interpretation** – Describes both parties have had the assistance of legal counsel and had the opportunity to fully negotiate the terms with the other party.

- **Notices** – Describes the need to notify the other party, typically in writing, if a dispute arises.

- **No Joint Venture** – Describes the license agreement does not imply a joint venture or partnership.

- **Severability** – Describes if it's later determined any part of the license agreement is ruled invalid, unenforceable, or illegal, that section can be removed from the agreement. The rest of the license agreement remains enforced.

- **Waiver** – Describes parts of the license agreement can be later be negotiated and changed when both parties agree in writing. By changing one part leaves the rest of the license agreement intact.

Please consult with an attorney to review your legal documents.

Index

For quantity purchases of this book, please visit Broadword Publishing www.Broadword.com.

For Invention Templates and other invention information, please visit the author's website www.ProductCoach.com.

LaVergne, TN USA
23 May 2010
183660LV00005B/60/P